SCIENCE AND RELIGION

SCIENCE & RELIGION

IN

CONTEMPORARY PHILOSOPHY

BY

ÉMILE BOUTROUX

TRANSLATED BY

JONATHAN NIELD

KENNIKAT PRESS
Port Washington, N. Y./London

SCIENCE & RELIGION IN CONTEMPORARY PHILOSOPHY

First published in 1909
Reissued in 1970 by Kennikat Press
Library of Congress Catalog Card No: 70-102563
SBN 8046-0723-0

Manufactured by Taylor Publishing Company   Dallas, Texas

PRÉFACE POUR L'ÉDITION ANGLAISE

C'est avec un vif plaisir que je vois mon ouvrage : *Science et Religion* introduit en anglais dans les pays de langue anglaise, auxquels m'attachent des liens si étroits de reconnaissance intellectuelle et morale. J'apprécie d'autant plus ce privilège, que le travail de M. Jonathan Nield n'est pas une simple transcription littérale du français en anglais, mais une véritable traduction, qui, remontant du texte à la pensée même, sait modifier la forme pour conserver le fond. J'ai lu en grande partie cette traduction, et l'ai trouvée très soignée, très nette, très exacte, très intelligemment et scrupuleusement fidèle. Je suis même redevable au traducteur de quelques corrections, pour lesquelles je lui adresse mes bien sincères remerciements.

J'espère que le point de vue où je me suis placé intéressera le lecteur anglais. Selon moi, l'esprit humain, désormais, ne peut plus se contenter de maintenir, côte à côte, la religion et la science, comme deux faits bruts, sans s'inquiéter de l'accord ou du désaccord qui peut exister entre elles. D'autre part, les anciens systèmes de conciliation rationnelle ne satisfont plus, ni le savant, ni le croyant, ni le philosophe. Ma position, en cette matière, n'est, proprement, ni celle du rationaliste dogmatique, qui impose à l'être, *a priori*, des formes données et immuables, ni celle du pragmatiste radical, qui ne consent à justifier le fait que par le fait, et qui ne voit dans une idée vraie autre chose qu'une idée empiriquement vérifiée. Je m'applique à distinguer, de la science positive, classification logique des faits réalisés et observés, la raison proprement dite, besoin spontané et perfectible d'harmonie et de convenance, et effort pour réaliser ces conditions dans la connaissance et dans la vie.

Au nom de cette raison vivante, je scrute l'idée d'une vie pleinement humaine. Et je trouve que, rapportées à une telle vie, comme à leur source et à leur fin communes, la science et la religion sont toutes deux également nécessaires, et se concilient quant à leurs principes essentiels. La science a trait aux choses sans lesquelles l'homme ne peut pas vivre, la religion à celles sans lesquelles il ne veut pas vivre.

ÉMILE BOUTROUX.

CONTENTS

INTRODUCTION

RELIGION AND SCIENCE FROM GREEK ANTIQUITY TO THE
PRESENT TIME

PART I

THE NATURALISTIC TENDENCY

CHAPTER I

AUGUSTE COMTE AND THE RELIGION OF HUMANITY

The encounter henceforth inevitable.

vii

CONTENTS

CHAPTER IV

PSYCHOLOGY AND SOCIOLOGY

Nature and natural phenomena : consideration of religious phenomena substituted for that of the objects of religion.

PART II

THE SPIRITUALISTIC TENDENCY

CHAPTER I

RITSCHL AND RADICAL DUALISM

Recognition of the fact that religion must come to terms with science.

CHAPTER II

RELIGION AND THE LIMITS OF SCIENCE

The dogmatic conception of science and the critical conception.

CHAPTER III

THE PHILOSOPHY OF ACTION

CONTENTS

CHAPTER IV

WILLIAM JAMES AND RELIGIOUS EXPERIENCE

PAGES

I. Doctrine of W. James on Religion—His point of view: religion as personal and inward life — Method: radical empiricism — The psycho-physiological soil in which religious feeling begins to grow—Mysticism—Religious experience properly so-called ; elementary belief—The value of religious experience—The pragmatistic point of view— The theory of the subliminal self as a scientific basis— Over-beliefs 306-323

II. Doctrine of W. James on the Relation between Religion and Science—Science and religion, two keys with which to open nature's treasuries—The psychology of the range of consciousness, replaced by the psychology of states of consciousness—Religion and science differ as concrete and abstract 324-332

III. Critical Remarks—Remarkable reinstatement of religion in human nature, and its strong position with respect to science — Difficulty: Has religious experience objective value ?—Universal subjectivism would not be a solution— Faith, the integral element of all experience—The essential rôle of symbols—The value of the social side of religion . 332-344

CONCLUSION

The inevitable encounter. The conflict is properly between the scientific spirit and the religious spirit.

I. Relations between the Scientific Spirit and the Religious Spirit — (a) The scientific spirit — How are facts, laws, theories, established ? — Evolutionism — The experimental dogmatist—(b) The religious spirit—Is it compatible with the scientific spirit ?—Distinction between science and reason—Science and man : continuity between the two—The postulates of life: they coincide with the principles of religion 352-378

II. Religion—Morality and religion : what the second adds to the first—Vitality and flexibility of religion as a positive spiritual principle — The value of the intellectual and objective element—The rôle of vague ideas in human life— Dogmas—Rites—The transformation of tolerance into love 378-400

INTRODUCTION

RELIGION AND SCIENCE FROM GREEK ANTIQUITY TO THE PRESENT TIME

I. RELIGION AND PHILOSOPHY IN GREEK ANTIQUITY.

II. THE MIDDLE AGES—Christianity ; the Schoolmen ; the Mystics.

III. SCIENCE AND RELIGION SINCE THE RENAISSANCE—The Renaissance —Modern times : Rationalism ; Romanticism—Science and Religion separated by an impassable barrier.

BEFORE coming to the study of the relations between Science and Religion, as they actually appear to-day, it is interesting to make a rapid survey of the history of those relations in the civilisations of which ours is the heir.

I

RELIGION AND PHILOSOPHY IN GREEK ANTIQUITY

Religion, in ancient Greece, had not to grapple with Science, as we now understand it, *i.e.* with the whole of positive knowledge acquired by humanity; but it encountered the philosophy, or rational interpretation, either of natural phenomena and life, or of men's traditional beliefs. Philosophy was born, in part, from Religion itself. The latter, in Greece, had not in its service an organised priesthood.

Consequently it did not express itself by hard and fast dogmas. It only imposed rites—external acts—which entered into the life of the citizen. It was, moreover, rich in legends, in myths, which charmed the imagination, trained the mind, and stimulated thought. Whence came these legends? Without doubt—it was believed—from forgotten revelations; but they were so copious, so different, so shifting, and, in many cases, so contradictory, childish, offensive and absurd, that it was impossible not to see in them the work of man as well as of divine revelation. To depart, in myths, from the primitive and the adventitious would have been a vain undertaking. Essentially an artist, moreover, the Greek was conscious—even when he spoke of the gods—of playing with his subject; and he scorned the proper meaning of the stories which he told. On the other hand, those gods who, according to tradition, had taught the ancients the rudiments of the traditional legends, were themselves fallible and limited: they knew but little more of these than men. So it came about that philosophy was developed very freely under the care and protection of the popular mythology itself.

She began, in the usual way, by disowning and striking her nurse. "It is," said Xenophanes, "men who have created the gods, for in these latter they find again their own shape, their feelings, their speech. If oxen knew how to depict, they would give to their gods the form of oxen. Homer and Hesiod have attributed to the gods all that, among men, is shameful and criminal." The stars, asserted Anaxagoras, were not divinities: they were incandescent masses, of the same nature as terrestrial stones. Some of the Sophists jested on the gods themselves. "It is not for me," said Protagoras, "to seek out either if the gods exist, or if they do not exist : many things hinder me from this, notably the obscurity of the subject and the shortness of human life."

So grew philosophy—critical, superior or indifferent in regard to religious beliefs, morally independent, and free even politically ; for, if some philosophers were suppressed, that was only for details which appeared to contradict the public religion.

This development of philosophy was nothing but the development of human intelligence and reason ; and thinkers were enamoured of reason to this extent, that they aspired to make of it the principle of man and of the universe.

The task given to reason, thenceforth, was that of proving its reality and power, as against the blind necessity, the universal flux, the indifferent chance, which appeared the sole law of the world.

Inspiration, during this task, was found in the consideration of Art, where the thought of the artist is seen struggling with a heterogeneous matter, without which there could not be any realisation. This matter—in its shape, its laws, its own tendencies—is indifferent or even impervious to the idea which one would make it express. The artist masters it, for all that : much more, he wins it over, and makes it appear supple and smiling in its borrowed form. It seems now that the marble aimed at representing Pallas or Apollo, and that the artist has only set free its properties.

Would not reason, in the face of Ananke, be in an analogous situation ? According to Plato, according to Aristotle, Ananke—brute matter—is not thoroughly hostile to reason and to measure. The more we investigate the nature of reason and that of matter, the more we see them approximate, invoke one another, become reconciled. In what is apparently the most indeterminate matter, demonstrates Aristotle, there is already some form. Matter, at bottom, is only form in potency. Therefore, reason is, and is efficacious, since, without her, nothing that exists would continue as it is, but would go back to chaos. We moan over the brutality of fate, over the miseries and iniquities of life, and that is just; but disorder is only one aspect of things : he who looks at them with reason, finds again reason in them.

The Greek philosophers were bent on making more and more important, more and more powerful, that reason whose rôle in nature they had thus discerned. And the more they exalted her, the more, in comparison with beings who partook of matter and non-entity, she appeared to merit surpassingly that title of Divine which popular religion had lavished at random. All nature hangs on reason, but all nature is powerless to equal it, said Aristotle ; and, proving the existence of thought in itself—of the Perfect Reason, he called this Reason " God." If, then, reason turned aside from traditional religion, it was to establish, through knowledge of nature itself, a truer religion.

The god-reason was not, moreover, reasoning in the abstract. It was nature's master, the king who ruled all things. To it belonged properly the name of Zeus. " This entire universe which turns in the heavens," said Cleanthes the Stoic, in addressing Zeus, " of itself goes whither thou leadest it. Thy hand, which holds the thunderbolt, submits all things—the greatest as the least—to universal reason. Nothing, anywhere, is done without thee; nothing, unless it be what the wicked do in their folly. But thou knowest how, from an odd number, to make an even number; thou renderest harmonious things that are discordant; beneath thy gaze, hate is turned into friendship. O God, who behind the clouds orderest the thunder, take men out of their baneful ignorance; disperse the mists that darken their minds, O father; and let them share in the intelligence by which thou rulest all things with justice, in order that we may render thee honour for honour, praising thy works without intermission, as it is fitting mortals should. For, unto mortals and gods alike, there is given no higher prerogative than that of praising eternally, in worthy speech, the Universal Law."

That was philosophical religion. Was it the irreconcilable enemy of popular religion? Was everything in those myths which Time had spared and consecrated only fantasy, disorder, and chaos according to its view? The multitude had deified the stars. But were not the stars, with the perfect regularity of their movements, direct manifestations of law, *i.e.* of reason, of God? The multitude worshipped Jupiter as king of gods and men. Did not this belief contain the sense of affinity which bound together all parts of the universe, making of them one single body subject to a common soul? Religion ordered respect for the laws, fidelity to duty, piety towards the dead; it lent to human feebleness the support of tutelary deities. Was it not, in that, the interpreter and helper of reason? Reason, the true god, was not unapproachable by man; he participated in it. Religion could, therefore, be at once human and worthy of reverence. It was the part of philosophy to penetrate the secret relations between traditional doctrines and universal reason, and to preserve, among these doctrines, all that contained some soul of truth.

Thus it was that philosophy became reconciled by degrees to religion. Already Plato and Aristotle had welcomed the traditional belief in the divinity of sky and stars, and, in a general way, had sought in myths some traces or rudiments of philosophical thought.

With the Stoics, reason—become, in a pantheistic sense, the part-mistress of the soul and the principle and end of all things—was, somehow, necessarily present in men's spontaneous and general beliefs, in everything that taught them to get away from their individual opinions and passions. Most certainly, myths, legends, religious ceremonies, in so far as they lowered the gods to the level of man or below man, deserved only contempt; but at the back of these tales, if one knew how to understand them, if from the literal sense one could disentangle the allegorical, there were truths. Zeus was the symbol of God binding all things together by his unity and his omnipresence; the secondary gods were types of those divine powers which were manifested in the multiplicity and diversity of the elements, of the earth's products, of great men, of the benefactors of humanity. It was the same Zeus who, according as one considered the aspect of his being, was by turns Hermes, Dionysus, Heracles. Heracles was power, Hermes divine knowledge. The worship of Heracles meant regard for effort, for intensity, for right judgment, and contempt of slackness and luxury. On this track the Stoics did not know how to stop, and the fancifulness of their allegorical interpretations exceeded all limit. It was that they had at heart the saving, to the largest extent possible, of popular beliefs and practices ; deeming that, if reason was to operate not only on a select few, but on all men, it should be clothed in sundry forms, corresponding to the variety of intellects.

The last considerable manifestation of the philosophical spirit of the Greeks was Neo-Platonism, which, speculating on the essence of reason, thought to be exalted, by its doctrine of the Infinite One, above reason itself. But the more the Deity was made transcendent with regard to things, with regard to life and thought even, the more it was judged necessary to introduce, between the inferior and superior forms of being, a hierarchy of intermediary beings. This intermedium it was which constituted the field of popular religion. Its gods, nigh to our feebleness, helped to raise us towards the supreme God. And Plotinus, but especially his disciple Porphyry, justified by degrees, from the point of view of reason, all the elements of religion : myths, traditions, worship of images, divination, prayer, sacrifices, magic. Symbols intercalated between the sensible and the intelligible, all these things were good and partaking of truth, through the necessary part they played in the conversion of man towards the immaterial and the ineffable.

II

THE MIDDLE AGES

Such was, as regards religion, the attitude of Greek philosophy. The Christian thought, which succeeded to it, shattered the framework of natural knowledge and action within which this philosophy was regulated.

Laden with an infinity of love and power which the clear genius of the Greeks had mistrusted, the religious idea was no longer limited to being the supreme explanation, the perfect model, the life and unity of the world. It was established, from the first, by itself above and outside things, in virtue of sole excellence and absolute supremacy. God was, because He was Power, Majesty and Independence—because He was Being. Henceforward the understanding would not ascend painfully, by way of induction, from the signs of perfection that our world could offer, to a Cause scarcely more perfect than these. The God of Christianity was revealed in and through Himself, exclusive of all the beings of this world ; these latter were only samples of His power, created out of nothing and that arbitrarily. Religion was going, therefore, to display herself quite freely, with look fixed on God alone. She would be herself as far as possible, while a religion based on contemplation of nature and man would always remain mingled with anthropomorphism and naturalism.

It was in this sense that Christ said to men : " You are troubled about many things, but one alone is needful"; and again : " Seek ye first the kingdom of God, and all else shall be added unto you."

It appeared that spirit itself, without borrowing anything from matter, was going to be realised in this world and to fashion there a supernatural body.

In fact, Christian thought had to reckon with the conditions of the world which it wished to conquer— that world with its institutions, with its customs, its beliefs, its traditions. In order to be understood, it had necessarily to speak the language of the men to whom appeal was made.

It was under the form of Greek philosophy that
Christianity encountered rational and scientific thought.
In a sense, it found in this encounter the opportunity
of acquiring a clearer consciousness of its own mind—
of developing and defining it.   To a doctrine of pure
light, in which God was only reckoned one with
universal law, in which the world was, of itself,
sensitive to the attraction of harmony and justice,
Christianity opposed faith in a supernatural revelation,
profound feeling for the misery and depravity of the
natural man, and the affirmation of a God all love and
pity, who was made man in order to save men.   But,
on the other hand, when pagan writers denounced these
ideas as against reason, the Christians, accepting their
adversaries' point of view, protested against that ac-
cusation ; and Origen, against Celsus, demonstrated
the rationality of the Christian faith.

In this manner was opened out the way which
necessarily led to what has been called Scholasticism.

Since Christianity aimed at mastering human life
outright, it had to secure satisfaction for the needs of
the intellect as well as those of will and heart.   But
intellect then stood for that *chef-d'œuvre* of clearness,
of logic and of harmony which was called Greek philosophy.   To go from faith to intellect, therefore, was to
rejoin that philosophy.   Truth could not contradict
truth : it was the same God, perfect and constant,
who was the author of natural enlightenment and
of revelation.   So, true philosophy and true religion
were only, at bottom, one and the same thing.

This view of Scotus Erigena, however, was too
summary.   The sources, therefore the compass, of
philosophy and of religion were not the same.   Between
philosophy and theology agreement was certain, but

each in its sphere. To philosophy would be restored knowledge of created things and of that portion of God's nature which could be deduced from created things; to theology, knowledge of the character and interior life of Deity. Reason and faith would share thus the domain of existence, as, in the community, Pope and Emperor shared authority. Not with equal right, however; reason and faith formed a feudal and Aristotelian hierarchy, in which the inferior owed homage to the superior, and in which the superior ensured the security and rights of the inferior. Philosophy demonstrated the preambles of faith. Grace did not destroy, but realised in their fulness the powers of nature and of reason.

This concordat between philosophy and theology implied mutual adaptation.

As regards Greek philosophy, those parts were cultivated, preferably, which served the development of Christian dogmatics : for instance, Ontology, which was especially regarded as a doctrine of natural theology. In Aristotelian logic, that mathematic of demonstration, was sought the theory of intelligibility; and, from this point of view, there was assigned to it an exclusively formal character which it did not have with Aristotle.

On the other hand, religion was submitted to a method of accommodation. That which, in the Gospel, was essentially spirit, love, union of souls, inward life, irreducible to words and formulæ, had —in order to tally with Scholastic conditions of intelligibility—to sink itself in rigid definitions, to be regulated in long chains of syllogisms, to be transmuted into an abstract and definitive system of concepts.

It was thus that in the Middle Ages Christianity satisfied the needs of the intellect, in assuming a form borrowed from Greek philosophy. This contingent combination could not last for ever.

Already, during this same period, certain Christians more or less isolated and sometimes suspected, called Mystics, had not ceased to demand, for the individual conscience, the right of communicating with God directly, above philosophical and even theological intermediaries. To dialectics they opposed faith and love; to theory, practice. Moreover, they did not aim at concentrating the whole of religion in pure spirit and bare potentiality. They showed that two ways were open to the soul: first of all the *via purgativa*, in which man purified himself from the stains of the natural life; then the *via illuminativa*, in which, from the bosom of God, sharing in His light and power, the soul realised itself and was revealed in a new form, the creation and direct expression of the spirit itself. Deeds, taught Master Eckhart, did not stop the instant that the soul attained holiness. On the contrary, it was with holiness that there began real activity, at once free and good—the love of all creatures and of enemies even, the work of universal peace. Deeds were not the method, but they were the radiance of sanctification.

While, in effusions sometimes vague, but living and fervent, the mystics maintained, against the abstract and rigid formulæ of the School, the free spirit of Christianity, Scholasticism, by a kind of inward travail, saw the separation of those two elements which it had reconciled and striven to unite harmoniously. The categories established by Greek philosophy had been destined by their

inventors to embrace and make intelligible the things
of our earth.   The Christian idea, except by renouncing itself, could not give way here positively.
On the other hand, philosophy became aware, in
Scholasticism, of its own bondage.   It was charged
with proving the Divine Personality and the possibility of Creation, the Immortality of the Soul, and
human free-will.   Was it certain that, left to its own
guidance, it would reach these conclusions ?   Besides,
was it consistent with the conditions of philosophical
knowledge that dogmas should be first of all laid
down, and that it should then be limited to the work
of analysis and inference ?

III

SCIENCE AND RELIGION SINCE THE RENAISSANCE

From the internal dissolution of Scholasticism, as
also from external circumstances, there resulted the
double movement which characterised the Renaissance
period.

On the one side, mystical Christianity, which put
the essence of religion in inward life, in the direct
relation of the soul with God, in the personal experience of salvation and sanctification, broke away
violently from the traditional Church.   And one
circumstance helped to give what was called the
Reformation, precision and settled purpose, without
which it would have remained, perhaps, a mere
spiritual aspiration, analogous to those which manifested themselves in the Middle Ages.   The need of
personal religious life which was the foundation of it,
came into line with that love of old texts, re-established

in their genuineness and purity, which Humanism had just initiated. Just as the Catholicism of the Middle Ages had associated Aristotle and the theology of the Fathers, so Luther combined Erasmus and the mystic sense. And, thus renewed, the Christian idea yielded fresh scope.

On the other side, philosophy broke the chains which, under the Schoolmen, had bound her to theology. Leaning, sometimes on Plato, sometimes on Aristotle himself, sometimes on Stoicism or Epicureanism, or on other like doctrine of Antiquity, she shook off, with uniform energy, the yoke of theology and the yoke of the Aristotle of the Middle Ages; and, in changing her master, she set out for independence. A Nicholas of Cusa, a Bruno, a Campanella proclaimed new doctrines.

That was not all : Science properly so called, the positive Science of Nature, emerged at this epoch, and aimed at unfolding itself freely. It culminated in the ambition to produce, to convert the forces of nature to its own use, to create. Previously, it was chiefly the Devil who had the pretension to intervene in the course of things created and governed by God, and to make them produce what they did not produce of themselves; also the alchemists, who sought to make gold, and were readily confused with sorcerers. Thenceforward, the idea of a Science, active and no longer merely contemplative—faith in the possibility of man's rule over Nature, was irresistible.

In his impatience to reach the goal, Faust, disabused of the barren learning of the Schoolmen, devoted himself to magic. What mattered the means, provided there was success in winning the unknown forces which produced phenomena, and in making them act at will?

> Drum hab' ich mich der Magie ergeben.[1]

Thus it was that, in the sixteenth century, the occult sciences furnished the prelude to Science. They were, moreover, joined, in the mind of that time, with a naturalistic pantheism, which called for a purely natural explanation of things and the employment of the experimental method.

.   .   .   .   .   .

To this period of confusion and of fermentation succeeded, with Bacon and Descartes, a new age—an age of discipline, of order, and of equipoise. Cartesian rationalism was the most precise and the most complete expression of the mind which then prevailed.

On the one hand, the experimental science of nature, already clearly understood by Leonardo da Vinci, was, with Galileo, definitely established. Towards 1604, through the discovery of the laws of the pendulum, Galileo had proved that it was possible to explain the phenomena of nature through binding them all together, without calling for the intervention of any force existing outside them. The notion of Natural Law was, from that time, established. And this Science, which made appeal to mathematics and experience only, having been (notably by Gassendi) recombined with the ancient Epicurean Atomism, was deemed incompatible with Christian supernaturalism by numerous intellects. Some daring logicians, frivolous or serious, the freethinkers, made use of Science to support Naturalism and Atheism.

On the other hand, Religious Faith, strengthened

---

[1] "That is why I have applied myself to magic."—GOETHE, Faust.

by its very trials, manifested itself with a new vigour —now on the Protestant side, now on the Catholic. For the one, as for the other, Faith could no longer be a mere trick of disposition, joined to secular traditions and practices. It had become an inward conviction, worthy of struggle and suffering.

What, in the spiritual jurisdiction of mind, was to be the harmony of these two powers, Science and Religion, which invoked seemingly opposite principles? This question was solved by Descartes in a manner which, for long, appeared to satisfy the exigencies of the modern intellect.

Descartes started with the mutual independence of Religion and Science. Science, limited to the domain of Nature, found its object in the appropriation of natural forces, and its instruments in mathematics and experience. Religion had to do with the super-terrestrial destinies of the soul, and rested on a certain number of beliefs—very simple, moreover, and having no affinity with the subtleties of Scholastic Theology. Science and Religion could not trouble or prevail over one another, because, in their normal and legitimate development, they did not meet. The time must never return when, as in the Middle Ages, theology could impose on philosophy the conclusions which the latter had to demonstrate, and the principles from which it had to start. Science and Religion were both autonomous.

But it did not follow that the human mind had only to accept them as two orders of truth foreign to one another. A philosophical mind could not put up with Dualism pure and simple. Cartesianism was just the philosophy of the connection or relationship established between two different things—irreducible in themselves to logical standpoint. In the principle he adopted—*cogito ergo sum*—Descartes intended to lay down a kind of conjunction unknown to the dialectic of the School. *Cogito ergo sum* was not the conclusion of a syllogism : on the contrary, this proposition was itself the condition and proof of the syllogism from which it was supposed to have issued. Being presented, in this proposition, with the copula *ergo*, one could translate the necessity which it expressed by a universal proposition such as *quidquid cogitat, est*, thereby rendering possible the construction of a syllogism ending in *cogito ergo sum*. The first and truly fertile knowledge was just this connection between two terms given as foreign to one another.

How was such a connection to be discovered? Experience, pointed out Descartes, offers us knowledge of exactly this kind. Now, from experimental connections, at first contingent, the mind—interpreting the experience of the senses with the help of a kind of supersensible experience, called by Descartes intuition —disengages necessary and universal knowledge. In ourselves there is a principle and foundation of necessary connection, and this principle is none other than what we call reason. Rationalism, a rationalism which attributed to reason a certain faculty of conjunction, a content, with laws and a power of its own ; such was the point of view that Descartes represented.

This was how he conceived the correspondence between Religion and Science.

Just as he had found in reason the basis of a view binding *sum* to *cogito*, so, in this same reason, Descartes thought he had found the relation of man to God, and of God to the world, whence resulted the radical harmony of Science, of Nature, and of Religous Beliefs. This result was obtained, in the case of Descartes, through analysis of the content of reason, and through certain deductions, no longer syllogistic and purely formal, but mathematical and constructive, proceeding from this very content.

It is clear, moreover, that there was no question here of the fundamental principles of Religion : God, His infinity, His perfection ; and our dependence upon Him. As to what concerned positive religion, philosophy had no competence to reason about it. When one thought of all the sects, heresies, disputes and calumnies to which Scholastic Theology had given rise, one could only wish for their complete disappearance. In fact, the simple and the ignorant gained heaven as well as the learned : their naïve beliefs were surer than the theology of the theologians.

Such was the Cartesian doctrine. In the bosom of reason itself appeared, according to this doctrine, both the germs out of which grew respectively Religion and Science, and the special bond which secured, along with their compatibility, their mutual independence. This original rationalism, which may be called modern rationalism, dominated the philosophical thought of the seventeenth and eighteenth centuries.

In a philosopher's category, this rationalism tends to become dogmatic. Confident in his powers, he seeks to constitute, on lines parallel with the science of nature, a science of divine things which will in no degree fall short, as regards evidence and certainty, of the physical and mathematical sciences.

C

With Spinoza, reason established the existence of the absolutely infinite Substance, which is God, and, from the essence of that Substance, deduced the principle of the universal laws of nature. In that way the attempt of science to reduce to law the apparently confused multitude of particular things was justified. On the other hand, encountering certain texts reputed sacred, such as the Judæo-Christian Bible, reason laid down the principle that Scripture ought to be explained by Scripture alone, in so far as it was a question of determining the historical sense of doctrines and the intention of prophets ; but that, once this work of exegesis had been accomplished, it was her province to decide whether our assent should be given to those doctrines.

Leibnitz, fathoming the distinction between the truths of reason and the truths of fact, which together constitute science, discovers their common principle in a possible Infinite which envelopes both necessary and actual existence, and which is none other than what we call God. According to him, while the sciences study the relation of things considered, in sense perception, as external to one another, religion is at pains to embrace, in its living reality, that internal and universal harmony, that mutual penetration of beings, that aspiration of each for the well-being and joy of all, which is the hidden spring of their utmost life and endeavour : and, in this way also, men are made capable of sharing in, and contributing to the glory of God as the very end and principle of every thing that exists or aspires after existence.

Subtile and metaphysical with a Spinoza, a Malebranche, a Leibnitz, dogmatic and objective rationalism

became more and more simple with Locke and the
Deists, who addressed themselves to men of the world
and to society. For the Deists, reason was not only
the opposite of tradition and authority : it shut out
all belief in those things which surpassed either our
clear ideas or the nature of which we formed part.
Thenceforward, reason banished systematically every
mystery, every dogma transmitted by the positive
religions. Nothing was allowed to stand but the
religion called natural or philosophical, which was
expected to provide adequate expression in the double
affirmation of God's existence as Architect of the
world, and the Immortality of the Soul conditional
on the fulfilment of justice. In professing these
doctrines, Deism regarded itself as occupying exactly
the same standing-ground as the natural sciences.
Entirely analogous, in its view, were physical truths
and moral truths. No action, moreover, was attributed to the First Cause, which could contradict
the mechanical laws proclaimed by Science. Deistic
rationalism rejected miracle and special providence.

The special quality of this rationalism was that it
more and more deprived Religion of its characteristic
elements, so as to reduce it to a small number of very
dry, very abstract formulæ, more calculated to furnish
occasion for argument than to satisfy the aspirations
of the human soul. Moreover, these so-called rational
demonstrations of the existence of God and of the
Immortality of the Soul were, in the eyes of an
unprejudiced critic, far from possessing the scientific
evidence that was pretended.

It was not, therefore, surprising that, in order to
define the relations between Science and Religion,
modern rationalism should have gone in quest of a

point of view other than that which was objective or dogmatic.

Pascal had already sought the elements of his proof in the conditions of human knowledge, of life, of action, *i.e.* in the sphere of the Knowing Subject, and not in that of Being taken in itself. He distinguished between reason in the narrow sense of the word, and the heart : the latter, still reason of a kind, *i.e.* order and connection, but a reason infinitely finer, in which the original faculties—scarcely to be understood—outstripped the range of the geometrical mind. This superior reason had for object, no longer logical abstractions, but realities. To work out fully all the required proofs was a task beyond our powers. Happily, this concrete reason expressed itself in us through a direct view of truth, an intuition with which our heart, our instinct, our nature was endowed. To despise the intuitions of the heart in order to restrict our adhesion to the reasoning of the geometrical mind, was contradictory ; for, in reality, it was already the heart or instinct which gave us the notions of Space and Time, of Movement and Number, the bases of our sciences. The heart was needed by reason, in order to get support for its reasonings. Moreover, just as it perceived that there were, in Space, three dimensions, so the heart, if it was not warped, perceived that there was a God.

The method called critical (previously practised by Pascal), which set out from the analysis of our means of knowing, and which, by the origin of our ideas, judged of their import and value, was clearly defined by Locke. That philosopher sets in relief a distinction upon which Descartes had already insisted : the

distinction between knowledge properly so called, and
assent or belief. There is knowledge properly so
called in the event of our possessing incontestable
proofs of the truth which we maintain. If the proofs
at our disposal are not of this kind, our adhesion is
only assent. Now it must be noted that, while
Science seeks and acquires genuine knowledge,
Practical Life rests, almost entirely, on simple beliefs.
The force of custom, the obscurity of questions, the
necessity, where action is concerned, of deciding
without delay—these create simple assent, or belief,
and not that knowledge which is the habitual principle
of our judgments. Not that we judge groundlessly :
we are guided by probability, especially by testimonies
deserving of credit. How, then, can we discard
religious beliefs, under pretence of their being only
beliefs ? They are all the more legitimate through
having for surety the veracity of God Himself. If
one is careful to retain only that which is indeed
Divine revelation, and to make sure that one possesses
the true meaning of it, religious faith is as certain a
principle of affirmation as knowledge itself.

This acute and broad " man of the world "
philosophy was the origin of the wise and profound
system of Kant. In the very constitution and in the
working of reason, Kant finds all the fundamental
conditions, both of Science and of Religion. Reason
constructs Science. She does not fashion it (an
impossible feat) with the sole elements which experience provides : it is from herself that spring the
notions of space and time, of permanence, of causality,
without which science would be impossible. But why
should not reason, which governs the given world,
purpose, not only to know, but to modify that world,

and to make it more and more the expression of her own nature, of her own will? Should not reason be able to assert herself, not only as theoretical and contemplative, but yet again as active, practical, and creative? And should she not be able to exercise her control, not only over the human will, but, further, over the external and material world, with which that will is in harmony? Doubtless such a possibility can be only a matter of belief, and not of science; but we have here to do with a belief that reason, integrally consulted, justifies, enjoins, and determines. Reason is entitled to the highest place: if we can labour to procure her rule, we ought to do so. And if certain ideas are, for us, by virtue of our constitution, practically necessary auxiliaries for the accomplishment of this task, we must adhere to these ideas. Now, such are the ideas of Freedom, of God, and of Immortality, understood in a sense, no longer theoretical, but practical and moral. Religion is the practical belief that the work of reason is realisable, an indispensable belief seeing that we give ourselves whole-heartedly to this work, which implies effort and sacrifice on our part. We must include, then, moral and religious beliefs. Thus it is that, for Kant, the same reason, by turns theoretical and practical, according as she aims either at knowing things or at ruling action, establishes both Science, and Morality, whence flows Religion; assuring to each of them an independent sphere, yet knitting them together through relationship to a common principle.

This connection is further strengthened and rendered clearer among the idealists succeeding Kant. Fichte tries to show that the real world presented to scientific observation is already, by nature, impregnated with morality and with rationality; that it is only, at bottom, pure spirit, transforming itself, by an act of unconscious intelligence, into object and image, in order to reach, by reflection on that image, consciousness of self. Hence, reason, justice, humanity are no longer in the world as strangers, seeking, by strategy, to establish themselves and to supersede one another in nature. The will that is free and good has, by virtue of itself, material consequences. Moral consciousness, that gleam of the Infinite, is the principle of the very life that we live in this world. Religion, which renders us sharers in the causality of reason, is to the merely verifying Science what the vapours of the sky are to the waters which fertilise the ground.

For Hegel, Science and Religion are nothing but necessary and logically successive "moments" of the spirit's development. Science is the knowledge of things in so far as they are external to one another, *i.e.* in so far as they are deprived of consciousness and of freedom. This condition is only a stage through which the Idea must pass in order to become personal and to labour in the realisation of spirit. Under its most complex form, which is the human organism, external and material being becomes capable of a special development, called History. And, by favour of that conflict of interests and wills, of that struggle against suffering and evil, of that rich invention of methods, of that continual experimentation, of that creation and accumulation of moral forces, which characterise History, new powers— conscience and freedom—are awakened and developed in man, *i.e.* in the world. Henceforward, that which was only matter becomes spiritual; form, without

ever breaking up or vanishing, becomes, more and
more, the free and complete realisation of spirit. The
individual, the family, the community, the State—
these are the successive moments of this development.
And the work of the living spirit is accomplished, to
the fullest possible extent, in art, in revealed religion,
in philosophy; this last being, in some way, religion
in itself, as it is when freed from the symbols with
which art and the various religions enveloped it.

The philosophy of Hegel requires us, in the last
analysis, to see God grow and gain consciousness of
Himself, in the world and by the world, and to
become ourselves the support and reality of this
same Supreme Consciousness. Science, as such, has
nothing religious about it, and remains a stranger to
religion. But for the philosopher, who follows the
internal and necessary evolution of the Idea, science
is only a moment in the progress of Being. She
(science) sets herself unwittingly towards a higher
stage of knowledge, of consciousness; and, in taking
the very direction thus indicated, thought arrives
logically at religion and at philosophy. Faith always
wishes to become understanding. That which, in
science, is only blind belief in a given matter, in art,
religion, and philosophy becomes expression, sentiment, knowledge of the principle of things.

Thus was developed, whether in the objective or
in the subjective sense, Cartesian rationalism. A
third development of that rationalism is what has
been called the philosophy of the Enlightenment.
Very different in its manifestations, this philosophy,
which flourished in the eighteenth century, had
this general character: it considered that the pure

intellect, separated from feeling, *i.e.* clear and distinct knowledge or science, ought to be sufficient guarantee for the perfecting and happiness of humanity. In France, La Mettrie, the Encyclopædists, Helvetius and d'Holbach combined Bacon with Descartes so as to form a kind of empirical or even materialistic rationalism, thoroughly hostile to religious beliefs. The progress of science was enthusiastically upheld, and a kind of religious faith in moral and political progress, considered as the natural and necessary consequence of scientific and intellectual progress, was propagated. The finest expression of this generous confidence in the practical efficacy of the Enlightenment is the celebrated work of Condorcet entitled, *Esquisse d'un tableau historique des progrès de l'esprit humain.*

. . . . . .

In opposition to the various forms of rationalism there appeared, as early as the second half of the seventeenth century, especially in England, a moral philosophy which found, in the irrational element of human nature, in feeling, in instinct, the primitive and fundamental fact. It is in this way that Shaftesbury, opposing to the philosophy of reflection the Hellenic sense of nature and harmony, places in an immediate and instinctive æsthetic sense the criterion of moral good. Butler gives this rôle to conscience, Hutchinson to the moral sense. The sceptical metaphysics of Hume lead up to an act of confidence in nature as the mother of custom; and his system of morals rests on the natural sympathy between man and man. Sympathy is yet again the principle of the economist Adam Smith. And the Scottish school, intending to re-establish, in every sphere, the rôle and value of intuition or immediate experience, in opposition to logic, glorifies common sense with its irreducible data whether theoretical or practical.

It is evidently with this new revival of the ancient naturalism in which instinct was placed above reflection, that the moral revolution, of which Rousseau was the exponent *par excellence,* allies itself. The enthusiasm with which his discourse of 1750 was received, shows to what degree the ideas therein supported were in the air. From his inward life, from his character, from his genius still more than from his lectures or from his philosophical meditations, Rousseau derived this precept, clear for him as a truth of actual experience : that feeling is, in itself, an independent and absolute principle, that it is in no way amenable to intellectual knowledge, but, on the contrary, is superior to it in the sense that our ideas are only, for the most part, logical constructions, fictions, invented too late to explain and justify our feelings. Adopting this standpoint, Rousseau believed that what were called progress and civilisation constituted, in reality, only corruption and error ; for the principle of that civilisation was, in contrast with the natural order, the supremacy of mind over feeling, of the artificial over the spontaneous, of science over disposition. Guided, originally, by nature, by instinct —the very principle of life—Humanity had sinned in eating the fruit of the tree of knowledge, of the proud intellect, that is, which thinks itself supreme. Henceforth the Race was dedicated to death, except through conversion and re-entrance into the path of nature. To re-establish in all matters the supremacy of feeling, of intuition, of immediate perception, and to govern the use of intellect on this principle—therein was safety, therein lay the means of realising an order of things as superior to the primitive Eden as a being who is intelligent and a man is raised above an animal that is stupid and restricted.

The ideas of Rousseau on religion are the application of his principles.

It does not much matter that he maintains nearly the same dogmas as the Deists, and that, seen from outside, his natural religion hardly differs from that of the philosophers. What is new and important is the source that he assigns to these ideas, the way in which he believes in them and professes them. They are no longer for him doctrines which are demonstrated by reasoning: they are the spontaneous effusions of his individual soul. I do not wish, says the Savoyard vicar, setting forth his profession of faith, to argue with you, nor even to aim at convincing you; enough if I can show you what I think in the simplicity of my heart. Consult your own during the whole of my address, that is all I ask of you. They tell us that conscience is the work of prejudice; nevertheless I know by my experience that she insists on following the order of nature against every law of man.

Thus religion proceeds from the heart, from feeling, from conscience, from nature, as from a first and independent source. She has in view the satisfaction of the heart's requirements, the enfranchisement, the control, the ennoblement of our moral life: everything outside this principle and this end is not only superfluous but harmful.

To have upheld these ideas with clearness and decision, while forcibly affirming their opposition to received ideas, was already a work of importance. What made this work a revolution was the enthusiasm animating it, of which the language of Rousseau was the expression. His writings were his doctrine realised : it was nature, with its irresistible dash ; it was spontaneity, life, passion, faith, action, breaking in upon a literature in which mind was supreme, and compressing or bending to its ends logic, ideas, facts, arguments, all the instruments of intellectual culture.

From this conception of religion there resulted two remarkable consequences.

Brought back to feeling, as to a principle radically distinct from knowledge, absolute and original, religion had no longer to do with science. Science and religion spoke entirely different languages : they could, then, be expanded indefinitely without risk of ever meeting.

In the second place, feeling had to behave quite otherwise than reason towards the positive faiths. Reason tended to dry up religion, to deprive it of the elements which only find support in imagination and feeling, in order to reduce it to that small number of ideas which can be methodically inferred from the most assured scientific and philosophical research. Thence came Deism, that thin substitute for faith which philosophical rationalists were wont to offer.

But feeling has other needs, other resources, and other ventures. Seeing that it is quite as original as reason, perhaps more so, why should its expressions be limited to the formulæ approved by science ? By nature the heart is creative : its overflowing life is poured out in images, in thought-combinations, in myths and in poems. Set at the core of religion, and declared autonomous, feeling will not be able to rest content with such a legacy of rational deism as that in

which Rousseau had thought he recognised its genuine
expression. Genius cannot be content with repeating
ready - made phrases. The inorganic, in the living
person, is either eliminated or transformed, so as to
become living itself. Hence, not only will feeling, as
Rousseau conceives it, replace the congealed formulæ
of the philosophers by living productions; but it is
clear, from its advent, that, as regards traditional
forms and symbols—rich after a manner other than
that of philosophical concepts—it will not maintain
the systematic hostility reached by the rationalists.
These forms speak to the heart and to the imagination :
indeed, to this fact they owe their origin. Why should
the heart reject them without testing their efficacy ?
I confess to you, says the Savoyard vicar, that the
sanctity of the Gospel is an argument which speaks
to my heart, and one to which I should even be sorry
to find any good reply. Look at the books of the
philosophers with all their parade ; how small they
are in comparison with this. You compare Socrates,
his knowledge and his intellect. What a distance
from him to the son of Mary ! If the life and death
of Socrates betoken a sage, the life and death of
Jesus betoken a god.

The work of Rousseau could not, any more in
religion than in politics, in ethics, or in education,
claim finality : it was a starting-point. Some of the
ideas which inspired it were calculated to bring about
religious restoration.

The witness and herald *par excellence* of this restoration was the author of *Le Génie du Christianisme.*
Falling back upon the principle of Rousseau—the
sovereignty of feeling—Chateaubriand wins for
individual and social life, no longer only the vague

abstractions of the religion called natural, but the dogmas, rites and traditions of Catholicism, in their precise and concrete form. Far from his seeing in these particularities any frivolous overplus, under pretence that they are impossible to deduce from the principles of pure reason, it is every detail of the outside appearances, as well as the moral contents of religion, which becomes, with him, the proof of its divine origin, inasmuch as every detail strikes the imagination and the heart, charms, moves, consoles, soothes, strengthens, exalts the human conscience. To-day, says he, the way to be followed is that of going from effect to cause, and of proving, not any more that Christianity is excellent because it comes from God, but that it comes from God because it is excellent. The poetry of bells constitutes a stronger argument than a syllogism; it is felt and taken into life, while a syllogism leaves us indifferent.

But, one must ask, do all these beliefs, all these customs, so eloquently described as charming and beneficial in their results, correspond, at least, with true and existing objects; or are they only the vain satisfaction of our desires and dreams? It is clear that for the author of *Le Génie du Christianisme* this question is without interest. His exposition makes us love Christianity for the beauty of its worship, for the genius of its orators, for the virtues of its apostles and its disciples: what more is wanted? Is not love itself a reality, perhaps the truest and most profound of all realities? Why should the truth which is established through its agreement with the conditions of love, of life, of being, prove less true than that which is built on the abstractions of the understanding?

These ideas, more or less clearly conceived, controlled the movement which has been called Romanticism. Feeling is therein the one rule : life, the consciousness of living and feeling, is the aim that the superior man sets before himself. He shuns the abstractions which have interest only for the perfectly bare reason. He surrenders himself to poetry, to passion, to enthusiasm, these being the things that stir the soul. He loves suffering and tears, which exalt self-consciousness to a marvellous degree. He is interested in all the expressions of life that the literatures of sundry peoples and the history of sundry times can offer. He wants to resuscitate, to bring home to his own experience, the ways of thinking and feeling that belonged to vanished periods. He has a predilection for religion, which enlarges his soul through awakening and sustaining in it the haunting sense of infinity ; and, if he follows the bent of his imagination, he is disposed to be specially sympathetic towards the concrete and positive institutions of revealed religion.

In thus giving way to feeling, is he running the risk of putting himself in opposition to science ? The pure Romanticist ignores that problem. The scientist analyses and infers, whereas he, for his part, lives, believes and loves. How would it be possible for science to take away his very self ?

This conception of things has been shown, notably in France, in the turn that college studies and philosophy have taken. Under the respective names of Sciences and Humanities, the culture of taste, of sentiment, of soul on the one side, and the knowledge of mathematics and of the laws of nature on the other, were separated and isolated. Not only was literature self-sufficing, but it readily claimed for itself the pre-eminence, since man, the heart, life were deemed superior to nature and nature's mechanism.

On the other hand, philosophy, so closely united with the sciences for a Plato, a Descartes, a Leibnitz, became—as officially taught—exclusively literary and sentimentally inclined; admitting, with Chateaubriand, that the value of her doctrines should be gauged by their consequences, according to the salutary or harmful character of their influence. Generally reserved over matters religious, in so far as she hoped to maintain the classical point of view of reason, she was, in fact, driven in the direction of religion, betraying in that manner the substratum of Romantic sentimentalism which was hidden under her prudent rationalism.

This considerable revolution, which had become all-powerful after Rousseau, but had been born before him, through an awakening of the Hellenic sense of nature, in opposition to abstract ideology, was not peculiar to France : it manifested itself, under various aspects, in all the countries of Europe. It seemed especially original and fruitful in German Romanticism; the motto—if one may say so—of this last-named movement was the saying of Novalis : *Die Poesie ist das ächt absolut Reelle* (Poetry is absolute truth).

Since the beginning of the nineteenth century, the romantic principle was placed at the very heart of religion by the great theologian Schleiermacher. Neither the intellect, nor the will, according to Schleiermacher, can bring us into the religious sphere. Religion is neither an act of knowledge nor a rule : it is a life, it is an experience ; and this life has its source in the deepest part of our being, viz. feeling. We cannot proceed through knowledge of religion to religion; this latter is an original fact.

The man who experiences religious emotion tends, besides, to make clear to himself, through his intellect, the nature and reason of his state of soul; and he finds that his feeling expresses, at bottom, the absolute dependence of the creature with regard to the Infinite Cause of the universe. In the development, in the spontaneous brilliancy of this feeling, is constituted the religious life. It has in view the exalting of individuality—what neither science nor morality could bring about. It tends to express itself, not through adequate ideas (that is impossible), but through symbols which can represent it in consciousness and make it yield communicable emotions. What is called dogma is nothing but an intellectual representation of the object or cause of these emotions. Sometimes the heart, enriching the intellect, creates symbols immediately by the power of genius; sometimes it makes use of the symbols offered by existing religions. But these same symbols it does not receive passively, it infuses life into them: it preserves for them, in that way, a religious character. Traditions, dogmas have only meaning, have only value, if they are constantly revivified by the feeling of individuals.

No obstacle, moreover, can be opposed by science to the creation or adoption of this or that religious symbol. Science herself is only a method of symbolical representation. She expresses in signs the endeavour of the mind to understand things, *i.e.* to perceive the identity of being and thought—an ideal which is for us unrealisable.

In short, with Schleiermacher, being excels knowing.

D

Truth is hand and glove with life ; the exaltation
of the superior life, of the life of the soul and of
feeling, is the highest truth of all. All that which
is formula, dogma, letter, thing, matter, has only
value as symbol of this super-intellectual truth.

More metaphysical in Germany, more literary in
France, the conception of religion corresponding to
Romanticism became the prevailing one in the course
of the nineteenth century. Religion, during that time,
rested essentially, not on the intellect, but on the
heart ; she had her principles, her arguments, her
works, which obtruded themselves on reason in the
name of a transcendent authority. Doubtless, there
were not wanting apologists of religion who caught
up again the rusty weapons of the great seventeenth-
century rationalists, or who endeavoured to forge
these anew, in order that they themselves, also,
might attack, in the name of reason, the adversaries
who invoked her. But life was on the side of those
who, without caring for science and independent of
reason, without anxiety for alliance with philosophy
and with temporal powers, unfolded religious truth
in all its originality and all its amplitude. What
flourished was free religion, based on its own special
sanctions—the heart, faith, tradition, and labouring
towards the development and exaltation of spiritual
forces.

On her side, Science had become accustomed to
ignore Religion. More and more distinctly did she
consider herself as resting on objective experience
entirely, and as having no other object than the
discovery of the immanent connections of phenomena.
What mattered to her those doctrines founded on

another principle and aiming at quite different ends?
The two points of view could exist in the mind of even
the same individual; they did not mingle at all. In
entering his laboratory, the scientist left his religious
convictions at the door, though he might take them
up again on leaving.

To sum up, the relation between Religion and
Science which had established itself in the course of
the nineteenth century was a radical dualism. Science
and Religion were no longer two expressions (analogous
in spite of their unequal value) of one and the same
object, viz. Divine Reason, as they were formerly in
Greek philosophy; they were no longer two given
truths between which the agreement was demonstrable, as with the Schoolmen; Science and Religion
had no longer, as with the modern rationalists, a
common surety—reason: each of them absolute in its
own way, they were distinct at every point, as were
distinct, according to the reigning psychology, the two
faculties of the soul, intellect and feeling, to which,
respectively, they corresponded. Thanks to this
mutual independence, they could find themselves in
one and the same consciousness; they existed there,
the one beside the other, like two material, impenetrable atoms placed side by side in space. They had
come to an understanding, explicitly or tacitly, in order
to abstain from scrutinising one another's principles.
Mutual respect for the positions achieved, and on that
very account, for each, security and liberty—such was
the device of the period.

PART I

THE NATURALISTIC TENDENCY

CHAPTER I

THE encounter henceforth inevitable.

There can be nothing clearer or more convenient
for the purpose of setting one's ideas in order and for
conducting an abstract discussion, than precise definitions and inviolable lines of demarcation. Shut up
respectively in the heart and in the intellect, as if in
the two separate compartments of a bulkhead, science
and religion had no chance of entering into conflict.
Enough that each of them allowed to the other the
liberty which was claimed and enjoyed by itself.
In this way the problem of the relation between
science and religion was solved, very easily, in the

world of concepts. It was quite another matter in
the real world.

In fact, neither science nor religion meant to limit
its competency and action, however big the province
assigned to it. The postulate of the maxim held in
honour at this time—"Render to Cæsar that which
is Cæsar's, and to God that which is God's"—was, in
the special sense given to it, not only that, in man,
the religious faculties have nothing in common with
the scientific faculties, but that in things themselves
there are two worlds, spirit and matter, a spiritual
province and a temporal province, which nowhere
clash. Now, this hypothesis may be a useful compromise ; it is not reality as given, it is nearly the
contrary of that reality. Where do we find, in man,
the dividing line between heart and intellect ; in
nature, the demarcation between bodies and souls ?
Hence it came about that religion, all the more eager
for expansion because she was declared independent,
found herself confined to the sanctuary of conscience,
and strove to conquer the visible world. And, on
the other hand, science, emboldened by her successes,
which were every day more striking, and by the ever-
increasing consciousness of her object and method,
proclaimed that the entire world of reality, in all its
parts, was henceforth open to her investigation, provided that she advanced by rule, in going, according
to the precept of Descartes, from the simple to the
compound, from the easy to the difficult, from that
which is immediately cognisable to that which we can
only reach mediately.

From that time the conflict, so skilfully set aside
in theory, was inevitable in practice. If religion
claims to rule over body and soul alike, and science

over soul and body alike, they are bound to come into collision, and the question of knowing how to settle the quarrel obtrudes itself.

Many, doubtless, will persist in thinking that the simplest way still is to maintain, by mutual discretion, a compromise which leads to peace; and, declaring that they themselves slumber very well on the soft pillow of indifference, they will complain of the noise that is being made on all sides, and threatening to wake them. There will remain others, who, pleading the intellectual superiority of a St. Thomas, a Descartes, a Malebranche, a Leibnitz, will ask why we should no longer fall back on the arguments that satisfied those thinkers, and will blame the progress of an unrestrained criticism for the grievous disrepute into which the classic compromises have fallen. But the human mind, considered in its permanence throughout the ages, is not to be confounded with the mental characteristics of such and such individuals, be these ever so numerous, and remarkable for learning and ability. The mind is a co-ordination, therefore a comparing of the sundry ideas that experience brings; it is an endeavour to establish agreement or harmony between them, either by the adaptation of some to others, or by the elimination of these for the benefit of those. That is why, when science and religion face one another, the mind is necessarily bound, sooner or later, to compare them, in order to know if it can, without contradicting itself, keep them together in some way, or if it must decide on rejecting the one so as to preserve the other.

And, in this reflection which obtrudes itself, it is clear that the mind can be inspired by such and such a doctrine formerly professed by a great intellect; but, in being thus inspired, it cannot revive the doctrine purely and simply, since it is quite unlikely that there will not be, in the phenomena sprung from great revolutions, any new element calling for change of attitude.

This sense of a necessary encounter between science and religion is generally found among the thinkers who applied themselves to these subjects from about the fourth decade of the nineteenth century. They may be divided into two classes, according as they show rather a naturalistic or a spiritualistic tendency. At the head of the first we place Auguste Comte.

I

THE DOCTRINE OF AUGUSTE COMTE ON SCIENCE AND RELIGION

The system of Auguste Comte consists in a methodical advance from science to religion by way of philosophy. The method according to which this advance is accomplished, and which determines the meaning and value of the conclusions, is called by Comte positive; and the system itself, more especially its religious culmination, receives from him the name of Positivism. This term signifies : firstly, that Comte aims at satisfying the real needs of the human spirit, and those only ; secondly, that he allows as sole means toward this satisfaction, a knowledge equally real, *i.e.* relative to facts that, in respect of human intelligence, are at once true and accessible—a knowledge which, itself, ought to be adapted to our genuine needs.

Utility and reality—these two words exhaust the contents of the term " positive."

From these two aspects, moreover, there follows a third—the organic aspect. For human knowledge and feeling, incapable of any fixed organisation so long as they are not submitted to their true standard, will form a definitive system, from the time of their being referred to an end that can be taken as both one and incontestable.

.   .   .   .   .   .

Of the two essential elements of a positive notion, the real and the useful, the first is found in science, and in it alone. Theology and metaphysics, which claim, in their turn, to make known to us the nature of things, are delusive methods. Science will, therefore, be the basis of positivism ; and, to enable us to systematise and turn to account all that is within our reach, positivism will insist on our viewing the whole of what is given in such a way as to comply with the limits of science properly so called.

As a matter of fact, human knowledge is far from presenting wholly, even now, the scientific form. If mathematics, astronomy, physics, chemistry are veritable sciences, biology scarcely begins to break loose from the swaddling bands of metaphysics ; the study of specifically human phenomena is still abandoned to scholars and historians—strangers to the idea of science.

The first need of all, then, is that of determining the idea of science, and of seeing how this idea can be applied to all the branches of human knowledge.

The method which Auguste Comte here follows is very remarkable. He proceeds from the concrete to the concrete, and not from an abstract principle laid down *a priori* in advance of its dialectical consequences. He starts, not from logic—the science of concepts—but from mathematics, real science as constituted here and now.

He will begin by determining the distinctive marks which constitute mathematics a science. Then he will set before himself the task, not of imposing these marks upon all other branches of knowledge, but of adapting them, by proper modifications and without impairing their essence, to the variety of objects that come under experience. It is this adaptation that he calls generalisation, extension. The same intellectual form will recur in all our knowledge, *mutatis mutandis*, and science will be both one and manifold.

Now, the science of mathematics, according to Auguste Comte, owes its definite form to the exclusive search after positive laws, *i.e.* after precise and unchangeable relations between given conditions. This, then, is the object, duly determined, which ought to be assigned to all kinds of knowledge. It is a determination which is reached : firstly, through seeking, in the thing to be known, an aspect which will enable us to range it under the laws of science ; secondly, through conceiving these laws themselves in a manner that accords with the proper nature of the object to be known.

Following these principles, Comte defines the form adapted to each order of science, and ends with the theory of a new science, called sociology, which will be to moral and social facts what physics and chemistry are to the phenomena of inorganic nature.

As regards sciences already in existence, he prescribes formulæ that carry an important philosophical meaning.

In physics there should be complete rejection of everything resembling those unverified influences to which appeal was long made for fantastic explanations. For the purposes of a real science, only the phenomenal conditions of visible phenomena need be specified.

Biology presents, in comparison with the physico-chemical sciences, a capital difference. The laws that she studies are the mutual relations of functions and of organs. In order to discover these laws, there is need, most certainly, for discarding the metaphysical hypothesis of vital spontaneity, and for considering vital phenomena as subjected to the general laws of matter, of which they present only simple modifications. But, on the other hand, we must guard against making biology the slave of the inorganic sciences. In the inorganic sciences the mind proceeds from the simple to the compound. The argument to be deduced from this example is, not that the whole of science ought necessarily to proceed in this manner, but that, in the category of phenomena considered by these sciences, the simple is more accessible than the compound, is known to us before the compound. But when living beings are in question, it is the contrary that takes place. Here the whole is more accessible to us and better known than the parts. While the idea of the universe can never become positive, seeing that the universe will always exceed our means of observation, in biology, on the contrary, it is the details which keep out of reach : beings that have life are the more easily known because they are more complex and more exalted. The animal idea is clearer than the vegetable idea, and the idea of man is clearer than that of

other animals ; so that the notion of man, for us the
only immediate one, is the point of departure requisite
in all biology. Thus, while the physical sciences
advance from the parts to the whole, biology, for the
very purpose of remaining, like the physical sciences,
a positive science, must proceed from the whole to the
details.

If the positive method has had to be submitted to
such a modification in order to conform to the conditions of the biological sciences, there need be no cause
for astonishment that, before we can enter upon the
study of moral and social facts, still greater modifications have to be made in it. The method will remain
positive, in spite of these modifications, should it prove
really effectual in enabling us to penetrate, through
the apparent disorder and the apparent spontaneity
of social and human life, to relations that are consistent
with the idea of natural law.

And, moreover, since society is a consensus or
solidarity, after the manner of the living body, the
same modification of method will be needed in regard
to it as obtained in the case of biology, and we shall
proceed from the whole to the parts. But the whole,
in sociology, will no longer be the individual, who, on
the contrary, is here only a member or part : it will be
society, and, in the highest classification, humanity.
The first theme in the study of human facts from the
scientific standpoint is the theme of collective facts.

That is not all. A distinction which needs to be
made in every science, but which, in the inferior
sciences, has only a secondary meaning, becomes here
important : that between statics and dynamics. On
the side of statics we study the consensus or social
organism as it is related to the conditions of its

existence, and reach the theory of order. On the side of dynamics we reduce to law all that is implied in progress—the human phenomenon *par excellence.*

Proceeding from the whole to the details, and following the method of social dynamics, we shall first of all determine the general progress of humanity. We shall employ, with that end in view, an appropriate mode of observation : the study of general history. This study scrutinises human facts under their collective aspect : those alone which are observable from the outside, those alone which are facts in the exact meaning of the word ; and, from the consideration of these facts, it extricates the general traits which characterise the different periods. By itself, however, general history would not suffice as the foundation of sociology. But, combined with the knowledge of fundamental and permanent tendencies innate in human nature, it will furnish those dynamic laws that require to be determined.

Auguste Comte, in this respect, does not reason merely as a theorist. He considers that he has discovered, in what he calls the law of the three stages, how to know—in the necessary succession of the Theological stage, the Metaphysical stage, and the Positive stage—the fundamental law of human progress ; and thence he infers *ab actu ad posse.*

In this way, when the notion of science has been at the same time determined in its principle and adapted to the diversity of the objects to be known, everything that is accessible, everything that is, for us, really existent can become the subject-matter of science.

. . . . .

But Positivism does not seek the real merely to attain the useful. How are we, with the help of the real knowledge furnished us by the sciences, to reach a stage of truly positive knowledge?

At this point the genuine rôle of philosophy begins. In order that the search after the real may coincide with that after the useful, philosophy must define the useful, and bring science to bear upon it; for the latter, left to herself, would not undergo the necessary discipline. .

In a general manner, the special end pursued by humanity is coherence, harmony, unity of conception and will. At the present time, Auguste Comte considers, this harmony, which was previously assured by the Church's rule, has been disturbed by the Revolution, and the object now to be sought is the regeneration of society through the establishment of a new system of co-ordination—immovable and definitive. The mistake which dogs us, lies in believing that we can re-establish this harmony immediately by means of political or religious institutions. Institutions are, indeed, essential, but these institutions must have a foundation; and the idea of the end to be reached, the practical idea pure and simple, is an insufficient foundation. Mere doing does not suffice in itself. We miss our aim when we make pretence of rushing straight away in its pursuit, without preliminary study of the means to be employed, without initiation. Art for art's sake is a chimera, theory for the sake of theory is vanity : what really counts is art for the sake of theory.

At this point the intervention of philosophy becomes necessary. If practical life were sufficient, the work of social regeneration would belong altogether to politics. If science, by itself, were competent, we could hand over the business of governing society to the scientists. But, both these hypotheses being equally false, we ought to institute a special investigation, in order to determine the conditions of the passage from knowledge to action. This investigation is the concern of science. The doctrine is of first importance for Auguste Comte, who, in virtue of it, believes that he can re-establish, for the welfare of humanity, the double character (at once theoretical and practical) of ancient wisdom.

The idea that, according to Comte, philosophy brings just here, is the vanity of looking for the moral and political convergence of human sentiment and action, unless we have previously realised logical coherence in thought and character. Intellectual unity is the condition of moral unity. The useful is, therefore, before all else, the realisation of intellectual unity. To establish this unity is, in a special sense, the task of philosophy.

Constituted quite uniformly according to the positive idea of natural law, the sciences possess a certain homogeneity, which might incline us to believe in their possible unification on the scientific field itself. But such an inference contains a dangerous fallacy. Analogous in their methods, the sciences are, for us, insurmountably separated from one another as regards their object. The very necessity of their resting satisfied, as regards method, with analogy, while renouncing identity, has its origin in an irreducible difference of subject-matter. One, in the sense of being a need of the human mind, science is perforce multiple and diverse in its realisation. It cannot be helped, but there is no purely one thing that we can

E

call Science.   There are, and there always will be
only sciences, the six fundamental sciences which the
Cours de philosophie positive has specified.

To rely on the scientists for the labour of procuring
the intellectual unity of mankind is, then, impossible.
So far as they are scientists, they exhibit tendencies
which run counter to this superior aim.   They affect
specialisation, parcelling out reality, and ignoring or
despising one another.   Or, yet again, deeming that
his own branch of learning is science *par excellence*,
each of them claims to impose his method, such as it
is, on all the other sciences.   That is the case with
mathematicians : infatuated by the success that they
have gained in their own domain, through proceeding
from the parts to the whole, they would like to
transfer their materialistic standpoint to biology and
sociology, whereas these sciences ought, on the contrary, to proceed from the whole to the parts.   The
mathematical mind — at once anarchical, narrow,
encroaching, and despotic — is the worst plague of
humanity.

Furthermore, the scientists have a tendency to
cultivate science for its own sake ; to go into raptures
over the ingenuity of their discoveries, even when these
cannot serve any purpose ; to search after a childish
accuracy in insignificant matters ; and to apply themselves, for the sake of showing off their virtuosity as
dilettanti, to innumerable factitious problems.

For all these reasons, science, or rather the sciences,
cannot be organised by themselves ; they must be
regulated by thought from the outside.

The immediate and objective synthesis of the
sciences being impossible, there remains for trial a
subjective synthesis, a synthesis effected, not from

the standpoint of things, but from the standpoint of man, who, with the help of the sciences, pursues his own ends. Now the science constituted last of all, viz. that just created by Auguste Comte, furnishes, he believes, the elements of this synthesis.

For the accomplishment of this work, sociology learns, through the example of theology in bygone times, how to unite minds by means of a subjective principle. But this principle was furnished by the imagination. What we have now to do is to resume the work of the theologians, at the same time trusting entirely to facts and to reason.

The principle of organisation will be the sociological notion *par excellence*—the notion of humanity. Humanity, in the spatial sense, exists only in its parts which are actual individuals ; but, regarded as a whole subsisting in time, it goes beyond its manifestation in space.

While the generalisation of the idea of science proceeded necessarily from the simplest sciences to the most complex, the organisation of the sciences ought to descend from sociology to the sciences of private life.

Social facts are, first of all, systematised through the notion of humanity. Scattered in space, they are all bound together by means of a special reference —the reference of connection or solidarity between the past, the present and the future. The connection between human events proceeds from two causes— external and internal. The external cause is that transmission of human attainment from generation to generation, which we call tradition ; the internal cause is our common instinct for improvement. The idea of progress by means of preservation and order, is the principle of the systematisation of social phenomena.

Again, this same idea can be employed in training, gradually, the inferior sciences. They also should take human happiness as their end and standard. They ought never to forget that they are made by man and for man. They will, therefore, set aside all speculation which is not calculated to improve the human lot, which is not human in its object. They will not bring to their examination of the laws of nature the curiosity of a mere amateur. Their motto will be : taking prevision for the sake of making provision.

Not only will they be altogether adjusted with a view to social welfare, but the special relation of end to means will be established between them. Each superior science will determine the problems that ought to be discussed by the inferior sciences, and the extent to which research may be carried on with advantage. In return, the laws established by the inferior sciences will be applied unrestrictedly to the superior, the irreducible peculiarity of the latter having for ground and condition of existence the very laws that are surpassed and supplemented.

It is in this way that natural laws will be determined in an entirely positive sense, i.e. from the standpoint of utility and reality. The relativity which critical philosophy has imposed on human knowledge will be maintained, moreover, not in the sense (negative and useless) that one phenomenon is conditioned by another, but in the positive sense that every kind of knowledge is relative to man, and only possesses meaning as instrument, immediate or remote, of his improvement. The consequences issuing from this doctrine are considerable : the science of mathematics, which some of us wished to make the royal science, falls to the lowest rank in the scale of our knowledge.

Such is the organisation of the sciences on which sociology is based. This organisation realises mental coherence, intellectual unity, without which the re-generation of society is impossible.

The sphere of philosophy extends as far as this. Can we be satisfied, then, with having reached intellectual unity, if moral and political unity are produced therefrom; or must we, in order to ensure the realisation of this supreme unity, furnish man with new resources, and make appeal to powers of another kind?

.   .   .   .   .   .

Philosophy, in her work of synthesis, while making use of the data that the sciences provided, has not concerned herself about these data themselves. She has found in sociology the principle of a systematisa-tion of the sciences, through which intellectual unity among men could be realised. She had not to inquire, on account of the work that she had in view, how it comes about that society exists, or what may be the nature of its scope and its principle. This inquiry, nevertheless, obtrudes itself before the man who wishes, effectively and not only in the way of theory, to regenerate society. The sciences furnish materials, philosophy regulates these materials. But the whole of this work remains abstract and conditional. Who can satisfy us that society, just as science imagines it, will exist and continue to be upheld?

History shows us realised communities. What has produced them? Can we point to either science or philosophy? Observation shows us that religion is the agent. It is to the persistent action of religion that sociology owes both its aim and its *raison d'être*. Will this aim subsist if religion disappears? When the cause has been removed, will the effect remain intact?

Let us consider human nature. The intellect, in its working there, cannot create or preserve the social bond. The cleverest of all the intellectual associations can only organise egoism and isolation. In a general way the intellect can do no more than regulate and systematise: it is unable to produce. That which creates is the heart. The heart is bound to be mentioned if we are to account for such a supreme creation as that of the social organism.

And the heart can never be confounded with instinct, with nature, with fact pure and simple. For it is a trait of the human nature immediately given to us, that its less exalted and more selfish instincts prevail over the nobler impulses of sympathy and altruism. Doubtless these impulses exist originally, even as the selfish instinct itself; but they get, from this instinct, neither energy nor perseverance. Now, it is the sympathetic affections which alone can engender and sustain the social state, through restraining the divergent promptings of individual instincts.

The existence of communities is, therefore, tied down to a state of things that neither instinct nor intellect can realise. It is a question of finding, for the sympathetic impulse in man, something that will help to strengthen it and render it superior to the selfish instinct. Help of this kind has, in the past, been procured for it by the various religions. They have, in their own way, made union of hearts a condition of intellectual union. The human subsoil of these ancient institutions ought to be taken up and preserved, even if the dogmas through which they were expressed are condemned to vanish. Religion, then, after being herself regenerated, will furnish the first principle of the regeneration of society.

The method to be followed in effecting this restoration is to disentangle, from the negative and decaying elements contained in the traditional religions, the positive, human, indestructible element of which they were the vehicle. In this way we shall consummate Positivism which reaches its culminating point in Positive Religion.

The whole teaching of religion is summed up in two dogmas : God and Immortality. What is the positive content of these two dogmas ?

The idea of God, so far as it interprets the real need of man, is the idea of a universal being, boundless and eternal, with whom human souls communicate : a being who inspires them with strength to overcome their selfish and divergent impulses in order that they may tend to harmonise and be united in him.

The positive idea of Immortality is the ascription of a share in the eternal life of the divine being to the righteous : i.e. to those who, already in this life, have shown towards God and their fellow-men a love that is real and efficacious.

Now, Positivism has no difficulty in finding a double object, real and accessible, for the satisfaction of these conditions. This object is not far from us, it is near and actually in us : it is nothing else than Humanity.

Humanity has often been conceived as a simple universal notion : in such a case it is the abstraction

of the Schoolmen, an empty and inert form. We
are still able to understand by Humanity the collection of actually existing men. In this sense it is a
reality ; but how can it prevail over actual individuals
to the extent of declaring the God and the Immortality
that they crave.

But Humanity, as presented to us in all its breadth,
differs altogether from a scholastic abstraction or a
spatial collection. Humanity is a continuity and a
solidarity in time. It is made up of all that men have
felt, thought and accomplished in respect of what is
good, noble, eternal. It is the supra-spatial being
in which the uncertain and transitory strivings of the
individual are brought to rest through purification
and organisation—in which immortal life and tutelary
influence are manifested.

Humanity, thus understood, is itself the God that
men demand : the real being, boundless and eternal,
with which they are in immediate relation, in
which they have being, movement, life. From the
reservoir of moral forces accumulated within this
being throughout the centuries are poured out great
thoughts and noble sentiments. Humanity is the
Great Being that raises us above ourselves, that
imparts to our sympathetic impulses the fulness of
power needed for their rule over selfish impulses.
In Humanity men love one another and enter into
communion.

So, in Humanity, individuals are able to enjoy,
in very truth, the immortality for which they long.
For therein is gathered, preserved and incorporated everything that is conformable to its essence,
everything that is calculated to render it greater,
more beautiful, more powerful. It is nothing but the

thoughts and sentiments of real men, and is more largely composed of the dead than of the living. As to the dead, they live in the remembrance of the actual generations—a remembrance that is stirring, vivid, and efficacious ; their influence is shown in the noble emulation which they never cease to arouse amongst the living, inciting these to render themselves deserving of reunion with their grandsires.

It is true that we cannot conceive of this God as personal, or of this immortality as objective. Positivism resents as imaginary the dogmas of the so-called revealed religions. But how does that injure religion in the true sense? What is a God who is limited, selfish, transcendent, capricious, in comparison with Humanity which is all in all, immanent, and, in its sublimity, truly one with the humblest? How can material persistence in space be compared with this survival in time and in consciousness which alone realises that dearest longing of the human heart—the union of souls in eternity?

If there is a religion which satisfies, in a sure and definitive fashion, the irreducible and indispensable religious instinct of human nature, it is Positivism or the Religion of Humanity.

This religion is not an abstraction, but a life : it is the positive development of altruism and love. But the method to be followed, in order to practise this religion effectively, is of capital importance. The older religions have had love, in like manner, for their object ; nevertheless, under their traditional form, they are doomed. The truth is, no institution can live which does not respect the law underlying the conditions of existence. Now, just as philosophy, in order to be positive and stable, must be preceded by science whence she receives the very subject-matter which it is her mission to organise, so religion, in order to be indestructible, must depend upon science and philosophy. It is in the real and rational world that the proper work of religion lies : therein will she look for the conditions of her action.

She will proceed, in the same way as science and philosophy, from the concrete to the concrete, and not from the abstract to the concrete. Away, then, with that banal philanthropy which has no motive power beyond the abstract and vague idea of mankind, an idle academic entity from which positivism has extricated us. Humanity, as an *a priori* supposition, would be nothing but a metaphysical principle, egoistic and revolutionary—one that would tend, in its application, to destroy those partial yet concrete expressions of humanity which the theological age had shown merit in realising.

Love cannot be communicated through an idea. It originates in personal relationship, and, singularly, in the relationship between man and woman. It is from this relationship that we must start, if we would see a living and efficacious love awakened and developed in the soul, and not be content with the mere concept of love, *i.e.* with a wretched logical abstraction. As the generalisation of the idea of science is accomplished through extending to the unframed sciences (saving the requisite corrections) the distinctive marks of the sciences already constructed ; as the philosophical organisation of the sciences is brought about through starting from sociology, the science immediately available, and through again descending the ladder of the sciences, considered as means with reference to the social end :

so love, originating—according to the law of nature
—in the relationship of the sexes, will become wider
by degrees and be made universal. And this will be
effected under quite real conditions, if, setting out
from its first object, it is directed, successively and
methodically, towards those increasingly wide and
complex objects which our universe provides for it.
Now there are four essential stages through which love
ought to pass in order to be realised in all its breadth
and all its power; these are individual relationship,
family, country, and humanity.

When, after surmounting the initiatory grades, we
come, in this way, to love Humanity with a love which
is at once very exalted and very real, then, and then
only, the Great Being lives in us, controls and governs
our existence. And under the irresistible influence
of this sovereign power our nature is transformed,
altruism prevailing over selfishness. In turning
Godward, our love for our fellows becomes practical
instead of theoretical, spontaneous instead of forced.
Our hearts are knit in God.

. . . .

Since, when love is in question, the reality is
everything and pure theory insignificant, we ought
not to overlook anything that can help to engender
and develop that reality. Now, it is not in vain
that the traditional religions have laid feeling and
imagination under contribution in the human soul.
Feeling and imagination are the motive powers of the
soul. They make it vibrate and live, while ideas only
affect it superficially. The mistake of the theologians
was that, lacking a theory of the real, they took the
fictions of the imagination for realities. But the man
who is firmly established in the impregnable strong-

hold of true science and true philosophy has no longer
to distrust imagination. He can restore to it a rôle
that the anxious metaphysician did not dare openly
to attribute to it. Fiction is no longer delusive when
we know that it *is* fiction, and when we are prepared
to restrain it, as soon as it is tempted to supplant
reality. And man is so constituted that fictions,
which are understood as fictions, have no less virtue
for him than those which are received as truths.
The imagination does not demand truth, but that we
should throw ourselves into things ; and, once moved
by agreeable representations, it communicates its
glowing intensity to heart and will.

Positivism, then, after having proscribed dogmas
in so far as they gave themselves out as truths,
will not shrink from reviving imaginative fetichism
as a practical auxiliary, subordinate to the rational
principle of religion. It will revive it as an aid
(conformable to human nature) towards producing
that concrete and effective systematisation of feelings,
without which the total synthesis needed for the
regeneration of society remains a simple idea.

The fetichism that Comte re-establishes will be,
in fact, purely poetical. It will consist in endowing,
under cover of hypothesis, the given types of natural
existence with active and beneficial wills—with wills,
that is, analogous to our own. Man feels himself too
isolated as long as nature is regarded merely as the
expression of laws that are blind and inevitable. In
order that he may act fervently and joyously, he
requires to consider himself as surrounded by friends
who understand and support him. It is, therefore,
expedient that he should imagine, under the forces
of nature, beings analogous to himself who sympathise

with him. For the perfecting of law, wills are necessary.

That is why the positivist's worship will not have to do only with the memory of the heroes of humanity. Its essential objects will be: the Great Being or Humanity, the Great Fetich or the Earth, and the Great Medium or Space. These three hypostases will constitute the Trinity of the positivist. And thus it will be possible for every natural law to be legitimately symbolised by a kind of pagan deity, calculated to interest the imagination.

II

THE INTERPRETATION OF THE DOCTRINE

Such is the doctrine of Auguste Comte in regard to the relations between science and religion. There is the reverse of agreement over the meaning of this doctrine.

Numerous interpreters deem that we ought to allow for what is not doctrine in the strict sense, but the expression of the man's own intimate and accidental feeling: that, if we rightly take away this element of anecdote, there remains, eventually, of the religion of Comte only what was already in his sociology: viz. man, more precisely, social man, as the measure and rule of human knowledge.

Others, deeming that the religious doctrines and institutions hold, in point of fact, a very large place in the achievement of Comte, and are, in themselves, clearly distinct from the strictly philosophical theories, acknowledge the special meaning that he has attributed to religion, but deny that his religious doctrine is connected logically with his philosophical doctrine.

. . . . . .

Does the religious part of Comte's work, when we compare it with the sociology, bring forward any principle that is really new ?

We will not allow ourselves, declare some, to be misled by words. Auguste Comte is speaking of the subjective, of feeling, of the heart, of morality, of eternity, of religion. In fact, it is only a question, in these theories, of mystical appearance, of the necessary predominance of the social and human standpoint in scientific research and in life. Believing that, from the point of view of things—from the objective point of view, the systematisation of the sciences is impossible, Comte describes as subjective the point of view which he recommends : it consists in organising the sciences for man's profit, *i.e.* it is a purely human point of view.

In like manner, what he calls the heart is only a traditional word, used to designate social feeling, the love of others, in opposition to self-love. The metaphysicians, according to Comte, have discredited reason, through identifying it with individual specu-lation. He, for his part, is going to employ the word heart (usually contrasted with reason) in order to denote the social point of view as distinct from that point of view which is metaphysical. And this subordination of the mind to the heart will not signify anything, in his case, unless it be the obliga-tion to base scientific research on social utility, under the influence of the social sentiment.

If this were so, the leap that Comte appears to take, in passing from philosophy to ethics and to religion, would not exist : there would, in reality, be nothing more in his ethics and in his religion than in his sociology.

Does this interpretation agree with the philosopher's own thought ?

The question would be quickly settled if we were really anxious to attach any value to the declarations of Comte himself. For he has told us, with all the vigour and insistence in his power, that from 1845 he discusses things under another aspect, following a new method—the reverse of the first. He speaks in many a place of his sentimental evolution, of his moral regeneration, of his second existence. He distinguishes, from the positive philosophy which was but preliminary, the positivism or religion of Humanity, which alone comprehends all the elements of social regeneration.

But, it may be said, his testimony is open to suspicion. In 1844-45 he met with Clotilde de Vaux, and the stormy passion then working in his heart was enough to unhinge his judgment. Moreover, he had been insane, and continued subject to relapses. His sickness took the precise form of a profound sentimental disorder. Self-deception was possible over the actual share of sentiment in the development of his philosophical thought.

We must, therefore, examine separately the different elements of the doctrine, and compare them.

If we look at the conclusions of the *Cours de philosophie positive*, we see therein the positive method presented as tending essentially to exalt the meaning of the whole over any partial meaning.[1] And, in accordance with this principle, the human

---

[1] Fifty-seventh lecture.

individual is treated as an abstraction pure and simple. Metaphysics constitutes the apotheosis of individualism; for, in giving the individual a higher reality, it consecrates and uplifts the egoism of the natural man. The Positive philosophy regards Humanity as the only real, especially in the intellectual and moral order.[1]

Thus do we find the matter stated in the *Cours de philosophie positive*. The language of the *Système de politique positive* is very different.

Comte is seeking therein the conditions which are to guarantee the persistent influence of the great servants of humanity. Vanished from the world of space, they yet maintain an existence in time. In this sense they form a veritable being that is continually augmented in proportion as new members of the elect press forward in their phalanx. But here we must avoid falling into the ontological aberration. Temporal or subjective existence is not sufficient. Each organ of the Supreme Being implies, of necessity, an objective and spatial existence. Man, therefore, gives support to Humanity, during his actual life, before serving as her organ after his death. We ourselves, in the act of living with our dead, keep them in existence. Their superior dignity does not exempt them from the need of our worship in order to become concrete after a fashion. The individual, indeed, is only of value in so far as he resembles the Great Being. But he is, himself, the actual depositary of existence, and, in virtue of this, something that is needful to the eternal.

Even in its subjective existence, the Supreme Being cannot be simply regarded as universal and impersonal.

---

[1] Fifty-eighth lecture.

For, in reality, it acts directly by means of objective organs alone : and these organs are the individual beings who have done best service in becoming, after their spatial existence, our world's legitimate representatives. The worship of certain individuals, of heroes, forms thus an essential part of the worship of Humanity.

In short, as, according to this view, these superior men constitute a certain personification of the Great Being, they are deserving of homage, in the literal sense even, provided that, in our thought, we set aside the imperfections which, too often, impair the best natures in this world.[1]

The new element that the religious doctrine introduces at this point, is manifest. The individual, after being debased by the positive philosophy, is exalted by Positivism or positive religion. He now plays a part indispensable as the condition of objective existence, of efficacious action and of development, to that Great Being which the sociology was content to imagine as abstract idea.

From this point, the terms subjective, moral, heart, religion, fully comprise, in their religious meaning, the notions that were lacking in the sociology.

The sociology was kept within the limits of proving that, without the preponderance of the affective faculties over the intellectual faculties, the notion of the social organism would be unintelligible. Wherein lay the reason of this preponderance ? Was it realisable, and, once realised, could it be maintained in a sure manner ? The sociology ignored these questions altogether.

We understand, now, that the heart possesses an

---

[1] *Syst. de pol. posit.*, *Statique sociale*, chap. i.

F

instinct called the religious instinct, in virtue of which the individual is able to live with the dead, and to assimilate their excellences; thus it is that he (the individual) becomes capable of overcoming his egoism and of gaining a living experience of the social sentiment. The sociology was only the abstract conception of the social bond, while religion is its realisation. Religion alone exhibits, in individuals, the conversion which is needed to make them the genuine props of a society which only exists in them and by them.

.   .   .   .   .   .

It appears, then, only right to admit the contention of Auguste Comte: his religious theory, compared with his philosophy properly so called, introduces something that is new and different. But another difficulty is now presented to us. Far from exaggerating, in his assertions, the originality of his religious doctrine, may not Comte have been too much in the right? Would not this very doctrine differ from his philosophy, just as, in reality, it had no sort of connection with the latter, but contradicted it outright—returning, finally, to those same theological and anthropomorphic tenets that the positive philosophy had irreversibly condemned?

If we compare the doctrines, the principles, the general tendencies of thought to be found in the earlier and later writings of Auguste Comte, we can easily gain the impression that the relation between philosophy and religion is, for him, no mere difference, but a decided opposition. On one side, the method of the intellect, and on the other, the method of the heart : there a scrupulous anxiety for demonstration, for the realisation of the idea of science : here inspiration, intuition, the immediate knowledge of the mystic;

there, regard for life, for action, for social profit : here
the heart set up as manager-in-chief of human affairs ;
love, not only distinguished from thought and action,
but placed above them.

Moreover, some one may urge, it is very difficult
to avoid looking upon these differences as the sign
of a veritable revolution, when it is noted that they
were put forward at the very time of that sentimental
occurrence which, on his own confession, unsettled
Comte entirely, viz. the meeting with Clotilde de
Vaux.[1] The sudden influence of his unhealthy love
for this insignificant woman, henceforth the preponderating influence of his whole life, while it
explains the philosopher's change of tone, marks, at
the same time, the gravity of the change. In fact
it becomes clear that two lives, two methods, two
doctrines, logically incompatible, are presented to us
in the story of the man who, besides being the
founder of the positive philosophy, was the worshipper
of Clotilde de Vaux.

It is true that Comte himself is never weary of
maintaining the contrary. He explains that the
great systematisation reserved for his century ought
to embrace the totality of human feelings as well as
the totality of ideas ; that the systematisation of
ideas ought to take precedence, and to rest solely on
the intellect, while the systematisation of feelings
implies a new adjustment, not only of thought, but
of the entire soul—feeling in its actual experience
being alone capable of realising it. Auguste Comte
has affirmed as clearly as possible the fundamental
unity that he himself attributed to his work, in
taking for epigraph to the preface of his *Système de*

---

[1] October 1844, then August 1845.

politique positive the saying of Alfred de Vigny : "In what does a great life consist ? In making the conceptions of youth the achievement of riper years."

But here again we cannot confine ourselves to the philosopher's own judgment ; for great thinkers excel in co-ordinating and harmonising too late the various phases of their intellectual life, be these ever so incongruous.

In order to know if Comte has contradicted himself, and if, in his religious doctrine, he has, not completed, but abjured the principles of his philosophy, we must consider his person and his work as one whole.

Now, we mark that, from the beginning of his philosophical reflection, when he had scarcely passed his twentieth year and was engrossed, like the men of his day, in the re-organisation of society, he had a clear idea of the decided mistake shown in bringing this question to the front : a question that, in reality, depended on several others which needed solution first. As early as 1822, at the age of twenty-four, he published a pamphlet entitled : *Plan des travaux scientifiques nécessaires pour réorganiser la société.* Therein is to be found the germ of his sociology. He sees distinctly that, instead of adopting the eighteenth-century maxim—Law makes custom—we ought to say, Institutions depend on custom, which, in its turn, depends on belief.

Thus, the scientific and theoretical studies which he is about to undertake, do not constitute, in his view, an end : they are the means (apparently indirect, but actually indispensable) required in preparing social re-organisation, which alone is the veritable end.

Doubtless, these theoretical studies ought, in his opinion, to occupy him only a small number of years. But there befell him something analogous to what had been illustrated in the case of Kant, when that philosopher, intending to write a critical introduction to metaphysics, took ten years in the composition of a work—the *Critique of Pure Reason* itself. Comte consecrated the years 1826-42 to the conception, revision and publication of the preliminary part of his undertaking.

In the course of these prolonged inquiries, the mind of the philosopher could not remain unchanged. He aimed at realising the unity of thought in himself and in humanity. He perceived, not without astonishment perhaps, that this unity was not to be gained through an objective systematisation of knowledge, effected with the help of a material principle. In the series of the sciences there is, evidently, a hiatus between the physico-chemical sciences which advance from the parts to the whole, and biology which proceeds from the whole to the parts. A new gap is seen between biology wherein co-ordination in space still prevails, and sociology with its essential law of continuity in time. In short, each science adds to the principles of the anterior sciences something really new; that is why the systematisation of the sciences is only possible, as a completed synthesis, from a point of view which belongs to it, intellectually, as a purely subjective synthesis. Philosophy is the science of this systematisation. It is a special activity of thought which, through unity of end, through the relation of means to end, binds together elements of knowledge that are, in themselves, irreducible. Philosophy is, in a way, something that is heterogeneous and irreducible with regard to the sciences.

Aware of the leap that he has been compelled to take in order to pass from science to philosophy, and understanding clearly that intellectual unity can be no more than a synthesis (a synthesis which is, not an object, but an activity of thought), why should Auguste Comte be bound, henceforward, to derive practice from theory, objectively, analytically, immediately? His chief idea is only to start on the task of political reform—a task that is practical in the true sense, after he has exhausted its conditions. He has already discovered that, in order to begin working for the political regeneration of society, the human mind must exchange the standpoint of the scientist for that of the philosopher. Would no other condition be required? *A priori*, nothing demands, nothing excludes the introduction of a new middle term.

In reality, the *Cours de philosophie positive* gives already the anticipation of a study bearing specially on the moral conditions of social reorganisation : the results of such a study cannot be determined *a priori*.

Already Comte sees very distinctly that the preponderance of the affective faculties over the intellectual faculties is indispensable, if the social organism that sociology implies is to be realised.[1] How can that preponderance be assured? Will the positive philosophy agree to a solution of the problem through a return to religion, *i.e.* to a mental form that the law of the three stages shows us as actually superseded ?

[1] Fiftieth lecture.

It must be noted that, in the law of the three stages, theology and metaphysics are considered exclusively from the standpoint of knowledge : they are proved impotent as regards our instruction in the laws of nature. But if there should turn out to be (not, doubtless, in theology, but in religion properly so called) some extra-intellectual element, related, not to knowledge, but to practice, that element would remain intact, even admitting the law of the three stages.

Yet again : the sociology has been founded on the idea of the solidarity of human generations through the ages, it has established the connection between progress and order—the need of destroying and replacing only those products of the past which are distinctly opposed to the positive spirit, and of religiously preserving, on the contrary, everything that paves the way for a higher state.

Since, then, Auguste Comte has already intercalated philosophy between science and politics, there is nothing to prevent him, now, from intercalating religion between philosophy and politics.

How has that intercalation been produced? It has been determined by the romantic passion of Auguste Comte for Clotilde de Vaux. This fact is incontestable. But it has not, necessarily, the significance that many have attributed to it.

The mediocrity of the beloved object and the extremely affectionate disposition of Auguste Comte, reduce this incident to the level of mere contingency.

Restrained, perhaps, by the severe intellectual task to which, as the philosopher of 1826 to 1842, he had applied himself, his sensibility was overexcited in 1845 under the influence of an ordinary event. It is a question, here, of understanding the use to which Comte was going to put this incident— so little philosophical in itself. The historical origin of ideas, while it may divert our scholarly curiosity, is generally of slight consequence when we want to determine their value. Would a theorem of geometry be less true through having been demonstrated by a madman?

It needs to be stated that Comte is not exactly an intellectualist or an apostle of science: he is a positivist. In this capacity, he allows only what is at once real and useful, but he rejects nothing that exhibits these two qualities. Now, following these lines, he has come to regard the religious phenomenon as a positive datum. In man there dwells a religious instinct, *i.e.* a certain faculty for perceiving and thinking. Love is sufficient for the manifestation of this instinct; for, of itself, it leads to adoration and worship.

Can this religious sentiment be brought into that rational harmony with the intellectual synthesis of knowledge which the general idea of positivism demands?

It should be noted that, once the intellectual synthesis has been achieved, a deficiency is discovered in the event of our wishing to be assured, no longer merely in regard to the theoretical possibility of sociology as a science, but in regard to the realisation of normal society. Provided that society is in existence, it is essential that, among individuals, altruism should prevail over egoism. But the intellect cannot, by itself alone, bring about this result. And, regarded as a natural endowment, feeling is, not only indifferent to order, but anarchical. If, in order to systematise ideas, we have to reconsider them, in the same way and with even greater reason, in order to systematise feelings, we must experience them.

Now, the void thus left by philosophy is quite filled up by religion as defined by the positivist.

Positivism sets out from the concrete : man will therefore begin with a determinate feeling. Positivism generalises through extension and adaptation— rising gradually from relatively simple realities to those that are more complex, but still concrete. Accordingly, man will extend to family, to country, to humanity (dignifying and in no way lessening the reality of each) the love that is at one time kindled within him by means of the natural and moral relationship existing between man and woman. From the standpoint of the end, positivism adapts and organises the means. That is why the idea of the religion of Humanity will discipline the feelings, and will allow society to recover, from the old religions, many a real and useful element which had perforce to disappear provisionally, along with empty theologies, when men lacked the power to discriminate between the good and the bad in traditional religions.

In this way there is established, gradually, a religious systematisation analogous to the philosophical systematisation. It is true that Comte is continually showing the connection between this systematisation and his love for Clotilde de Vaux. Let us give him credit for this. "To thee alone, my Clotilde, I have been indebted, during an unparalleled year, for the tardy but decisive expansion of the sweetest human feelings. A sacred intimacy, at once paternal and fraternal, and quite compatible with mutual respect, has enabled me to appreciate, amid all thy personal charms, such a marvellous combination of tenderness and nobility as no other heart ever realised in like degree. . . . The familiar contemplation of such perfection was bound (though this was hidden from me at the time) to increase my systematic passion for that universal advancement which we both regarded as the general purpose of human life whether public or private. . . . Together we conceived, in worthy fashion, the beautiful harmony existing between functions at once conjoined and independent . . . while the one led towards the establishment, in scientific method, of convictions that were active and masculine, the other led towards the development, in æsthetical method, of feelings that were profound and feminine. When two functions are thus similarly indispensable, any notion of precedence is out of the question." [1] Let no shallow critic come forward, now, with insinuations about the tediousness of this exceptional homage : " All thinkers who know how to appreciate the mental reaction of the sympathetic affections, will take sufficient note of the time employed in retracing and reanimating emotions of this pure quality."

Such was the love of Auguste Comte for Clotilde : the sum of it he has given us in his synthesis.

As to the re-establishment of fetichism, that is explained by the anxiety for realisation which was becoming more and more dominant with Auguste Comte. The imagination has a reality of its own, and that a potent one. Positivism, which preserves by means of adaptation, will not set it aside, but will make use of it. Enough that the imagination does not destroy the work of reason, that its fictions be

[1] *Syst. de pol. posit.*, Dedication.

not taken for truths. Similarly, the rationalism of
a Plato made room for myth as the auxiliary of
philosophy in practice.

It is not to be denied, however, that Comte has
started here on a slippery incline. Positivism rested
on a double principle—the real and the useful. Its
perfection consisted in maintaining an exact balance
between these two terms. Now, the evolution of
Comte seems to have consisted in first of all sub-
ordinating the useful to the real, ere coming, by
degrees, to subordinate the real to the useful. Such
an evolution is by no means accidental, seeing that,
from the very first, it was his avowed intention to
study the real with the sole object of finding use
for it. But there are, undoubtedly, considerable
difficulties in defining satisfactorily both the real and
the useful, as well as their relations—difficulties that
Comte has not sufficiently had in mind.

III

THE VALUE OF THE DOCTRINE

What is the value of this doctrine ? What lesson
can we derive from it ?

The Positivism of Comte may be defined as the
synthesis of science and religion, brought about by
means of the concept of humanity. Brought back to
the needs of man, science leads to religion, and it is
the latter, alone, that can secure the realisation of
those ends for which science supplies the means. On
the other hand, finding in humanity itself the fitting
object of its worship, religion accomplishes its task
without leaving the real world in which science moves.

Does this synthesis satisfy reason ?

It has been frequently remarked that the position of science in the system is one of singular embarrassment. Not only is it debarred from applying itself to inquiries of doubtful social utility, and from carrying its prepossession for accuracy beyond the limits that satisfy practical life ; but arbitrary hypotheses— mere fictions of the imagination—are imposed upon it, when its own bent towards positivism is not shown sufficiently. Comte arrives, in this way, at his definition of logic : the normal conjunction of feelings, images and signs for the purpose of suggesting to us those conceptions which harmonise with our moral, intellectual and physical needs. Free, independent science is more and more treated with suspicion and dislike. Science tends to specialise and to break up : she is, therefore, essentially anarchical. Her futile inquisitiveness — sheer mental concupiscence, her insufferable pride ought to be restrained. Science must be submitted to feeling. Her excesses may appear strange, but they are conceivable, if we understand that the office of science has been, from earliest times, to strive after the knowledge of things as they are, not as we would have them be : in fact to strip them, as much as possible, of that distinctive mark of humanity which it is the intention of Comte, before all else, to confer upon them.

Religion, in Comtism, is not less cramped than science. In vain does she seek to recover that mastery over philosophy which belonged to her under Scholasticism : she is tormented by a secret aspiration that she can neither curb nor satisfy.

She would like to retain, in all their fulness, those sentiments dear to the heart of man : love toward

God as the foundation of love toward man, and faith in Immortality as the pledge of communion with the dead. And Comte insists, more and more, on the reality and value of the extra-intellectual or subjective elements of our nature. Is not feeling a fact; is not the imagination a part of the human soul, quite as much as the senses or the reason? What can be more real than instinct — especially religious instinct, that irreducible ground of our being?

But reason, being likewise a principle of our nature, checks these effusions of the heart. If humanity properly so called (humanity as it appears in space and time) is itself the measure of being and of knowing, the eternity of the Great Being is but a word: the whole of God's reality is contained in the thought, actually present in certain individuals, of a certain collection of human facts; while Immortality amounts to no more than remembrance.

It is not without reason that we dispute over the value of the subjective in the scheme of Auguste Comte. He is at once willing and not willing to constitute it a genuine reality.

The embarrassment that he experiences is connected with the principle of his adoption. Humanity is an ambiguous notion, incapable of furnishing a first principle. There is man as visible, as seen from the outside—a collection of given facts, analogous to all other facts; and there is man as internal, *i.e.* as one who thinks, desires, loves and seeks. When, in spite of his proscription of psychology, he has taken clear note of the reality that belongs to man as internal, Comte offers the world of facts to his ambition, having previously constituted it an impassable prison in order to be quite sure that man could not get away from it; and he bids him rule over the world and find happiness therein.   But the barrier that he has raised between facts and ideas, between given realities and ideal possibilities, is illusory.   The human soul turns out to be precisely the effort to go beyond what is given, to do better, to seek after something else, to surpass itself.   Man, said Pascal, stands for what is infinitely above man.

It is not the closing up, once and for all, of metaphysical and religious inquiries that makes man the measure of things—it is the reopening of them.   For, what is man?   Can he be sure that he is, himself, only a datum, a collection of facts, a thing?

Philosophers, said Goethe, have torn in pieces the external and material deity who was throned above the clouds : what they have done amounts to nothing. Let man re-enter into himself, and he will find there the true God—internal as regards existence and not external, a creative influence and not a given phenomenon.

> Weh ! Weh !
> Du hast sie zerstört
> Die schöne Welt
> Mit mächtiger Faust ;
> Sie stürzt, sie zerfällt !
>
> .   .   .   .
>
> Mächtiger
> Der Erdensöhne
> Prächtiger
> Baue sie wieder,
> In deinem Busen baue sie auf ! [1]

---

[1] Goethe, *Faust* : Woe ! Woe ! Thou hast shattered it, the splendid world, with thy destroying hand ; it crumbles, it falls asunder. . . . Mighty son of earth, thou must rebuild it more glorious still ; build it in thine own bosom.

Comte, it is true, regarded human instinct as irreversibly fixed, in the same way as the instinct of animals. But science was bound to show that animal instinct is an unalterable datum. As to man, he is true man only if he takes his actual instinct as a starting-point from which to rise higher—not as a limit which he is forbidden to pass.

That is the debatable point in the doctrine of Comte. His positivism, with its fixity and arbitrariness, would be legitimate, if human nature were something given once for all. It is but the artificial fixing of a transient phase in the life of humanity, if man is a being who is ever seeking, modifying and re-creating himself.

Can we say that this creation of man by man is arbitrary? Man would be humiliated if this were shown him. For, in his wish to do better, he could, then, only bestir himself at random like an atom of Epicurus. But he believes that, while lacking a full pattern in what is given him, his work has, nevertheless, a regulating principle—one that, in a high sense, has its necessity, its existence and its value. That principle, which dwells at once within him and above him, is what he calls God.

It is thus that, in humanity itself, are found the germs of a religion in which the object goes beyond humanity. In order that man should rest content with man, it would be necessary for him to unlearn the γνῶθι σεαυτόν of ancient wisdom. He cannot go to the foundations of self without being made to recognise the strongest compulsion to enlarge the reality, the perfection and the value of humanity. Doubtless the legacy of past humanity, and the conditions therein prescribed, enter as an essential part into the ideal which is proper to man, and this ideal, in order to be practical, must remain close to given reality. But fact cannot succeed in governing idea, seeing that the overpassing of fact is just what is in question. Faith in the superior reality of an ideal object, irreducible to whatever is given, yet capable of being impressed on the given, has produced the very heroes whom Auguste Comte so rightly honours : they are the saints of his calendar, because they have not believed in his religion.

Positivism thus appears, throughout, to be placed in a position of unstable equilibrium. It knows only the real and the useful. But in the real and the useful are necessarily implied other and higher notions.

The scientist, to whom we look for inquiry into the real, soon discovers that all impressions of all individuals are equally real, and that his task lies precisely in distinguishing—from this same real— something that is more stable, more profound, less dependent on the conditions of a perception that is only individual and human. He claims as true that object which he can neither lay hold of nor define exactly : while his vague idea of it directs his investigations, and, by degrees, comes into shape before him under the influence of these same investigations. And, once in possession of this idea, he cannot subordinate it to any utility, be this ever so urgent. The truth itself is, in his eyes, a supreme utility. Science investigates by reason of her love for truth. It is her honour, her pride and her joy which she cannot allow to be stolen from her by any philosophical or political system. It is no question of understanding whether the interest of practical science herself can be best served in allowing theorists to believe that they are only labouring for the sake of theory. Science, as such, is a legitimate and absolutely noble activity which, through the agency of philosophy as guardian of the ideal, ought to be enfranchised and made aware of its capacities, instead of being left to, the bondage of any purpose that may appear.

In like manner, the man of heart and will, to whom is given the task of searching for the useful within the limits of the real, must not rest content with this object. What is the useful? What is the real? Man is desirous of determining the first, and of creating, in some way, the second. The useful may be defined as the means to be employed by me in realising the object which I have perceived, and which reason presents to me as worthy of man's endeavour. And the real, one may say, is something that I myself bring into existence through borrowing powers to be found in the very idea of the task that I set myself. In other words, man is constrained to put the good and the beautiful above the useful, seeing that in these we find the source and measure of the useful itself. The Good and the Beautiful, as well as the True, demand, in their turn, to be considered as utilities—as the utility *par excellence*.

So it comes about that the principle of Comte, the notion of the positive as union of the real and the useful, leads, of itself (as soon as man sets it in operation), to those superior objects in given reality that Comte had intended to eliminate. The real and the useful are, for us, an incentive towards the True, the Beautiful and the Good.

Vain is the attempt—in order to take from the

human soul the desire for what is beyond man—to
show that this desire is illusive in the sense of wast-
ing away and disappearing by degrees, as a useless
instrument : the real man does not recognise his
own nature in this description of it. Comte forbids
us to see anything, to look for anything, beyond the
world that we inhabit. This world, according to
him, suffices as our be all and end all. But Littré
soon discovers that this " all " is a mere island,
surrounded on every side by an ocean which we are
forbidden, says he, to explore, but which offers us a
spectacle as salutary as it is formidable.

Is it possible to enclose the infinite, and to
reckon on disuse as enabling us to lose the idea of
it ? Science and Religion are mutually inconvenienced
so long as we pretend to find room for both of them
in the finite world of human phenomena : would they
not recover their liberty and autonomy respectively,
if we were to allow—beyond the given world that
science claims—the existence of another world, open
to our desires, to our beliefs, to our dreams ? Would
such a doctrine run counter to the affirmations of
modern science, or would it not, rather, be demanded
by science herself ? This way of approaching the
problem was that of an illustrious English philosopher,
one of the principal contributors to the thought of
our time : Herbert Spencer.

CHAPTER II

HERBERT SPENCER AND THE UNKNOWABLE

In our estimate of what is most original in Herbert
Spencer's philosophy, we cannot include his speculations concerning religion. Roughly speaking, they
occupy only a small space in his works. But, if it is
always interesting to understand the ideas of a great
thinker in regard to this subject, there are special
reasons for seeking to know what Herbert Spencer
has written about it.

He belonged to a family of preachers and pro-
fessors, wherein religion was deemed the matter of
first importance. On his mother's side he was

connected with an old French Huguenot family—
that of Brettel. His great-grandfather was John
Brettel, who, as personal friend of John Wesley, the
founder of Methodism, applied himself to the task of
spreading that doctrine. His mother, Harriet Holmes,
was a woman of great piety : although a Methodist,
she rigidly observed the rites of the Church of
England. George Spencer, Herbert's father, was
keenly interested in religious matters. Originally
attached to Methodism, he seceded from it on the
plea of not finding therein the inward religion that
he needed, and went over to the Quakers. His
religious disposition was expressed in a veritable re-
pugnance towards ecclesiastical rules and ceremonies.

To these influences Herbert Spencer was far from
being insensible. In his *Facts and Comments*, as
well as in his *Autobiography*, he shows that religious
matters have an increasing hold upon his affection.
It is with reflections about religion that the *Autobiography* ends. In this way, the scientist who, by
means of his immense studies, rendered himself
capable of attempting that wonderful synthesis of the
sciences with which his name remains connected, was
no less qualified, on the side of life and thought, to
discuss the relations between religion and science.

It is not only because it expresses an important
side of the philosopher's own mind that the teaching
of Herbert Spencer in regard to religion is interesting.
That teaching is summed up in what Huxley has
called Agnosticism. Now, Agnosticism is one of the
most important forms of philosophical thought as it
exists to-day. What is Agnosticism ? For some, it
is a mysticism which is afraid of lowering God by
setting Him within our reach ; for others, it is only

an esoteric name behind which atheism is concealed. Agnosticism is a particular solution of the problem which the relations between religion and science involve; this problem we are bound to examine, and, if we are to study it in a concrete manner, we could not do better than consider it as expounded by Herbert Spencer.

I

THE DOCTRINE OF H. SPENCER ON SCIENCE, RELIGION, AND THEIR RELATIONS

It is essentially in the opening part of *First Principles*, entitled "The Unknowable," and in those parts of *The Principles of Sociology* which treat, at one time of the psychological data or bases of sociology, at another of the evolution of ecclesiastical institutions, that the passages concerning religion and its relations with science are to be found.

.   .   .   .   .   .

The last word of Herbert Spencer's philosophy may be expressed as follows : there is for us, incontestably, at the centre and origin of all things, an Unknowable — a principle, that is, which we can neither set aside nor reach. This doctrine binds together religion and science.

It often seems as if religion and science were opposed to one another : hence many people are driven to believe that the principles underlying these two are radically irreconcilable. For all that, we are compelled to note that both are equally given in experience as genuine realities.

It would be an error to regard religion as an artificial affair, manufactured by the mind through the accidental caprice of its imagination. Religion has been suggested to man by the very things of his experience : it is the spontaneous reaction of his thought, of his heart, of his soul, in response to the control exercised over him by the external world.

On the other hand, science, in like manner, is not the artificial and quasi-supernatural contrivance imagined (maybe through imperfect understanding) by those who glory in opposing it to the knowledge of the multitude. Science is common everyday experience itself, become, in the process of its natural evolution, more precise, more connected, more instructive, and far more capable than common experience of overstepping, in its affirmations, the limits of actual perception.

Science and religion have, then, one and the same origin : both are generated naturally in the human mind, by reason of its relation with the world ; they are, to the same extent, realities, spontaneous manifestations of nature : it is, therefore, nonsense to inquire if the existence of the one is compatible with that of the other. They are able to coexist seeing that they *do* coexist ! The only problem is that of seeking out the reason and meaning of this coexistence.

If we adhere to the examination of particular determinations, be these religious or scientific, we prove, indeed, flagrant contradictions between them, and we can only deem unnatural and feeble those efforts in the way of conciliation that ingenious exegetes strive to multiply. But the accidental cannot make us forget what is essential. In order to arrive at a clear appreciation of science and religion, we must consider, not their particular and contingent expressions, but their most general and most abstract propositions : perhaps, in this way, they will turn out to be quite reconcilable.

The special dogmas offered by the various religions (dogmas that often bring them into conflict with science) express, in reality, not supernatural revelations, but the endeavour of the human mind to imagine, in a manner agreeable to its categories and methods, what is absolute and infinite : this task is forced upon it by feeling. Now, all these formulæ —be they ever so learned, ingenious, or acute—turn out to be incapable of supporting the analysis. They appear satisfactory so long as we consider them from a poetical and sentimental standpoint, without strictly defining the meaning of words and the connection of ideas. But it is no longer the same when we seek to imagine them and to demonstrate them in a precise fashion.

For instance, let the question be in regard to the origin of the world—one of those questions which religion, in its various forms, usually attempts to solve. If we determine with precision the explanations that this problem allows, we find that they are reduced to three. We may assume, either that the world exists from all eternity, or that it has created itself, or that it has been created by an external power. Now, submitted to philosophical criticism, not one of these three hypotheses is really intelligible: each of the three conceals within itself logical incompatibilities, each is intrinsically contradictory. It is impossible *to realise them in thought*—to use the forcible English expression. These results have been, according to Herbert Spencer, definitely established through the criticism of Hamilton and of Mansel.

Examination of the other determinations that theology claims to impose on primal being—unity, freedom, personality, brings us to like conclusions.

That is why the object of religion, the absolute, in so far as we try to picture it as existent, is incomprehensible, *unthinkable*.

What shall we now say about science? Is it not, contrariwise, clear and obvious—from beginning to end—in its principles, in its reasonings, in its results? Not so, in Herbert Spencer's view! Science, in her definitive task of reducing quality to quantity, cannot dispense with such notions as space, time, matter, movement, force, seeing that they are the necessary conditions of quantity. But all these notions, if we attempt to realise them in thought, end, likewise, in contradictions.

Try for instance, to imagine clearly, *i.e.* to understand with precise and absolute determination, what existence implies, whether space or time. If space and time really exist, there are, with respect to their nature, only three possible hypotheses. They must be either entities, or attributes of entities, or subjective realities. But not one of these three hypotheses can be developed without contradiction. Spencer, once again, adopts the results of Kantian and Scottish criticism.

That which is true of space and of time is equally so of the other primary data of science. Do we endeavour, tracing back the course of universal evolution, to conceive matter as having existed originally in a state of complete diffusion? We find ourselves confronted by the impossibility of imagining how it has reached that state. Do we turn our gaze towards the future? We are debarred from assigning limits to the succession of phenomena spread out before us. If, on the other hand, man looks into himself, he finds that the two ends of the thread of consciousness are beyond his reach. He can only comprehend the production of a state of consciousness after that state has already slipped by ; and the disappearance of the conscious into the unconscious eludes him in like manner. The essence, the genesis and the end of all things are hidden from us. All our science leads to mystery in the long run.

There is, then, a resemblance, a bond, between science and religion. Both of these, when we dive into their principles, imply the unknowable, the unthinkable. Religion takes its rise in this unknowable, which it struggles fruitlessly to define. In vain, on its side, would science resolve on establishing itself within the region of the definable and knowable. The greater its progress and demonstration, the more obtrusive becomes that unknowable which it was bent on eliminating. Where religion begins, science ends. They turn their backs on one another, and yet they are reunited.

But would not the notion of the absolute, in which science and religion are thus reconciled, be a pure negation ? Would not this unknowable, this unthinkable be reduced to an abstraction, to a nonentity ? If this were so, the reconciliation that it effects would be only a word.

It is the peculiar merit and originality of Herbert Spencer to have established, as a positive reality, that Unknowable which, for his predecessors Hamilton and Mansel, was only a negation. He has declared, he has maintained that the Absolute is unknowable : he has not concluded thence that we can affirm nothing in regard to it. Between knowledge, properly so called, which grasps the thing in its full determination, and total ignorance which reduces the thing to a name devoid of meaning, Herbert Spencer has put an intermedium, viz. to know the thing in so far as it is perceived under its most general aspects.

In order to establish, in this sense, that the absolute can be positive and yet unknowable, Herbert Spencer distinguishes between positive consciousness and definite consciousness. We are mistaken in thinking that the first necessarily implies the second. This opinion rests on a logical error. A thing can, in reality, very well be at once positive and indefinite. And it is precisely to the affirmation of a consciousness at once indefinite and positive that we are led in examining this unknowable—the postulate of both science and religion.

When I say that the absolute is unknowable, unthinkable, I mean that it cannot be realised in thought, known under a concrete form, set up as an object of definite knowledge. What does this impossibility signify ?

Let us assume that the mind intends to think the absolute. It will necessarily be obliged to attribute to it certain determinations. For instance, it will have to suppose it either as limited or as unlimited. These two attributes are contradictory. The mind will, therefore, be bound to choose between them. Now, analysis demonstrates with uniform precision, on the one hand, that I am obliged to think of the absolute as limited since it cannot possibly be unlimited; on the other hand, that I am obliged to think of it as unlimited since it cannot possibly be limited. If, therefore, I try to imagine the absolute, I find myself in presence of two contradictory absolutes —the one limited, the other unlimited. But this result is not the last word in the analysis.

If the limited and the unlimited are opposed to one another, it is only in so far as there is, behind them, a subject which brings them together, compares them, and judges them incompatible ; in other words, it is in so far as there is a consciousness behind them. Accordingly, the limited and the unlimited, regarded no longer through the medium of words that isolate them from one another, but through the mental agency that is presupposed in every concept, are not totally inconsistent. After they have both been annulled, in so far as they are objects of definite conscious- ness, there remains the consciousness implied in this very fact of being aware : a consciousness indefinite and, nevertheless, positive. To affirm that definite consciousness of the absolute is impossible, is, *ipso facto*, to affirm the existence of a positive indefinite consciousness of that absolute.

The method of Herbert Spencer is, not that of formal and scholastic dialectics, but a concrete method of inference. He starts from what is empirically given, and eliminates therefrom all that cannot be imagined as existent. He stops when, like the chemist, he finds himself in presence of an irreducible residuum. Now, underlying the absolute, he discovers, in this way, an indefinite consciousness. Predicated by this consciousness, the absolute is, indeed, something that is real and positive, though unknowable.

And so, the reconciliation of religion and philosophy is effected, not by means of a word, but in a real manner : it is not negative, but positive. Whatever may be the intrinsic nature of their connection, there exists for us a living unity, viz. consciousness, which assures us of its reality.

Religion proceeds from the affirmation of the absolute, and she has truth on her side, seeing that we have a positive consciousness of this same absolute. Science cannot succeed in dispersing the mystery by which, in the fullest sense, she is surrounded ; and this incapacity is, indeed, irremediable, since we have, and must continue to have, only an indefinite consciousness of the absolute.

.   .   .   .   .   .

This doctrine of the relations between religion and science, nevertheless, is only in some degree the metaphysical introduction of the system. The system, properly so called, gravitates towards the idea of science. It aims at establishing the synthesis of the sciences by means of principles which are taken from the notion of the knowable.

The sciences class objects according to their resemblances—seeking for the reduction of those vague and incomplete resemblances which are qualitative, to the complete and exact resemblances which mathematicians call equality and identity. The sciences, by themselves, only attain to a partially unified knowledge. Philosophy tends to unify knowledge in a complete manner. Its instrument is the law of evolution, which the sciences exhibit, and which the analysis of our notion of the knowable makes good.

The sciences study facts, all the facts ; and, finally, incorporated in philosophy, they see these facts range themselves, in every province, under that law of evolution which is the common principle of being and of knowing. Following this law, taken in its most general sense, all things pass necessarily, progressively, from a state of incoherent homogeneity to a state of definite and coherent heterogeneity.

The various religions are submitted to the law of evolution in the same way as all other phenomena. Thus religion, which was set opposite science in *First Principles*, when it was a question of seeking for its ultimate object, is now—as a phenomenon given in space and time—ranged purely and simply among the wholly analogous things that science and philosophy study.

The problem to be investigated at this point, according to the philosophy of evolution, is the phenomenal genesis of ecclesiastical institutions.

The starting-point of religions after the historical method, the elementary fact which, through diversification, produces their infinite variety, is simply, in Herbert Spencer's view, the idea of what we call the *double*. Man sees his image or double in the water. Similarly, he sees himself in a dream, just as he sees in a dream the image of other men. This double, while resembling the original, is not necessarily identical with it : man's first impulse is to regard the one and the other as two distinct beings. Now, when sleep has passed away, what becomes of the double ? Man has a natural disposition to believe that he is not annihilated, that he is simply removed, that he will, perhaps, reappear in another dream. Consequently, when death comes, man readily believes that this mysterious self subsists, and that it remains more or less like his ordinary self—therefore, more or less like the visible being of which it was the double. Thence issues the belief in ghosts, in supernatural beings, in their power, in their influence over human life. Such is the historical origin of religions, according to Herbert Spencer : and, here, he is in agreement with the Epicureans.

From this belief are derived dogmas, rites, ecclesiastical institutions.

Every real being has its double, capable of being considered as a ghost. The inferior ghosts come, in time, to be grouped under the domination of superior ghosts called gods ; finally, these latter are themselves subordinated to a single God. These supernatural powers man has sought to picture to himself, in the act of rendering them accessible and propitious : out of this desire have sprung mythologies, forms of incantation, practices and organisations, which, being afterwards (according to the same law of evolution) developed for what they were worth in themselves, sometimes preserved only faint traces of their origin.

Thereafter, when they are no longer upheld on the ground of their first intention, by reason of the too definite evolution of men's beliefs, these institutions continue as social bonds : in this way evolution confers upon them a character of prime importance.   Henceforward, the religions of the world represent the continuity of social life ; and so there is, for individuals, a special concern in reverencing them.

The general trait of religious evolution is seen in the increasing preponderance of the moral element over the ritual or propitiatory element, as well as in the increasing elimination of those anthropomorphic qualities which were originally attributed to the first cause ; at bottom, this is the tendency to consider dogmas as pure symbols, and to replace them by the consciousness, at once indefinite and positive, of the absolute.

II

THE INTERPRETATION OF THE DOCTRINE

Such is the substance of Herbert Spencer's teaching on religion and its relations with science. What significance has it? Is this teaching, in view of his work as a whole, merely an accessory part, or is it the expression of profound ideas which are vitally connected with his system?

We are tempted to infer that speculation of this kind is of no moment in comparison with the vast synthesis of the sciences, which is Herbert Spencer's particular achievement; that, in short, its significance is chiefly negative.

Doubtless one can easily find, in *First Principles*, the materials of a theory of The Unknowable. But it must be noted that Herbert Spencer did not, originally, intend to preface *First Principles* by speculations in regard to The Unknowable. It was because of the fear that his general doctrine should be interpreted in a sense unfavourable to religion, it was in order to avert the reproach of atheism, that Herbert Spencer, on reconsideration, added that first part.

Moreover, this theory of The Unknowable, as its very name indicates, informs us that God, the first cause, and the special objects of religion, are entirely inaccessible to our understanding. Their reality, no doubt, is implied by the phenomena that we observe. But what is an existence deprived of every kind of being? What is an absolute that has to be described as absolutely unknowable? Do we not find therein (in spite of the philosopher's own denials) a mere abstract term—the wholly negative expression of an impossibility ?

So far as the doctrine relating to the historical genesis of religion is concerned, we are, indeed, presented with something that is precise, positive and developed. But is not an abstraction based on its scientific value (a value that is much contested at the present time) the very negation of a really objective foundation of religion ? Do we not see all the components of the various religions reduced, in this way, to a puerile and erroneous belief, viz. belief in the reality and in the survival of those phantoms which dreams suggest to us ? Does not religion thus become, purely and simply, a chapter in the natural history of man ?

In order that we may thoroughly grasp Herbert Spencer's thought in regard to these different points, we must apply to the interpretation of his doctrine that method of internal criticism—of explaining the argument by the argument itself—which Spinoza wished to see applied equally to the Bible and to Nature.

.   .   .   .   .   .

What are the considerations which have instigated the theories of Herbert Spencer concerning religion ? By examining the motives of his teaching, we are more likely to understand its genuine meaning.

If we consult the philosopher's *Autobiography*— so frank, so spontaneous, so spirited, so rich in details as regards the inner working of his mind—we see that these motives were as follows.

We note, first of all, the impression made upon him by the Bible and by the sermons of those preachers who expounded the sacred text. A thousand things, in this so-called revelation, appeared to him ground of offence. What an enormous injustice to punish the disobedience of the one Adam by condemning the whole of his innocent posterity! And how can it be right to make an exception in favour of a small number of men, to whom is revealed a plan of salvation which the rest of mankind have no means of knowing? How extraordinary is the assertion about the Universal Cause from which have proceeded thirty million of suns with their planets—that, on one occasion, it took the form of a man, and made a bargain with Abraham, promising to obtain territory for him, in the event of his rendering loyal service! How can God find pleasure in hearing us sing His praises in our churches, or get angry with the infinitely little beings of His own creation, because they omit to speak to Him constantly about His almightiness?

Such reflections appear frequently in Herbert Spencer's record. What motive inspires them? As to this there can be no doubt. Herbert Spencer is shocked by the disproportion that he discovers between traditional beliefs about God, and that character of infinity which his reason attributes to the First Cause. Can we call this an irreligious sentiment? Does it show indifference over matters of religion? The very freshness and quality of his diction manifest the serious and profoundly religious aspiration which suggests to him these attacks on religion.

This kind of criticism only concerns certain stories and dogmas belonging to a particular religion. Let us turn to criticism of another type, stated with insistence in the *Autobiography*. I possessed, says

H

Herbert Spencer, as innate in my mind, the consciousness of natural causality. "It seems as though
I knew by intuition the necessity of equivalence
between cause and effect—perceived, without teaching, the impossibility of an effect without a cause
appropriate to it, and the certainty that an effect,
relevant in kind and in quantity to a cause, must in
every case be produced." This mental disposition led
me to reject the ordinary idea of the supernatural;
and I thus came to regard as impossible everything
called miraculous, *i.e.* everything conceived as contrary
to the causality of nature.

The earlier motive was drawn from special
doctrines, put forward officially as religious. The
latter has its source in the nature of science: *a priori*,
science excludes the supernatural.

Is there, in the principle of natural causality
which Herbert Spencer here invokes, an insuperable
hindrance to religious beliefs? It is not likely; for
there are abundant examples of philosophers, who, to
a very clear consciousness of the natural connection
of phenomena, have added a very deep sense of
religion. We can point to the Stoics, in bygone
days, and—among men of modern times—to a
Spinoza, to a Leibnitz, to a Kant. As a set-off
we may instance the Epicureans, who, admitting
solution of continuity in the thread of phenomena,
denied all interference of the gods in the occurrences
of this world.

What, then, is the consequence of the doctrine of
natural causality, looking at it from the religious
standpoint? This doctrine forbids us to picture God
and Nature as two adversaries struggling in the lists
with a view to exterminating one another. It does

not allow us to think of the divine action as consisting in a destruction of natural forces, or to regard the action of created beings as a revolt against divine power. But a conception of natural and supernatural, wherein God and Nature are thus likened to two men in conflict, is manifestly childish; and it is not for casting aside such notions that we can be charged with irreligion. Besides, the doctrine of natural causality is by no means exclusive: for many minds it implies a universal principle of order, of unity, of life and of adaptation—a principle which, as regards the laws of nature, stands in a superior relationship, like that of cause to effect, or that of original to copy. Does the connection existing between the different moments of a mathematical demonstration exclude the existence of a mathematician, whom we presume to be the author of that demonstration?

In order that natural causation may admit of such an interpretation, a condition is, nevertheless, requisite. Nature, in the scientific meaning of the word, must not, herself, be considered as the absolute.

Now, this is just the position taken by Herbert Spencer. He himself declares that our natural laws (the world that is presented to us) are but symbols of Real Being, and that it would be contrary to all philosophy to set them up as absolute. There is, accordingly, room — beside his faith in natural causality—for faith in a principle which is superior to that causality : such a principle would be exactly at one with the object of religion.

Further, let it be noted that Spencer does not infer : I was bound to reject every idea of the supernatural ; he makes the simple admission : I was

led to reject that idea of the supernatural which
usually prevails. He classes himself with those who,
while they entirely disbelieve in miracle as violating
the laws of nature, consider themselves justified in
maintaining the genuinely supernatural principles of
religion — thinking, indeed, that they are, in their
disbelief, more religious than those who represent
God as a bad workman constantly engaged in amend-
ing his work.

.   .   .   .   .   .

But we cannot content ourselves with the examination of Herbert Spencer's own meaning : it is necessary
to consider in themselves his theory of The Unknowable and his theory of religious evolution. To several
expounders it appears that this latter, which is, in
short, the positive and scientific part of the doctrine,
does away with the objective value of the religious
idea, and that, in this way, it makes illusory and
purely verbal the former theory of an absolute yet
unknowable reality.

What, then, from the standpoint of scientific
philosophy, is religion, according to Herbert Spencer?
It is the natural development, conformable to the
general law of evolution, of the delusion about the
double : the development, that is, of an elementary
fact, which, besides being natural in itself, is even
vulgar and insignificant.

In order to measure the real consequences of this
argument, we must look at it from Herbert Spencer's
own standpoint.

Natural evolution, as he understands it, is no mere
mechanical phenomenon. Doubtless it is supplied
with materials in the shape of facts separated from
one another like atoms ; and it collects these materials

from the outside, grouping around an elementary fact those connected facts which are furnished by the surrounding medium. But it does not produce any aggregates whatsoever. It engenders pliant, modifiable beings, which are gradually adapted to one another. In reality, it is immanent in each element of nature as a tendency towards universal equilibrium and correspondence.

It follows thence that all the definite and relatively stable products of evolution have, in themselves, a certain value and dignity; for all represent a moment, or mode (the only possible and proper one in a given point of space and of time) of that universal mutual adaptation which is the supreme law of nature. We find here, it would seem, a principle familiar and dear to Anglo-Saxon folk: existence, simply as such, when it is sure and deep-rooted, when it is maintained and defended energetically, manifests or confers a right. And thus religious phenomena, in so far merely as they are, as they continue, as they appear endowed with generality and with vitality, give evidence, according to Herbert Spencer's teaching, of their conformity to the medium in which they subsist, of their legitimacy, of their value.

These same phenomena, moreover, in virtue of their existence and durability, are data or conditions to which the other modes of existence must be adapted. The opening part of *First Principles* is not confined to explaining how religion is bound to be reconciled with science. It shows, in like manner, how science ought to reverence whatever is essential in religion. While he condemns theology for making light of the laws of nature, Herbert Spencer is no less disparaging in regard to the pride of a science which pretends to abolish mystery—that sure token of the absolute.

Thus the very test of time, to which existing religions have been submitted, is a pledge of their value. But in what sense do these phenomena have a value? Are they calculated to interest the really religious consciousness, or must we see in them mere superstitions devoid of meaning, subsisting on the level of those mechanical forces or blind instincts with which we meet in the course of nature?

Herbert Spencer would appear to see no value—from the standpoint of religious consciousness—in the earliest stage of religious development: viz. primitive man's belief in the reality of the images presented to him in dreams. Would not this childish origin cast a slur upon the entire evolution? Do not beliefs and institutions which are only the development and adaptation of a clumsy superstition, remain (even while possessing some practical utility) imaginations without rational significance?

Perhaps this inference is less rigorous than it seems at first glance. Could not evolution, in the long run, transform this very origin, and change error into truth? That is not the reply, however, that Herbert Spencer makes. His own way of refuting the objection is to be found in that chapter of *The Principles of Sociology* which is entitled "Religious Retrospect and Prospect," as well as in certain articles contributed to *The Nineteenth Century* (1884). This refutation is as follows:

The inference would be right, if the premises were true. But, contrary to what, perhaps, most of my readers imagine, there is, in the primitive notion out of which religions spring, a germ of real knowledge. There is suggested to us in the primitive conception, be it ever so faintly, this truth—" that the Power which manifests itself in consciousness is but a differently conditioned form of the Power which manifests itself beyond consciousness." Our first impulse is to confound this Power with the image of self that certain natural phenomena introduce to us. Now this confusion is not an absolute mistake. For it is very true that there is an energy within us, and that this energy is one with the universal energy. The evolution that our primitive hypothesis ought to undergo in order to become a philosophical proposition, need not, therefore, be a complete transformation; it is sufficient if we eliminate from this hypothesis every anthropomorphic accompaniment. Reaching the last stage in our refining process, we recognise " that force as it exists beyond consciousness cannot be like what we know as force within consciousness "; and that yet they must be different modes of an existence which is one and the same.

The doctrine of The Unknowable is thus connected expressly, by Herbert Spencer himself, with the theory of evolution. In view of this it matters little that the philosopher did not, originally, have the intention of writing a chapter on The Unknowable as the foundation of his First Principles. The Unknowable may be termed the soul of evolution. For it is because Being, at bottom, is One, that the beings of nature find, in mutual adaptation, an end that is realisable.

But will this doctrine of The Unknowable, which

is all that Herbert Spencer offers to souls thirsting
for religious knowledge, succeed in depriving us of
every religious outlook that is positive, real, intelligible and efficacious ?   Is it any better than a hollow
formula—a residuum drawn from the discussion of
antinomies ?

Is not this doctrine, on further examination, quite
as abstract and void as it appeared at first sight ?

According to Herbert Spencer, consciousness brings
us to The Unknowable—that consciousness which is
the persistent and necessary ground of all our
conceptions, of all our reasonings, of all our analyses,
of even our most radical negations.   If this is really
so, it is likely that the system will be found to
contain some rudiments of a positive metaphysic.
And we actually meet with such rudiments in
examining it.

From the first we are aware of a pronounced
idealism piercing through our author's negations.
Let us turn to *First Principles*, and examine the
beginning of Part II. ("The Knowable").   We shall
see there that the starting-point of all our ideas (as
much those relating to the external world or *non-ego*,
as those relating to the internal world) is to be found
exclusively in our states of consciousness.   It is
pointed out that these states of consciousness are of
two kinds : vivid states or perceptions, and faint
states such as the phenomena of reflection, of memory,
of imagination, of ideation.   The first present indis-
soluble connections, and the unknown power which
they manifest we call *non-ego* ; the second present
dissoluble connections, and the power therein expressed
we call *ego*.   On both sides we see that consciousness
is the sole origin of knowledge.   Consciousness is the

channel through which the action of The Unknowable has to pass in order to be manifested to us. When Herbert Spencer shows that the phenomena of the *non-ego* can modify the phenomena of the *ego*, and that the converse is impossible, it is, with him, tantamount to saying that one of the two modes of consciousness can operate on the other.

In so far as it derives all our knowledge from consciousness, this system is idealistic. In its method of determining the relationship of the *ego* to the Absolute, it reveals a pantheistic tendency. We are informed, in the preface to *The Principles of Psychology* (1870), that the *ego* which subsists uninterruptedly in the subject of states of consciousness is a portion of The Unknowable. Moreover, speaking of the Eternal Energy from which all things proceed, Herbert Spencer declares, "It is the same Power which in ourselves wells up under the form of consciousness."[1] The *ego*, then, if it is not the Absolute-in-Itself, is the Absolute for us, *i.e.* the most immediate expression of It that is given us.

Herbert Spencer goes further still. As regards that which is beyond consciousness, and which we cannot reach—the Absolute-in-Itself, called by him The Unknowable, does he regard It purely and simply as unknowable? Will he say, for instance, that we do not know in the least whether It is Spirit or Matter, whether It is Personal or Impersonal? Herbert Spencer has put this question to himself, and he offers the following reply to it in *First Principles*:

[1] Quoted by A. S. Mories in *Haeckel's Contribution to Religion*, etc. (London, 1904).

"This [*i.e.* Agnosticism], which to most will seem an essentially irreligious position, is an essentially religious one—nay, is *the* religious one, to which . . . all others are but approximations. In the estimate it implies of the Ultimate Cause, it does not fall short of the alternative position, but exceeds it. Those who espouse this alternative position, assume that the choice is between personality and something lower than personality; whereas the choice is rather between personality and something that may be higher. Is it not possible that there is a mode of being as much transcending Intelligence and Will, as these transcend mechanical motion ?"

Does not this conception of Herbert Spencer recall to us how Pascal prescribed the threefold classification of body, mind and love, in the celebrated saying : " The infinite distance between body and mind typifies the infinitely more infinite distance between mind and love ? " And may we not say that the agnostic philosopher's system betrays, at this point, a spiritualistic and mystical tendency ?

That Herbert Spencer regarded these ideas as genuinely important, and actually set his heart upon them, is what his whole life attests.

If he has been repelled by the formal aspect of traditions, dogmas, rites, institutions, under which religion was presented to him, he has, all along, been on his guard against confusing form with essence ; and it is in the name of religious truth itself that he condemns superstitions and practices from which the spirit has departed.

Throughout life, he admitted the legitimacy of those beliefs which were based pre-eminently on feeling, so long as they were moral and practical, rather than theological, in character. He always alluded in terms of the greatest respect to the belief in immortality and future rewards. He speaks of "the truth, ever to be remembered, that during a state of the world in which many evils have to be suffered, the belief in compensations to be hereafter received, serves to reconcile men to that which they would otherwise not bear."[1]

In proportion as his thought developed, Herbert Spencer, far from becoming more indifferent, was more attentive in regard to religious matters, more impressed with their lofty import and their preponderating authority in the life of man. This is the way in which he introduces the notion of infinite Space, while he is tracing the progress of philosophical investigation:[2]

"And then comes the thought of this universal matrix itself, anteceding alike creation or evolution, whichever be assumed, and infinitely transcending both, alike in extent and duration; since both, if conceived at all, must be conceived as having had beginnings, while Space had no beginning. The thought of this blank form of existence which, explored in all directions as far as imagination can reach, has, beyond that, an unexplored region compared with which the part which imagination has traversed is but infinitesimal—the thought of a Space compared with which our immeasurable sidereal system dwindles to a point, is a thought too overwhelming to be dwelt upon. Of late years the consciousness that without origin or cause infinite Space has ever existed and must ever exist, produces in me a feeling from which I shrink."

Reading this passage, do we not again revert to Pascal in the recollection of some such thought as this: "If our sight fails at this point, let us pass

---

[1] *Autobiography*, vol. i. p. 58.
[2] *Facts and Comments*, 1902, pp. 204-5.

beyond it by means of an imagination that will sooner grow weary in conceiving, than nature in supplying. The entire visible world is but an imperceptible speck in the vast lap of nature."

And not only was the religious spirit, under its abstract and philosophical form, recognised by Herbert Spencer with increasing clearness. He made no secret of having become, in time, somewhat less severe in his attitude towards dogmas and institutions, *i.e.* towards the concrete and given form of religion. This change of judgment possessed him to such an extent that he was led to make it the subject of his concluding remarks in the *Autobiography*. These remarks may be summarised in the following manner :

Three causes, he tells us, have been at work in determining the important modification in my ideas about religious institutions.

The first lay in my sociological studies. These studies compelled me to recognise that, always and everywhere, in real life " the control exercised over men's conduct by theological beliefs and priestly agency, has been indispensable." In fact, the necessary subordination of individuals to society has been maintained only through the help of ecclesiastical institutions.

In the second place, I have learnt that it is necessary to distinguish between the nominal creeds of men and their real creeds. The former can remain more or less stationary ; the latter, as a matter of fact, change and are adapted insensibly to the fresh needs of societies and individuals. Now, it is the real creeds (far more than the nominal) that matter. That is why I am now of opinion that it is wise to respect, in a general way, the creeds of mankind, "and, further, that sudden changes of religious institutions, as of political institutions, are certain to be followed by reactions."

But, continues Herbert Spencer, "largely, if not chiefly, this change of feeling towards religious creeds and their sustaining institutions, has resulted from a deepening conviction that the sphere occupied by them can never become an unfilled sphere, but that there must continue to arise afresh the great questions concerning ourselves and surrounding things; and that, if not positive answers, then modes of consciousness standing in place of positive answers, must ever remain.

" We find, indeed, an unreflective mood general among both cultured and uncultured, characterised by indifference to everything beyond material interests and the superficial aspects of things. There are the many millions of people who daily see sunrise and sunset without ever asking what the Sun is. There are the university men, interested in linguistic criticism, to whom inquiries concerning the origin and nature of living things seem trivial. And even among men of science there are those who, curiously examining the spectra of nebulæ or calculating the masses and motions of double-stars, never pause to contemplate under other than physical aspects the immeasurably vast facts they record. But in both cultured and uncultured there occur lucid intervals. Some, at least, either fill the vacuum by stereotyped answers, or become conscious of unanswered questions of transcendent moment. By those who know much, more than by those who know little, is there felt the need for explanation."

At this point Herbert Spencer calls up the mysteries inherent in life, in the evolution of living beings, in consciousness, in human destiny—mysteries, says he, that the very advance of science makes more and more evident, exhibits as more and more profound and impenetrable; and then comes this final passage :

"Thus religious creeds, which in one way or other occupy the sphere that rational interpretation seeks to occupy and fails, and fails the more the more it seeks, I have come to regard with a sympathy based on community of need: feeling that dissent from them results from inability to accept the solutions offered, joined with the wish that solutions could be found."

III

THE VALUE OF THE DOCTRINE

Such being the real meaning of Herbert Spencer's doctrine, what shall we say as to its value?

According to several contemporary philosophers, belonging to the school of advanced positivism, it is very certain that the philosophy of Herbert Spencer reveals a decided religious tendency; we are quite justified in identifying his Unknowable with the creating God or Providence of actual religions. But that very fact indicates the weak side and obsolete part of the system—the part which it is the critic's special business to distinguish and eliminate.

In reality, say these philosophers, The Unknowable of Herbert Spencer is not a scientific principle: it is a residuum, a late survival of that imaginary entity which, under the name of God or First Cause, has, from time immemorial, formed the basis of religions and of metaphysical theories. And it is not a residuum that can be passed over. For, if maintained in the way suggested, it upholds what was essential in religion and metaphysics: viz., the inaccessible presented as object for man's speculation and possession. In truth, even the reservations and negations of Herbert Spencer are delusive. In so far as the initial error is maintained, the entire philosophy is compromised. So long as the source of infection continues, the disease only awaits the opportunity of breaking out and pervading, yet again, the whole organism. Accordingly, it is but too true that Herbert Spencer remains a theologian. To this extent he belongs to the past. His Unknowable ought to bear company, in the realm of nothingness, with all those phantoms which human reason has cast out. For, the only unknowable is the unknown, *i.e.* something that to-day we know not, but that to-morrow we shall, perhaps, know.

This objection, which has its origin in the very doctrine of evolution, was, of course, familiar to Herbert Spencer's mind. He, as much as any man, was accustomed to see the truth of yesterday become the error of to-day. But he acknowledged limits in the possible alteration of men's beliefs. According to him, the sheer impossibility of imagining the contrary of certain propositions imposes on the mind —whatever this may involve—adhesion to those propositions. We know, he has told us, that a proposition presents the highest degree of certainty, when its negation is inconceivable. Now, it is precisely in regard to The Unknowable, that he recognises such an inconceivability. Henceforward, for him, The Unknowable is a datum, it is given along with our mental constitution itself.

Is the impossibility thus felt by Herbert Spencer a delusion of his fancy, an indolence of his mind, a consequence of his individual temperament? It is remarkable that we find a similar attitude, a like insurmountable resistance to negation, not only in the experience of a Luther or of a Kant, but in the experience of many a contemporary thinker. Let us look, for instance, at the way in which Professor William James closes his famous book, *The Varieties of Religious Experience* :

"I *can*, of course, put myself into the sectarian scientist's attitude, and imagine vividly that the world of sensations and of scientific laws and objects may be all. But whenever I do this, I hear that inward monitor of which W. K. Clifford once wrote, whispering the word 'bosh!' Humbug is humbug, even though it bear the scientific name, and the total expression of human experience, as I view it objectively, invincibly urges me beyond the narrow 'scientific' bounds. Assuredly, the real world is of a different temperament,—more intricately built than physical science allows. So my objective and my subjective conscience both hold me to the over-belief which I express. Who knows whether the faithfulness of individuals here below to their own poor over-beliefs may not actually help God in turn to be more effectively faithful to His own greater tasks?"

Herbert Spencer is by no means alone in realising the impossibility of allowing either that science is self-sufficient or that it is sufficient for us. But, it may be said, we have to do, here, with a phenomenon which is explained psychologically—one to which we cannot attribute any importance. It is simply the application of a law which governs the relations existing between reason and imagination. A celebrated English moralist, Leslie Stephen, has stated this law as follows : *The imagination lags behind the reason.* When the reason has already demonstrated the fallacy of an opinion, the imagination, *i.e.* the heart, enamoured of this opinion, perseveres therein during a more or less lengthy period. Their evolution, in fact, requires an amount of mental labour which, though it has to be accomplished eventually, cannot be accomplished all at once : for harmony of the mind with itself is the supreme law, and, of the two powers thus brought face to face, reason is that which will not change.

The *non possumus* of Kant or of Herbert Spencer rests, such critics declare, on nothing but the law enunciated by Leslie Stephen. Without doubt, it is very real and very sincere ; but, in view of the progress of human reason, it is bound to succumb.

Is this estimate really made good ?

In the first place we may ask ourselves if it does not imply a vicious circle, if it does not take for granted, in advance, the negative solution of the very problem that Herbert Spencer raises. He (Spencer) wonders if the condemnation of certain traditional elements of religion involves the condemnation of their principle. The critics make reply : Since the various religions offer the appearance (even as regards their first principles) of hopelessly decaying structures, they ought to be utterly demolished— their very ruins should be cleared away and consigned to oblivion. And, since every religious belief is entirely empty and delusive, the constant effort to find therein something good and true can only come, it is evident, from the tardiness of imagination and feeling in following the lead of reason. Such a reply is not a demonstration ; it is only an argument put forward as the contrary of another argument.

Moreover, is it true that the impossibility affirmed by Herbert Spencer proceeds exclusively from feeling, and has no sort of rational basis ?

There can be no doubt that Herbert Spencer has given, in his philosophical doctrines—especially in those which have a practical bearing, an important place to

I

feeling. With the majority of Englishmen, he saw in reason, properly so called, an instrument rather than a principle of action, and reserved to feeling the power of instigating the soul. But it does not follow that his theory of The Unknowable rests exclusively on feeling.

The groundwork of the theory of knowledge taught by Herbert Spencer is to be found in the radical identity of the most precise knowledge and the ordinary ideas of the multitude. As ordinary ideas disclose a mingling of feeling and of reason, it cannot be doubted that every kind of knowledge, for Herbert Spencer, necessarily contains these two elements which are only disunited through a logical abstraction. And when the question is raised as to the final ground of certainty, there is, for Herbert Spencer, only one possible answer :—that, alike in the sphere of science and in the sphere of metaphysics, certainty rests on feeling, on feeling which is truly natural and not to be coerced.

Our only course, apparently, is to join Herbert Spencer in affirming that a radical separation of reason and feeling cannot be upheld, unless we mean to confine reason to dialectical reasoning alone, and to re-establish that circumscription of the human soul which modern psychology has taken so much trouble to refute. Reason, as we know it in experience, determinate and efficacious, is not something given once for all—an isolated attribute (eternal and immutable) of the human soul. It is something that becomes and grows, that is fashioned and trained. It is cultivated through being supplied with truths, as Descartes saw. It receives a twofold training in science and life. It contrives, prescribes, condenses and determines relatively whatever tends to make more real, more beneficial, more human, more striking, the development of man's complete powers —experience, feeling, imagination, desire, will. Thus it ought to be our supreme guide in practice as also in theory.

It is certainly to reason understood in this manner, rather than to disconnected feeling conceived in the blind and sluggish sense of an abstract rationalism, that Herbert Spencer makes appeal, in order to learn if it is possible for man to deny The Unknowable. Even though, in his opinion, it would not be strictly illogical to affirm that the phenomenal world is sufficient—that science has the power and the right to scatter all mysteries, such a contention would be unreasonable, extravagant. Man would have to renounce his highest faculties, those which, more than all the rest, make him man, before he could be brought to allow that what he knows or can know is the sum-total of being and perfection.

It is, then, foolish to reproach Herbert Spencer with having contradicted himself in maintaining a supersensible reality as object of religion, over against the given world as object of science ; foolish to have recourse to the theory of residuary organs and biological survivals in order to explain this so-called contradiction. As soon as it is seen that Herbert Spencer relies, not upon science pure and simple, but upon science interpreted by reason, this contradiction vanishes. For upon human reason itself, as it has become in contact with things, is inscribed the affirmation of an invisible reality—a reality which surpasses all that can be given us in experience.

.   .   .   .   .   .

But the supersensible of Herbert Spencer — regarded as transcendent and inaccessible—possesses this kind of being, in the highest degree. Herbert Spencer calls it The Unknowable. We are debarred from *realising it in thought.* We fall, he is persuaded, into insoluble contradictions—we can no longer see our way, when we go beyond the simple affirmation of the First Cause. Therein, perhaps, is to be found the debatable side of his doctrine.

In fact, as we have several times had occasion to remark, Herbert Spencer could not maintain that absolute transcendence and unknowableness of the fundamental Principle to which his inferences led him. His Absolute is force, power, energy, the infinite, the source of consciousness, the common ground of the *ego* and the *non-ego*, that which transcends intelligence and personality. Having regard to such terms, can it be claimed that this Absolute is entirely unknowable ; and, if the predicates that Herbert Spencer has fearlessly attributed to It are legitimate, is it certain that these rudiments of knowledge are incapable of progress and development ?

In order to estimate the value of Herbert Spencer's agnosticism, we must examine its principle. That principle is objectivism. Herbert Spencer is bent upon the employment of an exclusively objective method as the condition of all science, of all real knowledge. He sees in facts the one source of knowing ; and we are only justified in calling " fact " whatever is perceived or perceptible as an external thing, placed opposite the knowing subject : whatever can be grasped as a complete entity—fixed and separate : whatever is clearly expressible by a concept and by a word.

When once this doctrine of knowledge has been admitted, we are, of course, impelled towards the view that the supersensible, if existent, is unknowable. For it is evident that we cannot here assume one fragment of being beside other fragments—an object, in the meaning that adherents of objectivism give to that word. Between it (the supersensible) and the world of science thus conceived, there is no possibility of transition. If the supersensible exists, it must hover in vacuity, infinitely removed from all those objects which are accessible to our means of knowing. For the objectivist, therefore, the Absolute either is not, or is, literally, outside the world and transcendent.

We have now to ask if absolute objectivism is a possible and legitimate standpoint. Doubtless, the possibility of such a standpoint is the postulate of science : in virtue of it she sets herself to extract from nature certain distinct and quite limited images which she can arrange beside one another, compare, graduate, put in opposition, assimilate. But, can it be said that science reaches that complete objectivity which is her aim ? Must we not rather hold that she herself, like everything else human, furnishes an example of compromise between the possible and the ideal ? Does she ever obtain data entirely free from subjective elements, or results in which the concrete meaning implies no borrowing of feeling ? Even if, in the mathematico - physical sciences, the human mind approaches perfect objectivity, and sometimes delusively infers therefrom that the " perfection " has been realised, does it follow that what succeeds in one branch of knowledge is possible and adequate in all the other branches ? Why should all the sciences be constructed after the same pattern, and why should the said pattern be necessarily physical? Is a single case, then, sufficient for the establishment of an induction? Why should science make exception to this rule : that the human mind has to mould its conceptions in accordance with realities, and must not make realities depend on the shaping of its conceptions? Why, in science itself, should not the method be adapted to the object?

It is not clear that, in the physical sciences, all employment of the subjective method is actually eliminated, or that it ever can be eliminated. But we see plainly that the sciences dealing with things moral would be impoverished and perverted, if we really sought to treat them according to a purely objective method. How, in particular, could we know by such a method what is specific and distinctive in religious phenomena? To consider these from the outside would be to reduce them, in so far as they concern the individual, to certain nervous phenomena ; while, on the social side, they would be merely a collection of dogmas, of rites and of institutions. We should try to explain them by some elementary phenomenon borrowed from every-day experience, such an experience, for instance, as the naïve belief in the abiding reality of the double. But are there only elements of this kind, *i.e.* phenomena that are external, disconnected, definite and measurable, in actual religions—in the whole series of the religions which have been developed throughout the ages, in religion as it prevails in our very midst? Are we to reckon as nothing the inward life of Buddhist or Christian—a life of such intensity, such depth, such fruitfulness? Is not Mysticism a form of the religious

life? Is Protestantism without interest? And is it
not time, at this point, to bring forward once again
Shakespeare's famous lines :

> There are more things in heaven and earth, Horatio,
> Than are dreamt of in your philosophy.

Religion would appear, then, to be essentially the
connecting link between the relative and that Absolute
—Infinite and Perfect—which Herbert Spencer conceived. It is, at the same time, the endeavour to
develop, and bring nearer to perfection, subjective
life and knowledge : the conviction in regard to the
communion of a being that is external, particular,
limited, uncertain, with the common Source of all
existence—that Source which, according to Herbert
Spencer, wells up, and is, in some way, presented to
us in consciousness.

We cannot rest content with objectivism, because,
in reality, subject and object are nowhere actually
separated. In order to grasp the object separately,
we have to abandon ourselves to an artificial consideration of it, after the manner of a mathematician stating
the terms of a problem. As we find them given by
nature, in other words as they *are*, the object and the
subject make but one. In order to bring itself into
harmony with things, the human mind effects many an
abstraction, many a reduction of beings to concepts,
of which, for the most part, it can give no account.
Now, religion is the secret consciousness of the reality
of life, *i.e.* of the soul, and its connection with those
beings which, as perceived by our understanding,
seem to impinge on each other mechanically, like the
atoms of Democritus.

For this reason, religion cannot be made to consist

purely and simply in the mute recognition and adoration of that which is Unknowable and Transcendent. Herbert Spencer offers us too much or too little, and the extreme naturalists not unreasonably reproach him on that account. If the Humanity (Grand-Être) of Auguste Comte is an incomplete and unstable conception, seeing that man is, in essence, a being who goes beyond self, there is still greater reason why we cannot, with Herbert Spencer, place men in presence of the Being whence all things proceed, and then tell them that they can neither understand nor depend upon this Being in the smallest degree.

Let us call to mind the sentence already quoted : " Is it not just possible that there is a mode of being as much transcending intelligence and will as these transcend mechanical motion ? "

In the act of stating such a proposition, we go beyond it. How, if we imagine that such a mode of being is possible, are we to refrain from wishing that it may be, not only possible, but real ? How can we refrain from seeking the means of converting this possibility into reality ? What is reason, what is the human will, if not the attempt to symbolise that which is ideal, and to bring it within the limits of our world and of our life ? Is not the natural and necessary complement of Herbert Spencer's saying to be found in that other saying : ἐλθέτω ἡ βασιλεία σου, γενηθήτω τὸ θέλημά σου, ὡς ἐν οὐρανῷ καὶ ἐπὶ γῆς,[1] in other words—Let us pray and do our utmost that this divine kingdom of truth, of beauty and of goodness which human reason comprehends so imperfectly, may not be an ideal only ; that it may come within our reach, that it may be realised, not

---

[1] Thy kingdom come. Thy will be done, as in Heaven so on Earth.

simply in the Unknowable and in the transcendent region of the Absolute, but in the world wherein we live, wherein we love, wherein we suffer, wherein we labour; not simply in Heaven, but on Earth—καὶ ἐπὶ γῆς?

CHAPTER III

HAECKEL AND MONISM

I. THE DOCTRINE OF HAECKEL ON RELIGION IN ITS RELATIONS WITH SCIENCE—The conflicts between religion and science— Evolutionary Monism as a solution, both scientific and rational, of the enigmas which are the *raison d'être* of religions—The religious need—The progressive advance of existing religions, in so far as they possess utility, towards Evolutionary Monism as religion.

II. THE VALUE OF THE DOCTRINE—(*a*) The idea of a scientific philosophy : how does Haeckel pass from science to philosophy ? (*b*) Scientific philosophy as the negation and substitute of religions : how does Haeckel pass from Monism as philosophy to Monism as religion ?

III. SCIENTIFIC PHILOSOPHY AND ETHICS AT THE PRESENT TIME— Scientific philosophy : the obscurity or looseness'of this concept —The ethics of solidarity : the ambiguity of this term— Persistency of Dualism touching the relation between man and things.

NEITHER the system of Auguste Comte nor that of Herbert Spencer can be regarded as sufficing to obtain for the mind a state of permanent equipoise. Man, the king of nature, the organ and support of the Great Being, finds himself ill provided with room in the purely human universe of Auguste Comte. The Unknowable of Herbert Spencer cannot remain in the limbo to which he would consign it : if it exists, it must seek to unveil itself and to put its mark upon the real world. Moreover, these systems are thoroughly dualistic. Comte tends to consider man, more and more, apart from nature, while, for Herbert Spencer, the absolute is confronted by the relative. Now, if it were found possible, at length, to overcome this dualism completely, and to establish, once and for all, the fundamental unity of all things, should we not be able (taking this same unity as our starting-point) to settle in a definitive manner the tormenting question of the relations between religion and science? The position just indicated is that of Ernst Haeckel.

The distinguished Professor of Zoology in the University of Jena is not only the learned and original author of the *Generelle Morphologie der Organismen* (1866), the creator of Phylogeny. In such works as *Natürliche Schöpfungsgeschichte* (1868), which has been translated into a dozen languages; *Der Monismus als Band zwischen Religion und Wissenschaft* (1893); *Die Welträtsel* (1899); *Religion und Evolution* (1906), he has given expression to philosophical views which, beyond the value appertaining to them through the author's distinguished personality, possess this interest—that they represent, in a striking way, a state of mind very prevalent to-day, especially in the scientific world.

I

THE DOCTRINE OF HAECKEL ON RELIGION IN ITS RELATIONS WITH SCIENCE

It is time, so Haeckel believes, to have done with this method of mutual watchfulness, of abstract and metaphysical controversy, which always leads, one way or another, to our making a merely verbal reconciliation between the concept of science and the concept of religion. We must, once for all, bring them face to face : not science in itself and religion in itself—those idle scholastic entities, but religion and science as they are when, desirous of genuine meaning and concrete reality, we look at the conclusions which they both declare, the principles upon which they rest. That, for instance, is what J. W. Draper has done in a well-known book, entitled : *The Conflict between Religion and Science* (1875); that is what Haeckel intends to do, in his turn, when he comes to determine with precision the conditions of the conflict, and the method that ought to be followed in order to bring it to an end.

Let us push aside, says he at the beginning of his *Riddle of the Universe*, ultramontane Popery, as well as the orthodox Protestant sects which come little short of it in ignorance and gross superstition. Let us repair to the church of a broad-minded Protestant pastor who, thanks to a good average education and an enlightened perception, can make room for the claims of reason. Even here, amid moral precepts and humanitarian sentiments that are in complete harmony with our ideas, we hear expressed—on God, on the world and on man—propositions thoroughly inconsistent with scientific experience.[1]

Let us take a few examples of such inconsistencies.

Man, for our pastor, is the centre and goal of all terrestrial life — indeed, ultimately, of the entire universe.

[1] *Die Welträtsel,* chap. i.

The existence and preservation of the world are explained by what is termed Divine Creation and Providence. This Creation resembles the performance of a mechanician, who, aware of his capacity, thinks of putting it to some use, conceives the idea of a more or less intricate machine, sketches it in outline, and actually realises it through the employment of suitable materials. Then he watches it at work, and preserves it from wear and from accident.

Since this God is fashioned after the human pattern, it is quite easy to think of him as having, himself, created man in his own image. Thence arises a third dogma, which consummates the apotheosis of the human organism : man's nature is twofold, he is a compound of material body and spiritual soul—the product of the divine breath. And his soul, endowed with immortality, is but the temporary guest of his perishable body.

These dogmas form the groundwork of the Mosaic cosmogony. They are to be met with, as regards their essential elements, in the various religions. They consist, to put the matter shortly, in an anthropomorphic conception of nature : of nature, that is, regarded as only the artificial working of a supernatural power. Nothing within nature can be considered as proceeding from her. The transcendent god rules over her, just as he has created and preserved her, and he does whatever he pleases with the laws of her existence : those very laws are but the arbitrary caprices of the creator.

The foundation of these dogmas is the tradition, or transmission, through the ages, of notions relating to a supernatural revelation.

Such are the affirmations of religion : what has science to say on these same matters ?

We must carefully decide upon the attitude which the scientist ought to take, before we reply to this question.

Metaphysicians are accustomed to say that these matters with which we are now dealing are not the concern of science—that they altogether go beyond the range of its knowing powers. And a number of scientists, happily at work in their laboratories, show themselves indifferent to problems that cannot be solved by the aid of instruments and calculations. Our knowledge is confined to facts, say they, and so it comes about that they cannot see the wood for the trees. That is the origin of the misconception which endures among men of intelligence. By reason of this abstention on the part of professional scientists— whether through timidity, contempt, or indifference, theologians and metaphysicians continue to dogmatise with impunity. It would seem that science and religion do not move in the same world, that their assertions never bring them into contact. This state of things will subsist as long as science, limited to empirical research, omits to treat of philosophical problems. Science began with the study of details : that was only fitting, and it is through such procedure that she has obtained definitive results. But the time has come for her to generalise, in her turn, and to bring forward, with regard to those questions of origin which exercise the human mind, the demonstrations of experience and of reason against dogmas that are based on sentiment and imagination. At last the time has come to establish a scientific philosophy or rational interpretation of the results of science, and to deal therein with the questions which, up to now, have been left to theologians and meta-physicians.

That is, in Haeckel's view, what follows from the general state of modern science, as it is presented in the works of such men as Lamarck, Goethe, and Darwin. Thanks to the discoveries and speculations of these great men, we are able, henceforward, to see clearly what are the main laws of nature, and what meaning is to be gathered from them.

The philosophy which is the outcome of science is summed up in two words : Monism and Evolutionism. On the one hand, being is one, and all modes of existence are of one nature, so that every difference between them is one of degree merely, *i.e.* quantitative. On the other hand, being is not motionless, but possesses a principle of change ; this change, in itself purely mechanical and subject to immutable laws, is the origin of the various kinds of existence, and these are, accordingly, the result of an entirely natural creation.

It is from the standpoint of this philosophy that science, henceforward, ought to approach the questions with which religion is occupied.

Now, starting in this way, science puts forward conclusions which are absolutely hostile to religious dogmas.

Man, according to scientific philosophy, cannot be the centre and aim of the universe. Man is a link in the chain of being, a link which is just as surely connected with the rest of existence as worms are connected with the protista, or fishes with worms. His superiority is but an instance of the extraordinary manner in which the vertebrates have got ahead of their congeners in the course of universal evolution.

In place of the world's artificial creation, science maintains the theory of natural creation. Nature contains in herself all the forces requisite for the production of every kind of existence that is to be found within her realm. The species are born from one another, through transmutation, in accordance with laws and with an order that can, hereafter, be determined. And thus, for the myth of creation, science substitutes the natural history of the world.

The dogma of the immortality of the soul is no less contrary to science, which regards the human individual as only a transitory combination of material particles, analogous to all other combinations.

The general principle of religious dogmas is found in anthropomorphism, artificial creation, and the supernatural. Instead of these notions science suggests those of naturalism, continuity, and natural creation. There is nothing in nature which cannot be explained by nature. She cannot be preceded by anything, nor can anything go beyond her. For the man who enters into the meaning of her laws, especially those of Natural Selection and Evolution, nature is, herself, the author of her existence and of her progress. In this way science is to religion what Darwin is to Moses.

This opposition of doctrines is in keeping with that of the actual bases. Religion rests on revelation : Science knows nothing beyond experience. No idea, according to the scientific view, has value, unless it is either the immediate expression of facts, or the result of an inference determined by those natural laws which govern the association of ideas.

Religious delusion cannot, therefore, prevail in the future, unless we deliberately blind ourselves. If we consider actual science, as constituted by Lamarck and Darwin, there is a direct contradiction, an absolute incompatibility between the affirmations of science and those of religion, as regards the fundamental problems of being and of knowing. It is, then, impossible for an enlightened ·and consistent mind to approve both at the same time. The choice must, necessarily, be made between them.

Now, the Monistic philosophy—the philosophy of evolution, *i.e.* of science—which causes the conflict to break out, furnishes at the same time the means of deciding it.

According to that philosophy, wherever this conflict springs up, no mind cast in a scientific mould can hesitate. That belief of ours in revelation, in faith—a belief which is really based upon the emotion and feeling, not only of our subjective states of consciousness, but of our very knowing faculty— represents an inferior stage of intelligence that man has already overpassed. Man, in the existing period of his development, realises that knowledge is supplied to him exclusively through experience and ratiocination, which together constitute what is called reason. Reason, it is true, does not belong to all men in equal degree, but is developed in the human mind by means of educational progress; and, even to-day, a man devoid of modern culture possesses about as much reason as our near relatives among the mammalia— apes, dogs, or elephants.

These principles once admitted, man cannot fail to acquiesce in the conclusions of scientific philosophy. For these conclusions, which, up to the time of

K

Lamarck and Darwin, were mere guesswork, have become, thanks to the labours of these two scientists, actual truths of experience—as much so as the laws of natural philosophy. The great achievement of the nineteenth century, an achievement analogous to that of Newton in the seventeenth, consisted in referring biological phenomena to laws which were clearly as mechanical and natural as those controlling brute matter. To-day, by observation and experience alone, we know for certain that the same great laws —eternal and irreversible — operate in the vital processes of animals and plants, in the growth of crystals, and in the expanding power of vapour.

The universal naturalism that science substitutes for the supernatural creationism of religions is no longer a mere hypothesis agreeable to the scientific mind—it is plain matter of fact.

This conclusion may appear over-bold to some. From the fact of our now being able to explain mechanically, *i.e.* scientifically, a number of phenomena which formerly seemed to call for supernatural agents, can we infer that all things will be, henceforward, explained or even explainable in the same manner? Is it true that science has completely and once for all abolished mystery? But if mystery remains, if it may conceivably remain, in any part of the universe, to all eternity, is there not still room for religion, for the emotions and the revelations belonging to it? How comes it, after all, that the human mind is surrounded by impenetrable mysteries unless we allow a supposition of this kind? Why does man appeal to revelation if not because it sets at rest certain questions which his reason cannot solve?

Now, says Haeckel (speaking as recently as 1880, before the gathering held in honour of Leibnitz at the Berlin Academy of Sciences), Professor Emil Dubois-Reymond has made the assertion that the universe involves seven enigmas, and that, of these, four at least are absolutely insoluble, so far as we are concerned. *Ignorabimus!* That, he declared, was to be the last word of science in regard to these matters. The four transcendent enigmas were, according to Dubois-Reymond : the essence of matter and force, the origin of movement, the origin of simple sensation, and free-will (unless, indeed, subjective freedom is to be considered as an illusion). The three other enigmas, viz. the origin of life, the apparent finality of nature, and the origin of thought and language, could only, with extreme difficulty, be stated in terms of scientific mechanism.

Such an assertion, in Haeckel's opinion, cannot be too energetically combated ; for it means that everything is called in question again. Once we allow mystery to come in, there is nothing to prevent its entry at all points. We must declare that science is, from this time, justified in proclaiming unequivocally : The world, from the standpoint of man, has no more mysteries to offer.

The difficulties here suggested arise, in the first instance, through our putting forward, under the term matter, an indescribable something—amorphous and inert—and then going on to ask how, from this nothingness, such powers as force, movement and sensation are able to spring. But the hypothesis from which we thus start, is arbitrary and imaginary. Such a substratum is neither given nor conceivable. Science, in her knowledge of facts alone, cannot allow a principle of this kind. That which is given irreducibly, and which, in consequence, is of prime importance for her, is not an indeterminate and passive substance, incapable of entering upon movement and action unless stirred and quickened from without; it is an essentially animated substance, at once extension, *i.e.* matter, and energy, *i.e.* mind.

"We hold with Goethe," says Haeckel, "that matter cannot exist and operate without mind, nor mind without matter. And we approve the comprehensive monism of Spinoza : Matter, or infinitely extended substance, and mind, or feeling and thinking substance, are the two fundamental attributes or special qualities of the divine essence (universal substance) which embraces all things."[1]

These concepts have nothing mystical about them. They rest : firstly, upon the laws of the persistence of matter and the persistence of force, conceived originally by Lavoisier, and afterwards established by Mayer and Helmholtz; secondly, upon the unity of these two laws, a unity which science is led to admit, and which, in the last analysis, necessarily proceeds from the very principle of causality. Goethe has shown, in his *Wahlverwandtschaften,* how the affinities in human experience are only those which, in greater complexity, are found existing between the molecules of the body : how the irresistible passion which drives Paris towards Helen, and which makes him violate every rule of reason and of morality, is the same unconscious power of attraction that impels the spermatozoon to open for itself a passage into the ovum in order to realise fertilisation—the same impetuous movement which combines two atoms of

[1] *Die Welträtsel,* chap. i.

hydrogen with an atom of oxygen in order to form a molecule of water. Let us not, then, be afraid of saying (like Empedocles of old) that Love and Hate control the elements. This guess on the part of genius has to-day become matter of experience.

And thus, in our view, it has been shown that the atom itself is not without possessing a rudiment of feeling and of inclination—the germ, in fact, of a soul. The same argument applies, equally, to molecules, which are composed of two or more atoms, as well as to the compounds, more and more complex, of these molecules.[1]

The mode of these combinations is purely mechanical; but, even by virtue of mechanism, the psychical element of things is complicated and diversified with their material elements.

Once in possession of these principles, science solves—or, at any rate, knows that she is on the way to solve—all problems.

First of all, opposite ponderable, inert matter, she sets the ever-moving ether or imponderable matter: at the same time premising, between the ether and ponderable matter, eternal action and reaction. And these two elements, representing the twofold division of universal substance, suffice to explain the most general phenomena of nature.

Science, however, labours in vain so long as she fails to grapple with the greatest and most difficult problem which the mind of man is called upon to face—that relating to the origin and development of things. Now, she can, henceforward, for the purpose of solving this problem, make use of a magic word that Lamarck and Darwin have taught her, viz.

---

[1] *Die Welträtsel,* chap. xii.

Evolution. By virtue of the laws of evolution, the
various forms of existence are connected with one
another through natural descent; their development,
their creation is explained by the simple action
of uniform mechanism. And, though a thousand
problems still remain unsolved, we are able, in the
light of those which we have already succeeded in
overcoming, to realise that all partial questions bearing on creation are linked together indivisibly, that
they represent a cosmical problem which is one and
all-inclusive, and that, therefore, the key to one
problem is necessarily the key to every other.

But what is the origin of evolution itself? Must
we attribute it to the action of a supernatural
principle, and thus leave present in the whole that
very element of miracle which we have driven out of
the parts?

We should be brought to this extremity if we
took for our principle a matter destitute of energy
and, on that account, incapable of evolving by itself.
But the animated substance that we have put forward, has, within itself, a principle of change and
of creation. It does not exclude God, it is, itself,
God—a God intramundane and identical with Nature.
It ought to be understood that, if the scientist rejects
Theism, he no less rejects Atheism. For him, God
and the World are one. Pantheism is the scientific
conception of the Universe.

In this way vanish, before the search-light of
modern science, the so-called enigmas regarding the
origin of matter and force, of movement and of
sensation. As to the question of free-will, which
has kept the world busy for two thousand years, and
which has produced so many books that encumber

our libraries and accumulate dust therein — this
question, also, is no more than a memory. Of what
value are vague suggestions based upon sentiment,
in comparison with scientific deductions ? The will,
indeed, is not an inert force. It is a power of auto-
matic and conscious reaction, which is regulative
and actively influential. But the inclinations that
are inseparable from life itself explain this attribute ;
and, as to the mode of action inherent in the will,
we only consider it free because, following the abstract
and dualistic method of metaphysicians, we isolate
this faculty from the conditions which determine it.
We have not, first of all, to consider the will separately,
and then to examine the circumstances wherein it
acts. The will as given is burdened with a thousand
determinations that heredity has settled upon it.
And each of its resolutions is an adaptation of its
pre-existing inclination to actual circumstances. The
strongest motive prevails mechanically, by virtue of
the laws which govern the statics of emotion. If,
then, the abstract and merely verbal will appears
free, the concrete will is determined like everything
else in the universe.

All the enigmas of Dubois-Reymond are, therefore,
solvable, or rather, from this time forward, they are
solved. The unknowable has no existence. The
word stands for nothing but the unknown ; and it
is no longer the principles of things, but their details
only, of which, in future, we can remain in ignorance.
The philosopher is little concerned that the extent
of this ignorance is enormous, and must always
continue to be considerable.

Still, it would be a mistake to assert purely and
simply : there is no longer any enigma. One enigma

remains, and necessarily remains, viz. the problem of substance. What is this prodigious energy that the man of science calls—Nature or Universe, the idealist—Substance or Cosmos, the believer—Creator or God? Can we affirm that, thanks to the wonderful advances made in modern Cosmology, we have solved the problem of substance, or that we are in sight of its solution?

In truth, the last foundation of Nature is as unattainable by our minds as it was by the mind of an Anaximander or an Empedocles, of a Spinoza or a Newton, of a Kant or a Goethe. We must even confess that this substance becomes, in its essential constitution, the more mysterious and the more enigmatical in proportion as we penetrate further into the knowledge of its attributes and of its evolution. We do not know the "thing-in-itself" which lies beneath knowable phenomena.

But why should we trouble ourselves over this thing-in-itself, since we have not the means of studying it, since we cannot even be sure whether it exists? Let us leave the barren task of brooding on this unintelligible phantom to the metaphysician; and let us, like genuine scientists and realists, take pleasure in the immense headway that has been made in our science and in our philosophy.[1]

.   .   .   .

In short, the comparison between science and religion leads to the recognition that they are contradictory in their affirmations; and the philosophical examination of their respective doctrines leaves no room for the dogmas of religion in opposition to the conclusions of science. Does it follow that we have

[1] *Die Welträtsel*, Conclusion.

only to consign religion to the past, among those things which time has cut down and which are to be traced merely in the pages of history?

We are, perhaps, disposed to subscribe to that opinion, if we regard religion and science as two abstract doctrines—if we disengage them from that human soul which is their common ground. But religion has not been invented solely with a view to the vanity of theologians: its real aim is to satisfy certain primary needs of man; and, so long as it cannot be shown that these needs find elsewhere full and entire satisfaction, religion will reappear—no matter how thoroughly it has been suppressed—and will reappear justifiably as an essential factor in human life.

These demands are peculiar to the human mind, and cannot be evaded; one of them is concerned with the explanation of the origin and nature of things. To this demand science undoubtedly paid no attention, so long as she confined herself to the mere record of phenomena and to the study of particular laws. But scientific philosophy is now able to bestow on science her full width of range, and to infer, from her experimental discoveries, the solution of the great enigmas of the universe. Thus, on the side of theory, the elimination of religion is already an accomplished fact.

Now, man has not only theoretical needs, but those, also, which practice brings to light. He has to reckon with affection and sentiment as well as reason; and, since the emotional element of his nature is not less real and essential, its wants, also, ought to be met. Science will only have the right to dimiss religion on the day when, more surely and better than her rival, she shall have learnt to satisfy man's heart, as well as his intellect.

The scientist who, through reflection, has become a philosopher, and who has discovered the rational secret of carrying the inductions begun by science to the very end, feels no anxiety in this respect. The practical range of science is not, in his eyes, less wide than its theoretical range. He is ready to show that science, through her doctrines on the universe and on life, is capable (indeed, that she alone is capable) of bringing emotional satisfaction to man.

But he cannot deny that these considerations are still mainly theoretical. The practical achievement of science is not to be realised, down to the veriest detail, in a day. In her exposition there will remain, for a long time to come, certain gaps of which the various religions will make the most. And not only will these religions be actually maintained so long as science shall fail to perform all the tasks that she has undertaken ; but their preservation, during that period, ought to be regarded as salutary and good in some respects.

It is not, then, sufficient to declare that, in principle, religious beliefs have been abolished. They are, in truth, still with us, and they have a service to discharge for many a long day. Science ought, therefore, to come to terms with them, and to find a bond of union between Religion and Science.

Now this bond is furnished by that very philosophy which ensures the exclusive ascendency of science in the future, viz. Evolutionary Monism.

This philosophy, followed up to its practical consequences, ends in the threefold cult of the True, the Good and the Beautiful—a real Trinity offered in place of the Trinity that theologians have imagined.[1]

In connection with this formula of a trinity, what is to be the attitude of Monism towards that faith which is generally regarded as the highest of all religions—Christianity?

As regards Truth, we ought not, according to the Monistic view, to preserve anything in religious Revelation so called. This revelation teaches a "beyond" which has no meaning for us, and it lowers to the rank of unstable phenomenon, that which we have come to consider as the only reality.

As regards Beauty, the contradiction is particularly flagrant between Monism and Christianity. For Christianity teaches us to despise nature, to withstand her charms, to do our part in battling against the inclinations that she inspires. It extols asceticism—the emaciation and disfigurement of the human body. It challenges the arts, seeing that their creations always threaten to become, for man, idols capable of serving as a substitute for God. In fact, what is called Christian art has never been anything but the protest of the imagination and of the senses against the ultra-spirituality of the Christian standpoint. How are we to reconcile the grandeur and beauty of Gothic cathedrals with a religion that regards the earth merely as a vale of tears? Christian art is a term involving contradiction. Monism, on the other hand, is essentially naturalistic, and a friend of Beauty, which it recognises as an end in itself. Consequently it will oust Christianity from the domain of art, no less than from the domain of science.

We have still to consider the cult of Goodness.

---

[1] *Der Monismus als Band*, etc.

Here Monistic religion agrees, for the most part, with the Christian religion. We are now alluding, of course, only to Christianity in the pure and primitive form depicted for us in the Gospels and in the Pauline Epistles. Most of the teachings of Christianity, as therein presented, are precepts of charity and forbearance, of pity and comfort, and to all of them we firmly adhere. These precepts, moreover, are not the discoveries of Christianity : they can be traced much further back. They have been carried out by unbelievers, quite as much as they have been disregarded by the faithful. Furthermore, as practised among the adepts of revealed religion, they are not without a touch of exaggeration, often exalting altruism to the prejudice of self-reliance. The Monistic philosophy, on the contrary, adjusts the balance between these two tendencies, both equally natural to man. But, if restricted to measuring the value of its main principles, the Christian religion may become an auxiliary of Monism and promote moral advancement; and—understood in this sense—it ought to be actually supported in the name of Monism itself.

Thus we find in Monism the connecting link between religion and science after which we have been groping.

The course to be taken will consist, shortly, in making an intelligent use of religions, so as to get rid of their unnecessary co-operation by degrees : just as, in order to cross a river, we make use of a footbridge, and have nothing more to do with it when we have reached the other bank.

Adopting this method, we shall, first of all, bring about the complete separation of Church and State, in order to take away from the Church the factitious

support of the State, and to make it dependent upon
its own resources alone.

The positive complement of this negative measure
is educational reform : such a complement is, indeed,
indispensable.   Education is the most important
question of all for a society which is anxious to
extricate itself from religious beliefs.   The object of
a genuine education is to shape man, *i.e.* man in his
entirety : to care for the emotional side of his being
as much as the intellectual side, for his religious soul
as much as his scientific mind.

Public education cannot allow any religious
formularies : she shuts out such formularies from the
school, abandoning them to home instruction.   Public
education directs and makes use of the principles of
scientific morality, *i.e.* of the practical teaching which
proceeds from Evolutionary Monism.   It does not
ignore existing religions, but it takes from them the
subject-matter of a new science—that of Comparative
Religion.   The myths and legends of Christianity are
considered therein, not as truths, but as poetical
fictions, analogous to Greek and Latin myths.   The
ethical or æsthetical value that myths may contain
will not be lessened through being traced to their
real source in human imagination ; such value will be
thereby increased.

The man of a later day, in possessing science and
art, will possess religion : consequently, he will not
be obliged to shut himself within that walled portion
of space which is named a church.   Everywhere
throughout the great world, besides the fierce struggle
for existence, he will discover signs of Goodness, of
Truth and of Beauty ; and in this way his church will
be the Universe.

But there will always be men to whom retirement into richly decorated temples, for the purpose of a common cult, will appear desirable; and we may, therefore, expect that—in line with what took place in the sixteenth century when a number of Catholic churches fell into the hands of the Protestants—there will, at some future time, be a still larger transference of Christian churches to Monistic communities.[1]

II

THE VALUE OF THE DOCTRINE

The doctrine of Haeckel on the relations between religion and science is very precise. According to him, the uncertainty which prevails, even to-day, upon this subject, has its origin in the antipathy of scientists towards those speculations which outstrip their own immediate and particular investigations. Let science, seeing that she is quite ready for such a course, adopt the rôle of philosophy, and she will then be able, not only to refute, but to take the place of existing religions.

This doctrine raises two main subjects of inquiry : (1) The idea of a scientific philosophy ; (2) Scientific philosophy considered as the negation and substitute of religions.

.   .   .   .   .   .

The idea of combining philosophy and science was quite simple in the Greek world. Science, as then defined, was keenly alive to the principles of order, of harmony, of unity and of finality which were the common foundation of reason and things : she was,

1 *Die Weltätsel*, chap. xviii.

accordingly, metaphysical in essence. And philosophy was the mind, recognising its own æsthetical and rational principles in those of nature and of human life.

For men of to-day the outlook is different. Science has more and more got rid of everything connected with metaphysics. She is (or wishes to be) entirely positive : in other words, she intends to confine her survey to facts, and to those inductions which are exclusively determined by facts. A scientific philosophy would, therefore, be a philosophy devoid of all metaphysics—finding in facts its necessary and sufficient ground. Is such a philosophy possible ?

Philosophy, according to Haeckel, is essentially inquiry into the nature and origin of things. We can distinguish it from science properly so called through seeing that it is not satisfied with investigating the peculiar nature of such and such a body, or the approximate cause of such and such a class of phenomena, but that, generalising problems, it considers whether there are, indeed, common and universal principles, capable of explaining both the laws of nature collectively and the origin of all existence. Now, if for a long time science has not succeeded in supplying philosophy with data that can be regarded as adequate for the examination of these problems, the situation, according to Haeckel, has become altogether different since the labours of Laplace, Mayer and Helmholtz, of Lamarck and Darwin. To-day, science—in the real sense of knowing facts—has made such ample progress in studying the problems of essence and of origin, that philosophy can accomplish her task through scientific co-operation alone. We need only interpret, rationally, the great discoveries of modern scientists—following, in this respect, the example of such men as Lamarck, Goethe, and Darwin.

What is the real gist of this line of thought, which has to justify humanity in preserving philosophy, while entirely repudiating metaphysics?

Haeckel's purpose is, evidently, to conceive scientific experience and philosophical interpretation as being simply, at bottom, one and the same mental process. After quoting those lines of Schiller wherein the poet exhorts scientists and philosophers to become united in effort instead of being divided, he declares that the end of the nineteenth century saw a return to the monistic attitude which the great poet of realism —Goethe—had presciently adopted, at the beginning of that same century, as the only one that was healthy and permanent.

We are now wondering, perhaps, if Haeckel has been able to carry out his intention in very truth.

Treating—in the first chapter of his work, *Die Welträtsel*—of the philosophical methods through which the riddles of the world may be solved, he says that these methods are not actually different from those used in purely scientific investigation. They are (as in science) experience and inference.

Experience comes to us by way of the senses, while inferences are the work of reason. We must take care not to confuse these two modes of knowledge. Sense and reason are the functions of two entirely distinct portions of the nervous system. As, moreover, these two functions are equally natural to man, the exercise of the second is no less legitimate than the exercise of the first, provided that it take place in conformity with the dictates of nature. If metaphysicians are wrong in isolating reason from the senses, scientists err just as much in pretending to eject reason. It is quite a mistake to declare that philosophy has had its day, and has been replaced by science. How are we to describe the cellular theory, the dynamic theory of heat, the theory of evolution and the law of substance, except as rational, *i.e.* philosophical doctrines?

The explanations given by Haeckel would seem to throw hardly sufficient light upon this transition from science to philosophy which, according to him, ought to decide all problems. In order to justify this transition, Haeckel draws attention to the joint presence of reason and sense in those animals which are beneath man in the scale of existence. He maintains that the reason differs from the senses through having its seat in other parts of the nervous system; and he asks why we should be debarred from using our reason in conformity with nature any more than from using our senses. But how does all this prove that, in reason, there is no principle of interpretation apart from scientific inference properly so called, and that, in viewing things from a standpoint other than that of the scientist, the mind is unquestionably at fault? In order to arrive at this conclusion, we should have to be provided with a survey of the contents of reason, and for such a survey we look to Haeckel in vain.

Possibly, indeed, a precise theory of reason, whatever it were, would be embarrassing at this point? Scientific philosophy, as it is conceived by Haeckel, must differ, in some way, from science; its conclusions are bound to go beyond those of science pure and simple, though connected therewith according to the relationship of continuity. Now, if it be assumed that there is, literally, nothing more in reason than what the scientist turns to account, the philosopher, notwithstanding all his efforts, will nowise be able to outstrip science, unless, above a science that is exact and true, he decides to place a science that is inaccurate and false. In this hypothesis, only science is legitimate ; and all philosophy is but science under another name, or mere literary caprice. On the other hand, if there are, in reason as naturally constituted, certain principles besides those of which science makes use, we must abandon the hope of establishing a continuity between science and philosophy ; we must acknowledge, between the two, a distinction, not only of degree, but of kind.

But doubtless the very system that Haeckel has constructed, reveals, by itself, the possibility of realising a purely scientific philosophy. If this philosophy exists, and if its working proves that it really possesses scientific certainty, though inexplicable in terms of the scientific method pure and simple, why trouble ourselves because we cannot altogether see in theory how, from science, we are to derive a philosophy which may or may not be science ?

This system is Evolutionary Monism. Accepting the laws discovered by a Newton, a Lavoisier, a Mayer, or a Darwin, Monism is not restricted to adopting, defending, determining and enlarging these laws—in fresh cases—with originality, penetration, daring or recklessness : that would be merely to continue a specifically scientific task, subject to control, to rectification, to modification—like every other theory of science. Monism sets up as dogmas the formulæ that it has drawn out, announcing that the conception of the world therein presented is enjoined upon us once for all, as a logical necessity, by the recent advances in our knowledge of nature. It would claim for those very propositions which are deduced scientifically, a certainty beyond that of science—a truly metaphysical certainty.

A first characteristic to be attributed to its principles, to its substance—one implied in its twofold nature and in its law of evolution—is absolute determination, fixity, eternity. Now, we could not, by the aid of merely scientific logic, definitely ascribe eternity to even the most fundamental principles of the sciences; for, in science, fundamental principles are functions of particular laws, and these laws can never be considered as determined in an unalterable manner.

Haeckel assigns universality as a second characteristic to his principles. But he cannot call scientific, or analogous to scientific induction, the generalisation through which he extends to all possible kinds of existence the properties that actual science claims for those beings which have come under her observation. The induction of which he here avails himself is that *inductio per enumerationem simplicem*, destitute of analysis and criticism, which in science is quite valueless. The beings of our observation present, in a portion of time, certain phenomena which cannot be summed up in words about unity of constitution and of evolution (words, moreover, which do nothing more than express general ideas, admitting of very different determinations): existence is, therefore, one, and subject, in the totality of its manifestations, to one and the same law of evolution. We have to do here, not with an induction, but a transmutation of the particular into the universal.

Does the system, when all has been said, leave to the words *unity* and *evolution* a scientific and experimental sense? It is difficult to grant this.

The One of Haeckel dominates ether and ponderable matter, brute matter and living matter, extension and thought, the world and God. It is essentially alive, sentient, capable of action, endowed with reason in the deepest sense. As to evolution, on the one hand, Haeckel pronounces it strictly mechanical, though, apparently, it exceeds the forces known to science (actual science at least); on the other hand, he knows that, in spite of cases of reversion to lower grades, advance towards perfection predominates, though this, likewise, is something more than a generalisation.

He describes his system [1] in terms of Pantheism, thus indicating that God is not outside the world, but at the very heart of it—that He works from within, through force or energy. The rational interpretation of things, Haeckel declares, is the monistic conception of the unity of God and the world.

Here again, the distinction between " within " and " outside," between a transcendent force and an immanent force, sets one thinking about metaphysics much more than about science.

In fine, after having promised to reduce everything unknowable to the unknown—to an unknown, similar, in its essence, to the knowable—Haeckel brings us to a law of substance which, according to him, becomes increasingly mysterious as we penetrate further into the knowledge of its attributes.

[1] *Die Welträtsel*, chap. xv.

It is, then, impossible to consider his philosophy as a simple extension of science. We were told at the start that it would have regard not only to the senses, but to the reason : that it would really illustrate the method of the philosopher, and not only that of the scientist. Its method, most assuredly, is philosophical as well as scientific ; but the philosophical elements which it contains are clearly borrowed from what in metaphysics is termed dogmatism.

.   .   .   .   .   .

Does this philosophy, as we find it set forth, perform the task which Haeckel assigns to it—the task of refuting and replacing religion ?

In order to pave the way for a complete and definitive refutation of religions, Haeckel undertakes, in the first place, to exhibit their fundamental principle. He finds this principle in Dualism. The various religions have beheld on all sides, as the outcome of a radical duality, a struggle of natural forces and of supernatural forces. The innumerable applications to which this idea has given rise, can be summed up, according to Haeckel, in two main contentions : the duality of God and the world expressed in the doctrine of design, and the duality of man and nature expressed in the doctrine of human freedom.

In his philosophy, Haeckel finds the process of reasoning necessary for refuting these two erroneous beliefs which lie at the root of all others.

Theology, says he, starts from the hypothesis (based on superficial analogies) of a world that is but an inert machine. Now, a machine calls for an artificer, and a machine that is incomparably more perfect than all human machines requires, in like manner, an artificer infinitely superior to human artificers.

This anthropomorphic reasoning breaks down as soon as it is realised, in harmony with the teaching of Monism, that the world is not a machine, but an essentially living being.

Similarly, the delusion of free-will arises through our failing to take note of the obscure impulses which determine our acts, and through our believing in self-activity simply because we do not perceive the forces that are driving us : hence, theoretically, we isolate action from the conditions of its exercise. Thus set apart, our activity appears to us as indeterminate. But Monism proves that a bare activity is an abstraction ; that, in reality, activity is simply one with matter wherein lie the conditions of its exercise ; and that, consequently, every given activity is entirely determined.

In this way, declares Haeckel, the props of the traditional religions—those very props which were deemed so unshakable—collapse in presence of Evolutionary Monism.

But is it quite certain that, in destroying the Mosaic doctrine of the creation and the Scholastic doctrine of the liberty of indifference, Haeckel has, at the same time, destroyed everything that gives support to religions ?

Haeckel knows but one kind of design, viz. external and transcendent design as illustrated in the altogether mechanical relation of the manufacturer to his production. In showing that this conception of design cannot be applied to the world, he imagines that he has done away with every kind of teleology. But this conception, which, after all, scarcely suggests the supernatural except in name (seeing that God is therein likened to terrestrial beings), cannot be considered as representing the philosophical doctrine of design in an adequate manner. From Aristotle to Hegel, philosophy has conceived, more and more clearly, a design that is not external, but internal; not mechanical, but dynamic; not fixed, but living— a design which does not consist in any sudden overthrow of the natural order of things, but which, inwardly developing life and the struggle for something better, is manifested in the actual laws of nature.

Again, the theory of freedom to be found in the teaching of an Aristotle, of a Descartes, of a Leibnitz or of a Kant, hardly resembles that which Haeckel restricts himself to considering and refuting. Those philosophers have professed the very doctrine that Haeckel puts forward in opposition to them—the doctrine concerning the unity behind freedom and its conditions of action in the will as real and given; and, far from their having been satisfied with the imaginative and mechanical conception of an artificer making use of forces external to himself, the tendency of their speculation has been towards conceiving this unity, with growing confidence, as dynamic and living.

In short, the conceptions of design and freedom that we find among representative philosophical thinkers, obviously tend, in their turn, towards a doctrine of unity. In carrying out this aim, would they have shown themselves at variance with the religious disposition? And would Haeckel have been right in pronouncing such a disposition thoroughly dualistic?

Haeckel's assertion constitutes an expression of

opinion rather than an authentication of facts.
Many religions rest precisely on the hypothesis
of an original unity embracing the human and the
divine.   In religion we are to find the means of
translating this unity into life, and of re-establish-
ing it where it has been broken off.   Far from
dualism being the essence of religion, *unity* is the
fundamental dogma which is revealed in the highest
examples, and there are plenty of passages to prove
this.   One of the best-known and most significant is
the Stoic maxim taken over by Christianity : " In
Him we live, and move, and have our being."

Still, it is quite true that religions teach a dualism,
a separation of God and nature, while tending to
reunite them.

They teach an actual duality, when the unity
represents to them what is right and what ought to
become fact.   " Thy kingdom come.   Thy will be
done, as in heaven so on earth ! "   This means : let
the separation which is actually found between
creatures and the Supreme Being come to an end,
and let the hidden unity underlying all things be
realised !

This conception of an actual duality, coexistent
with the essential unity of being, contains nothing,
in principle, which can give offence to Haeckel ; for
it is in this way that he himself apprehends the world
and human life.   After having shown how substance
is, at bottom, necessarily one, Haeckel goes on to state
that it is manifested under two essential aspects
which are opposed to one another : vibratory ether
and inert matter.   He is even of opinion that this
dualism might furnish a rational basis to religion.
It would be sufficient for this purpose, he says, to

consider the universal vibratory ether as the creating deity, and the inert ponderable mass as the matter of creation.[1] Similarly, human nature—fundamentally one—is realised, according to Haeckel, under the double form of emotion and reason, which are given as opposite expressions. The search after truth, for instance, is the concern of reason alone : we are therein debarred altogether from feeling. Philosophical progress consists in accurately describing the dualism of feeling and reason, and in completely separating the latter from the former.

Speaking generally, Haeckel's turn of mind is dualistic. All truth is for him on one side, all error on the other. Human life is symbolised in the story of Hercules, set between two opposite ways. Dualism or monism, immanence or transcendence, science or religion, reason or emotion, natural or supernatural, liberty of indifference or absolute determinism, artificial purpose or thorough-going mechanism,—all is presented, for Haeckel, under the form of an alternative which necessitates choice.

Dualism is, then, the actual standpoint from which Haeckel views human life. His philosophy aims at establishing unity therein through abolishing one of two contraries.

If, therefore, the system of Haeckel is radically opposed to traditional religions and crushes them beneath the weight of its criticisms, this result is only gained, in reality, by strangely limiting or even altering the meaning of these religions. It is their formal confessions rather than their essence that Haeckel has attacked, and these confessions he has taken in a narrow and material sense that would be rejected by

[1] *Der Monismus*, etc.

many religious minds. This refutation, then, has really left standing more than one reconstructive principle of religious doctrines.

There is no cause for astonishment at this. Haeckel cannot mean to destroy everything that upholds religions ; for he himself believes that the religious need, connected by him with feeling, is a natural need of man, just as feeling is a distinct and natural faculty ; and he is of opinion that this need must necessarily be met, no less than the scientific need. His philosophy, in fact, is bound to solve this practical problem. Does it succeed in doing so ?

In order to face religion properly, science has merely, according to Haeckel, to enlarge her compass and to convert herself into philosophy. As a matter of fact, Haeckel has only carried out this development to the extent of presenting science with a certain number of concepts borrowed from metaphysical dogmatism. Now, it would appear that in order to render this philosophy, in its turn, capable, not only of refuting, but of replacing the various religions, Haeckel would have been obliged, likewise, to furnish it from the outside with embellishments that could not have been obtained from its own resources.

He is fond of reiterating that what science and art possess is equally the possession of religion. And he terminates his confession of monistic faith by an invocation to God as the common principle of Goodness, Beauty and Truth. In Truth, Goodness and Beauty we have, he says, the three sublime aspects of deity before which we may bend the knee in devotion. It is in honour of this ideal—a God genuinely one

and threefold—that the twentieth century will erect
its altars.

And in order to justify the ascription of such a
meaning to his philosophy, he invokes the authority
of Goethe, the greatest genius of Germany.   It is
this very Goethe who has said :

> Wer Wissenschaft und Kunst besitzt,
> Hat auch Religion ;
> Wer jene beiden nicht besitzt,
> Der habe Religion ![1]

Now, what are we to gather from this saying?

Art, with Goethe, stands for the ideal, in so far as
it is separated from the real.   And this ideal is not
simply an effluence or reflection of the real, but its
principle.   Upon it we must rely, from it we must
receive inspiration, if we would overpass ourselves.
*Das Vollkommene muss uns erst stimmen und uns
nach und nach zu sich hinaufheben:*[2]   Perfection,
as if by prevenient grace, must, first of all, give us
the right disposition ere raising us by degrees toward
itself.

Thus, by adding Goethe's authority to that of
Spinoza just as he had already supplemented Darwin
by Spinoza, Haeckel thinks that he can satisfy, not
only philosophical requirements, but the specially
religious and ideal aspirations of humanity.

How is this new accession incorporated into his
system ?   That, it must be admitted, is by no means
clear.   Haeckel rests satisfied with saying : the man
of to-day, besides the fierce struggle for existence,
discovers everywhere traces of Truth, Beauty and

---

[1] He, who possesses science and art, has religion also.   He, who has
them not, may have religion.

[2] *Eine Reise in die Schweiz*, 1797.

Goodness; but what connection is there between these two aspects of reality? How comes it that, while teaching us to regard the law of the struggle for life as the fundamental law of nature, science is able to persuade us that Truth, Beauty and Goodness are everywhere present in the world, and ought to be the aim of all our longings and endeavours?

Evidently Haeckel, with a view to replacing religions, has introduced at this point certain obligatory concepts over and above experiential concepts, or—what amounts to the same thing—has imparted a value to the imperatives subjectively given in our consciousness. But a subjective and imaginary injunction, thus set up as constituting real knowledge and obligation, is nothing else than what we call revelation. And so, through the introduction of an alien principle, analogous to religious revelation, Haeckel is able, in the end, to join with Goethe in reaching out towards truth, goodness and beauty.

But once we are allowed to find room again in philosophy for beauty, truth and goodness as ideals to be pursued, what is there that we may not restore? How is the God of religious beliefs expressed if not in the attempt to picture truth, beauty and goodness? These objects are not concepts of a fixed and calculable kind, like the idea of a triangle or the notion of a vertebrate. All the metaphysical and religious speculations of mankind have been suggested by the strange nature of these three objects, which are not materially given, but which the mind seeks, in endless progression, to bring within its range—rising, in this effort, above itself, and striving to be at one with what it calls God.

It would be difficult to say with precision to what

ethical scheme, to what form of religion, the monism
of Haeckel would have led, if it had not, with sheer
inconclusiveness, drifted towards the ideal of Goethe.
So long as the philosophy of Haeckel was limited to
combating religions, it laid particular stress on the
fundamental unity of the various kinds of being, on
universal mechanism, on the fatality of the struggle
for existence, on the emptiness of our subjective convictions, on the absolute solidarity which links each
being with the totality of the universe. Can we,
from these principles, infer anything resembling what
we call freedom, personal worth, humanity, fraternity,
search after ideals ?

Just as there was for science (as Haeckel conceived
it) a paradoxical problem in connection with its
conversion into philosophy, so the conversion of this
same philosophy into religion is a change so slightly
indicated by the system's own principles that it
presents the appearance of the supernatural.

The only satisfactory explanation to be given is
that Haeckel has raised science to the rank of philosophy in such a manner as to find in it the means of
overthrowing religions ; and that he has afterwards
brought his philosophy to the level of these same
religions, in such a manner as to render it capable of
replacing them. And the end, as a heterogeneous
principle, has created the means !

III

SCIENTIFIC PHILOSOPHY AND ETHICS AT THE
PRESENT TIME

We must distinguish, in Haeckel's system, between idea and execution. The execution is characterised by an eclecticism which is decidedly embarrassing to criticism. Haeckel compares rather than unites Darwin and Spinoza, Spinoza and Goethe. But the idea is not necessarily affected by the objections that execution suggests. Perhaps the eclecticism to which Haeckel has recourse presents merely the same degree of obscurity as any new idea that we cannot grasp at once.

The idea which Haeckel has clearly conceived, and which he has cleverly upheld, may be expressed as follows. Man, henceforward, has one genuine certainty, viz. Science ; and, the more he reflects on the nature of this certainty, the more it becomes clear to him that he does not possess—and, indeed, cannot possess—any other. He would deceive himself, therefore, and build only crumbling structures, if he sought, for any of his theories whatsoever, other foundation than that of Science.

But, while moulding his thought in compliance with things (as rational integrity demands), man is not disposed and does not feel it right to renounce, in any degree, what—according to his conviction, according to an invincible feeling — links him veritably with the nature of things, and constitutes his nobility, his superiority, his self-reliance, his happiness.

To all this, it will be said, science is indifferent.

That is so, observes Haeckel, and at this point we come upon his cardinal idea, that in science we can find nothing else than science. Consider what is involved in science—interpret, with the help of reason, her principles, her methods, her results; in short, create, by means of the very faculties with which science set out, a scientific philosophy; and science thus developed, thus extended, without thereby changing her special nature, will furnish you with all the theoretical knowledge, all the practical teaching that a well-ordered mind demands, and that a purely empirical science was impotent to procure.

In this manner the traditional religions will become useless, being superseded. The religion of the future will be the religion of science.

Defects of execution, then, have nowise compromised Haeckel's idea. As a rule, it is not because a principle is indifferently or badly applied, vehemently contested and disproved a hundred times, that it falls away and disappears; it is because it is without any real content, without vitality and without energy. The idea that Haeckel upholds is one of those which to-day rule the intellectual world.

Various attempts have been made to think out this idea so as to avoid the defects that, in Haeckel's case, seemed on the way to compromise it. Can it be said that these attempts have ended in success?

The philosophy called scientific is, just now, in high favour. It seeks increasingly to deserve its name. Now, the furtherance of the scientific method consists in setting aside, more and more, every metaphysical or subjective datum, in order to rely exclusively upon fact understood in a certain way—fact as identical for every observer, objective fact, scientific fact.

Consequently, scientific philosophy is specially desirous of being established apart from any metaphysical hypothesis. She would like, literally, to have no other foundation than science, no other organ than reason, and to be strictly tied down to the logical methods that science asks of her.

Scientific philosophy, then, without relinquishing her hold on the problems which are more general and more far-reaching than those with which science in the strict sense deals, is bent on adhering, ever more closely, to science; she is minded to continue this adherence even when she seems to be going beyond the scientific limit.

This attitude leads—among those who take its requisitions seriously—to the withdrawal of scientific philosophy from speculative and, in particular, from practical problems which are rightly the subject-matter of religion. If religion is affected by studies on such subjects as the nature of the scientific hypothesis or the principles of physical chemistry, that can only be very indirectly and in a slight fashion. The biological sciences, it is true, seem in themselves more akin to things moral and religious, since they have to do with the conditions of existence, of development, of competition, of adaptation, of communities and of progress. But their method, like that of all science, consists in reducing the higher to the lower. Now, while allowing that the concepts which are here in question have, in the natural sciences, a practical meaning analogous to that of our moral concepts, who would willingly resign himself to the spectacle of man shaping his conduct exclusively in accordance with the life of creatures beneath him in the scale of being, without seeking to provide satisfaction for the conscience and for the aspirations that belong to man as such? If animal society is the starting-point of human society, does it follow that human associations cannot and ought not to differ from animal associations?

That is why, in general, professional scientists say goodbye to methodical analysis and deduction, as soon as they go beyond the philosophical problems that are somehow included within the strictly scientific sphere of knowledge, in order to enter upon those wide generalisations called by the Germans *Weltanschauungen*, and to reach thereby the questions that are of genuine interest to the moral and religious consciousness. They do not state their views on the religion of science in the same scientific manner that is customary in stating a general law which is evolved from the particular laws based on observation. Nay rather, in set speeches, in prefaces, in conclusions and in lectures, are they wont to celebrate with eloquence the blessings of science: how great and beautiful it is—how it calls forth and develops the virtues of patience, of abnegation, of tenacity, of sincerity, of sociability, of brotherhood, of devotion to humanity; and they wind up glowingly by claiming for science the supreme dominion. Henceforward she alone is in possession of the moral vigour needed to establish the dignity of human personality and to organise future commonwealths. It is science that will usher in the golden age of universal equality and fraternity based on the sacred law of toil.

The scientist thus offers us, in place of religion, his own nobility of life and depth of thought, the prestige of his personality and of his genius, rather

M

than definite doctrines scientifically established through the discoveries of actual science.

.   .   .   .   .   .

Further, we are not to be content with the indistinct conception of a scientific philosophy, intervening between science and religion.   Instead of contrasting religion with a science defined as unifying principle and as philosophy, many thoughtful people have wondered if it were not possible to constitute a determinate science, in harmony with the general notion of scientific knowledge, but specially conceived so as to fulfil, in human life, all the requisite or useful functions that have hitherto been fulfilled by religion.

The particular science which appeared capable of being constituted in this way, was that of ethics ; and on all sides the idea of a scientific morality was extolled.   This idea was not only embraced with fervour ; the attempt was made to realise it.   One of the most remarkable results of this effort is shown in the ethics of solidarity.

Solidarity is a scientific concept, unlike Christian charity or Republican fraternity.   Solidarity is a law of nature—gravitation, for example.   It is the condition underlying the existence and prosperity of every human community.   At the same time and on that very account, solidarity is desired, explicitly or implicitly, by every reasonable man for whom the idea of living outside the conditions of existence is impossible.

Hence solidarity constitutes just that convergence of theory and practice, that natural transition from fact to activity, which it was necessary to discern before we could dispense with religion.   Life, in the really human sense, is in need of a rule. So long as science was incapable of furnishing this, we were obliged to look for it in the region of sentiment. Thanks to *solidarisme*, the deficiency has at last been supplied : science appears under a new aspect as coincident with life. Moreover, the principle which this aspect of coincidence expresses, is sufficient. Let us analyse all the obligations that an enlightened judgment imposes on man : the obligations of justice, of help, of self-improvement, of tolerance, of devotion towards family, country, society, humanity—all are explained and determined by the single scientific notion of solidarity.

The ethics of solidarity, according to adepts, will play the very part that Haeckel attributed to monism regarded as religion. For the present, through the tolerance that it recommends, as well as through the analogies that it offers with what is reasonable in the various religions, this ethical teaching will serve to reconcile religion and science. But, by degrees, along with the development of its applications and with its growing acceptance, it will tend to replace the old religions ; for it will perform, not only all the useful tasks which they succeeded in carrying out, but other tasks of a still wider and loftier kind, obligatory for minds trained according to the methods of scientific culture.

The *solidaristes* are confident that, in this way, they have determined the exact concept necessary for the establishment of scientific morality as genuinely one and homogeneous—no longer merely the eclectic combination of two heterogeneous courses of discipline.

The importance of a discovery like this is scarcely to be exaggerated ! In the early stages of modern science, Descartes found in extension—at once observable and intelligible—the connecting link between the material world and the mind.   Can we, in the same way, discover a connecting link between the world of science and the world of action?   It is this last-named link that *solidarisme* provides.

What is the real value of such a standpoint?

Solidarity, it is said, is a scientific datum.   Most certainly science shows us how a concourse of beings, of phenomena depend upon one another.   It is even part of its office to discover relations involving solidarity.   The law of action and reaction is a law of solidarity.   But science is not less desirous of seeking and establishing relations of independence.

Pascal has written : " The parts of the world are so linked and interconnected, that we cannot, I believe, understand one without another or without the whole." Perhaps this statement as to universal solidarity is theoretically legitimate.   But it is, at least, certain that the practical admission of such a principle would render science impossible.   The work of science has only been effectual through the belief that certain parts of nature are sensibly independent of the rest. What is called a law, a species, a body is a particular solidarity which is relatively constant, *i.e.* relatively independent as regards the rest of nature.   The discovery of Kepler's Laws and of the law of universal attraction has only been possible because the solar system was taken as forming, in some way, a whole by itself.   The very terms of Newton's law indicate that the action of certain bodies on others can be disregarded.   It is through eliminating all the other given circumstances that we have found how, in

barometrical experience, to make the rise of the liquid
column depend on the pressure of the atmosphere
alone.   Assuredly, science is on the look-out for
solidarities.   But the problem that she undertakes is
to know what solidarities she ought to allow—what
apparent or conceivable solidarities she ought to
reject; and she can only discover solidarities where
nature itself has presented certain connections of
phenomena sensibly independent of other phenomena.

It would, then, be very arbitrary to adhere to the
notion of solidarity without referring to the opposite
notion.   A *solidariste* who really takes science as his
guide is not less anxious to dismiss solidarities that
are purely apparent and accidental, than to determine
those which are true and genuine.   He labours at
establishing relations of independence and autonomy,
not less than those relations which imply solidarity
or mutual dependence.

But even though this parting of false and true
solidarities were realised, the *solidariste* would then
be only at the beginning of his task; for he cannot
rest content with the solidarities that nature offers
him.   He is compelled to look for the well-being, the
righteousness, the happiness of men.   Is he, then,
going to restore the anthropomorphic dogma so vigor-
ously denounced by Haeckel, and to allow that, in
the solidarities of her own making, nature has actually
in view the satisfaction of the human conscience?
It is evident that what the *solidariste* borrows from
science is simply a framework, the abstract form of
solidarity.   Into this framework, he reserves to
himself the right of putting what will satisfy his
moral needs.   He will preserve a considerable part of
what science offers him, but just in so far (to adopt

the phrase of Descartes) as he may find it amenable to reason.

Hence it would seem that the principle of the *solidaristes*, though apparently one, is in reality two-fold. A single word proves, in this case, to conceal two ideas. On the one hand, we have physical solidarity, *i.e.* solidarity as naturally given, indifferent to righteousness, rudely · out of keeping with the humane point of view that is man's special prerogative ; on the other hand, we are shown moral solidarity, free and equitable—an idea which presents man with an object worthy of his struggles, and which he will realise (in harmony with the rest of his ideal experience) through making proper use of the materials that he finds in nature.

In other words, the connecting link between science and practical life of which we are in search, is not provided by the scheme of the *solidariste*. This scheme embraces fact and idea after the manner of eclectic doctrines, and, putting them under a single name, it declares that they are one.

It is true that many are prepared with this reply : It is wrong to discuss moral solidarity from the stand-point of pure idea, and on that account to place it opposite physical solidarity. It also is a fact, an experimental datum, a scientific truth, for it has its root in human instinct. It is simply the perception, by consciousness, of a law peculiar to human nature, analogous to physical laws. The human individual, like the animals, is born and lives within a particular association of certain beings. What is called moral solidarity is merely the knowledge and theory of this special solidarity.

The postulate of this explanation involves the

likening of consciousness to a mirror which can only
give a passive reproduction of the objects placed
before it. A metaphor becomes a theory. But, in
point of fact, man finds himself in presence of a great
multiplicity and variety of given solidarities. Between these solidarities we have to make our choice :
here we ought to annul, there to maintain. It is
even a question of establishing solidarities that are
not given in any visible sense, *e.g.* solidarities based
on righteousness and happiness. Why these struggles
and endeavours, this generous and untiring fervour,
if we are only to take note of actual existence, and to
uphold it for what it may be worth? Clearly, in
order to choose between given realities—in order to
get beyond them—we must possess or try to find a
criterion of truth and value distinguishable from these
realities themselves. Whence shall we procure this
criterion ?

The reply is made : From instinct, from conscience,
from the moral needs of human nature ; for these, also,
are facts.

The ambiguity underlying the theory becomes
evident at this point. It is forgotten that we have
to do with fact *and* fact. The suspension of the
mercury in the barometrical tube is a fact : the consciousness of the idea of righteousness is likewise a
fact. But these two facts are very different in kind.
The first can be reduced to clearly defined, objective
elements which will be represented in all minds by
obviously identical ideas : the totality of such elements
is what we call a scientific fact. The second is the
representation of an ideal object. It contains, in very
truth, an objective element, viz. the existence, in the
knowing subject, of a certain idea—or rather of a

certain feeling. But it is not this element which is here in question. There are in us a thousand other feelings, to which we do not attribute the same value: what we really want is to secure for this feeling the pre-eminence over the rest. It is not, therefore, to feeling, as such, that we make appeal : it is to the issues which are involved in it—righteousness, happiness, humanity, ideal solidarity. But righteousness and happiness are not objective and scientific facts. These are immediate, subjective representations, which, being incapable of analysis, cannot be described as scientific facts. They are crude notions, really comparable with those that science undertakes to criticise and to reduce, if it be possible, to fixed and measurable elements. They are even data which, if we believed in the verdict of consciousness upon which they are assumed to rest, would be irreducible to scientific facts, inasmuch as they express the claim of the human mind to correct reality, and to offer, for the investigation of future science, facts that are beyond the purview of actual science.

After long and careful peregrinations, we discover that we have been brought back to the point reached by Haeckel. In order to satisfy both the scientific demands and the moral demands of human nature, Haeckel placed side by side Darwin and Goethe, the struggle for life and the cult of Truth, Beauty and Goodness ; and his system, in spite of its monistic title, assumed a dualistic character. With a view to obtaining the longed-for unity, we conceived, as a synthesis of knowledge and action, the ethical doctrine termed scientific ; and up to now we have hardly done anything, by means of this formula, beyond securing the juxtaposition of two words. If, following its guidance, we apply ourselves to science—to science worthy of the name—we do not reach morality; if, again, we set out from the moral claims of man, we are unable to rejoin science. The mere assumption of a name does not entitle us to use it.

This dualism, into which we are continually relapsing, be our endeavours to surmount it ever so great, is, it would seem, inseparable from the very problem to which we have devoted ourselves. The formula indicating this problem has been expressed very well by Haeckel : to satisfy, by the aid of scientific method, the needs—no less practical than speculative—of human nature.

Now, science is the knowledge and the organisation of scientific facts in their entirety. The requirements of human nature are only scientific in their physical basis—not in their purport, with which we are exclusively concerned at the moment. How, then, should we know *a priori* that science is able to bring man satisfaction ? Are we not debarred with good reason, in the name of science, from all anthropomorphism, from every theory of pre-established harmony between man and things ? Do we not constantly take up a defiant attitude toward conscience, toward feeling and desire, all of which are said to be out of harmony with objective reality ? The dualism in which we are landed originates merely in the terms through which we have sought to harmonise science and the needs of man.

Both the religion of science and scientific morality demanded a critical estimate that these systems have failed to supply : an estimate of the intellectual and moral needs of the human spirit. Before endeavouring to satisfy these needs, it was necessary to inquire into their actual nature and value. If we had been able to show that they, also, are only facts : that everything in them which seems to be ideal or superior to the given, is illusory, *i.e.* reducible to this same "given" in accordance with natural laws, then indeed there would have been for us nothing but facts capable of being brought into line with other facts—with facts of a scientific character. Under such a view, all that recalls the supernatural, the absolute, the unknowable, the ideal, would then be definitively eliminated : science in the strict sense would be, for us, the relatively adequate representation of all existence ; she herself would be our supreme requirement, our absolute, our ideal.

CHAPTER IV

PSYCHOLOGY AND SOCIOLOGY [1]

NATURE and natural phenomena: consideration of religious phenomena substituted for that of the objects of religion.

I. PSYCHOLOGICAL EXPLANATION OF RELIGIOUS PHENOMENA—Religious phenomena considered subjectively, objectively. The historical evolution of the religious sentiment—Religious phenomena explained by the laws of psychic life.

II. SOCIOLOGICAL EXPLANATION OF RELIGIOUS PHENOMENA—The advantages of the sociological point of view—The essence of religious phenomena: dogmas and rites—Insufficiency of the psychological explanation; religion as social duty.

III. CRITICISM OF PSYCHOLOGY AND OF SOCIOLOGY—The ambition of these systems—Are the explanations that they supply really scientific?—Are the human *ego* and human society resolvable into mechanical causes?—Psychology powerless to explain the feeling of religious obligation—Sociology, in its appeal to society, not only real, but ideal.

In the different systems which have hitherto occupied our attention, science and religion are set opposite one another like two given things, and the question raised is that of knowing to what extent and

[1] The terms "Psychology" and "Sociology" are used, in this chapter, with a special significance; hence Monsieur Boutroux writes "Psycholog*isme*" and "Sociolog*isme*." Our author is examining the respective claims of those who systematically maintain that the psychological, or the sociological explanation of religious phenomena, is adequate.—*Translator's note.*

171

how, without infringing the principle of contradiction, the mind can allow their coexistence. This conception of the problem is not the only one possible.

When, in the seventeenth and eighteenth centuries, science was definitely established on the double basis of mathematics and of experience, she asked herself what attitude she ought to take in regard to such entities as nature, life and the soul—these being generally regarded as given realities, though very different from the objects of experience and of mathematical demonstration. After having hesitated for a time, she thought of a distinction which seemed to solve the difficulty once for all. Instead of considering nature, life and the soul as entities, science adopted the notion of them as physical, biological and psychical facts, given in experience; and, as to the universal essences of which these phenomena were the manifestation, she decided on ignoring them. The classic names of Physics, Biology and Psychology have been preserved, but they have now come to mean nothing more than the science of physical, biological and psychical phenomena respectively. With this change of standpoint, science has been obliged to bring within her own sphere certain realities which, as represented by tradition, seemed of necessity to be permanently inaccessible.

Can we not realise, in regard to religion, an analogous change of standpoint? Whereas, in considering religion and its aims as a single and universal entity, science appeared to be indefinitely restricted to furnishing an illusory explanation, what would happen if, in the place of religion, we put religious phenomena? These phenomena, in short, are the only thing that we find directly given. They can be observed, analysed, classified—like other phenomena. We are able, in respect of these phenomena, as in respect of others, to find out if they admit of being brought within the compass of experimental laws. Why should not religion, thus envisaged, become an object of science, as nature became on the day when this word was used simply to indicate the totality of physical phenomena?

Would the reduction of religion to religious phenomena involve the loss of any essential element? Only by the aid of such an element would it be possible to maintain the belief that, outside natural phenomena, *i.e.* physical objects, there is something which answers to the name of nature, and which, in some way, is capable of being grasped by us. In fact, for every mind liberated from metaphysical prejudices, if religious phenomena can be described with precision, and reduced to positive laws analogous to the laws of physics or of physiology, the problem of the relations between religion and science is no longer in existence : it re-enters into the general problem of the connection between science and reality —a problem that is, indeed, more verbal than real, seeing that science, as henceforth constituted, is just the fullest possible expression of reality.

When this method of regarding things is adopted, what becomes of those imperious needs—whether moral or religious—which human nature exhibits, and which have, in the end, won the respect of an Auguste Comte, of a Herbert Spencer, and of a Haeckel?

I

Moral and religious needs are expressed in accordance with principles that appear to consciousness as evident and necessary. Such principles are those relating to the dependence of the finite upon the infinite, to the moral order of the universe, to duty, to equitable compensation, to the triumph of right. Now, an acute philosopher of the eighteenth century, David Hume, has shown, with respect to the principle of causality, how such a proposition, which seems to be imposed upon the mind as an absolute truth, may really be nothing more than the abstract interpretation and intellectual projection of internal modifications within the conscious subject. When I affirm a causal connection between A and B, I seem to be applying a principle given *a priori*, which I call the principle of causality. But this principle, as soon as I come to formulate it and to subject it to analysis, raises insoluble difficulties. In reality I yield to a habit, created in my imagination through the reiterated perception of the sequence A B. By reason of this habit, every time that A is presented, I expect to see B appear. And it is this habit that my mind expresses, in its own way, by the concept of causality. There is nothing real in what I call the principle of causality except the psychical disposition of which it is the formula. Already, through analogous reasoning, Spinoza, in criticising the feeling of free-will, had referred it to ignorance of the causes which determine our actions, combined with the consciousness that we have of those same actions.

In thus explaining certain ideas, no longer by realities distinct from thought, but by phenomena shut within consciousness, these philosophers inaugurated a veritable revolution—the transformation of Ontology into Psychology.

It is in accordance with this method that several thinkers, even at the present time, seek to bring all that concerns religion within the domain of the positive sciences.

The problem, so presented, consists primarily in observing and analysing the religious phenomena furnished by experience; and, then, in seeking the explanation of these phenomena in the general laws of psychical phenomena.

It cannot be said that at present we find complete doctrines, capable of being described as common to all specialists, and of being established on a definitely scientific basis. These investigations, still in the early stage, give rise to great differences of opinion. Accordingly, it is necessary to consider the methods, the questions and the hypotheses suggested, rather than the results that have been definitively obtained.

. . . . . .

The starting-point of these investigations is the verification of facts as they are presented in the religious consciousness itself. Setting aside every preconceived idea, every theory, every system, the specialists analyse both past and present religions; and, from actual data, they deduce those psychical states, practices and institutions which are characteristic. The conception of religious phenomena reached in thus adopting the very standpoint of the religious consciousness, may be termed subjective.

The main inference to be drawn from the religious

phenomenon, in this sense, is that man learns thereby to consider himself as having intercourse with a superior and more or less mysterious being, to whom he looks for the satisfaction of certain desires.   This initial conviction gives to all his emotions, to all his experiences, their special aspect and significance.

For the man who experiences faith alone, and who knows nothing of mystic feeling, union with God is the object of thought, of desire and of action, but it is not realised here and now, and can only be realised very imperfectly in this world.   The mystic, on the contrary, is conscious of union with God as something that is a natural constituent of the human soul, and his task lies in the endeavour to keep it in mind and to make it the foundation of his entire life.   While the simple believer proceeds from idea and action to feeling in order to attain union with God, the mystic starts from this very union and regards it as determining, first his feelings, then his ideas and actions.

The union with God which the mystic begins to enjoy in this life, is completely realised in a special experience called rapture or ecstasy.   During this state the soul is distinctly aware of being alive in God and through God.   Not that it acknowledges annihilation.   According to the doctrine of the great mystics, it is, on the contrary, conscious of existing in the fullest sense of the word.   Its life is so much the more intense through being in closer unison with the source of all life.

Such is the appearance that religious phenomena present when they are regarded from the standpoint of the religious consciousness itself.   It would, doubtless, be very difficult—it might even appear impossible—to discuss the value of the assertions implied in these phenomena, if we were only able to consider them from this wholly intuitive standpoint. How can we prove to the man conscious of freedom that he is not conscious of freedom? How are we to contest a man's right to declare his sense of communion with God?

In order to criticise the spontaneous judgment of the mind, Hume (as we have seen) has conceived a way of observing the psychical phenomenon other than subjective intuition. He looks at the phenomenon from without, objectively; and he wants to know if what man assumes as existent has actual existence —if the object that he pictures as the cause of his feeling exists apart from the feeling that pronounces its existence; or if that object is merely the interpretation and imaginative projection of the psychical phenomenon itself. Similarly, it is through studying religious phenomena, no longer merely from the subjective standpoint of the religious consciousness, but from without and objectively, that the psychologist can hope to strip them of their supernatural semblances and to group them under the laws of science.

In this manner, psychology effects the reduction of religious phenomena in their entirety to three main categories: beliefs, feelings properly so called, and rites.

Beliefs are the representations of objects, of realities conceived as external to man. Viewed from the outside, they appear to have a close connection with the ideas, the knowledge, the intellectual and moral conditions of the period in which they are put forth, as well as with the particular opinions or longings of

N

the individuals who profess them. In a general way, man fashions his gods after his own likeness, as the ancient Greek philosopher, Xenophanes, pointed out. St. Teresa expects the Lord to dictate what she ought to say from him to the bare-footed Carmelite Fathers. Now, the four very explicit recommendations that God orders to be put before them, are in such exact conformity with the prepossessions of St. Teresa herself, that we cannot escape the impression that God is, in this instance, only the echo of her own consciousness.

The study of religious feeling, as distinct from beliefs, raises a multitude of questions. What are the elements of this feeling? We are able to distinguish therein : fear, love, longing for happiness, the inclination towards fellowship with other men. These elements, moreover, are mingled in very different proportions, and present well-nigh innumerable aspects, according to the beliefs with which they are associated.

The culminating point of inward religious life is ecstasy, or the feeling of an immediate union with God. Seen from outside, this state consists: firstly, in concentrating the attention upon a single idea, or upon a limited group of ideas ; secondly, in rapture, *i.e.* in the abolition or transformation of the personality. At the same time, the nervous system is in an abnormal state, characterised by the more or less complete suspension of sensibility and of movement. Ecstasy is not, moreover, an isolated phenomenon : it is that which sets the seal on a period of excitement, which alternates with a period of depression. Intense religious feeling is thus submitted to a more or less regular rhythm. God draws nigh, and then absents himself; phases of rapture are followed by phases of emptiness, and *vice versâ*. And we notice that these phenomena coincide with the states of excitement and of nervous depression.

Rites—which are the third element in religions—appear as phenomena realisable by man and possessing a virtue called supernatural, *i.e.* the special quality of being (after some unknown and unknowable fashion) the causes of other phenomena which are not directly within man's reach.

For the mystics, rite is, not an instrument, but a consequence. It originates in a certain state of the soul. This state, experienced as union with the divine omnipotence, engenders and determines, not only other psychical phenomena such as the transformation of the passions and of the character, but, further, physical phenomena—actual deeds.

In a general way, the religious rite expresses the idea of a causal relation between the physical and the moral, between the moral and the physical : the *how* of this relation is unfathomable by us.

It is such results as these that have been gained through observing religious phenomena from the objective standpoint. By adopting this same standpoint, we are enabled to trace the historical evolution of the religious sentiment.[1]

We may take as our starting-point, for example, the predominance of fear and of imagination, whence is derived the conception of divine beings especially powerful and terrible. After this, love and joy are gradually developed and gain the preponderance, while intellect and reason regulate the conceptions of the imagination. The deity is then incorporated,

[1] Th. Ribot, *La Psychologie des sentiments.*

and, at the same time, becomes kind and gracious :
religion, metaphysics and ethics are knit together into
one rich and harmonious whole. It is the apex of
religious evolution. At last, in a third phase, the
intellectual element becomes, in its turn, preponderant,
the equilibrium is disturbed, and religion is gradually
supplanted by science—that science which is framed
exactly with a view to satisfying the intellect.

.   .   .   .   .   .

In proportion as they extend further and deeper, it
is clear that objective examination and analysis of
religious facts lead us towards that psychological
immanent explanation which the thorough - going
psychologist seeks to establish.

The question set for his consideration is as follows :
Should religious facts be explained (as the consciousness of the believer insists) by supernatural and
mysterious interventions, or should the general laws
of human nature offer a sufficient account of them ?

Now, whatever phenomenon we consider, when
once we have strictly reduced it to its objective and
given content, when we have started definitely from
the fact that science ought to retain, and from the
manner in which this fact is represented in the subjective consciousness of the believer, we find—following
the system which we may term psychology—that the
phenomenon contains nothing which cannot be explained through the laws of ordinary psychology.

The feelings to which the religious sentiment is
reduced—dread, attraction, self-absorption, desire of
fellowship—are feelings natural to man. The mono-
ïdeism and rapture which characterise ecstasy, together
with the rhythm of which they form part, are only
the exaggeration of the traits which belong to the

affective life in general. It is in the nature of passion to concentrate on a single object all the energies of the soul. And alternation of excitement and depression constitutes the very law of the affective life. Phenomena analogous or even similar to mystical manifestations are easily recognised in certain nervous affections. Religious obsessions, the conviction as to the influence of God, of the Holy Virgin or of the devil, the delirium resulting from scrupulosity, the abiding notion of sacrilege, the mania of remorse and of expiation, are natural accompaniments and exact symptoms of definite hysterical states.

Intellectual or imaginative phenomena: beliefs, ideas, visions, revelations are also explained by mere psychical modifications of the subject, without our finding it necessary to suppose any transcendent reality whatsoever, of which they would be the effect and representation.

Transcendent explanations originate through the ignorance of the subject, and through the attempt of the imagination, guided by tradition and custom, to make up the deficiency. For the man who, thanks to temperament, to acquired notions, to personal experience and to the condition of the subject, possesses sufficient knowledge, the beliefs of this subject—the revelations and the visions of which he is conscious —no longer present anything new and miraculous. It is simply from the recesses of his memory that, unwittingly, man draws all the objects which appear to him as supernatural. God, speaking to St. Teresa, tells her what, unwittingly, she makes him say. Our desires, our fears, our prepossessions, our knowledge, our ignorance, our habits, our affections, our passions, our needs, our aspirations, furnish the substance of the beings that we bring down from on high to enlighten us and to give us succour. We fling ourselves forward — stronger, greater, better — in order to augment our powers through union with this other self. God is the self-aim that is here indicated. The method adopted in thus creating him, is unconscious. The *ego*, therefore, does not recognise itself in its creation; and if, perchance, an abnormal state of the nervous system determine within it a certain degree of exaltation, this creation will be for it the object, not only of belief, but of hallucination, of vision and of dread—quite on a par with what happens to the rest of our perceptions under certain conditions.

It is, then, no longer necessary to explain the mutual action of feeling, of belief and of rites upon one another, through the appeal to some supernatural intervention.

We may allow that, feeling being the one fundamental phenomenon, ideas are only an intellectual interpretation of it. There exists, at the present time, a wide-spread theory which reduces the rôle of the intellect to transforming into representations the feelings—unthinkable in themselves—of which we are conscious. To think a thing, is to explain it, *i.e.* to refer it to a cause, to a model, to an end of which the concept pre-exists in us. Our intellect, in order to explain our feelings, seeks thus some suitable principle which may be familiar to it. Since our activity is that which is most familiar to us, it is a cause analogous to our activity that the intellect first assumes. Then, in proportion as we know more about things, it draws in a curious manner from that treasury which we call our memory, in order to present us with objects and causes as proportioned as possible to the feelings which stir within us.

If we deem that it is, rather, ideas which, in the matter of religion, determine feelings, there is no need—as Pascal used to think—of divine grace, in order to bring down into the heart a truth recognised by the intellect. Human feeling is not alien to the intellect, it is only human in so far as—even under its humblest forms—it already partakes of intellect and idea. The endeavour to act on the feelings and on the conduct of man through ideas, through reason, is what we term philosophy. The very word reason has, in its common acceptation, a value that is at once theoretical and practical. Now, who would wish to maintain that all philosophy, all belief in the efficacy of idea and reason, is but scholarly prejudice? We experience every day how an idea, a doctrine, a system moulds our feelings, our affections, our passions. Is it not on actual record that the teaching of Rousseau produced a new way of loving and feeling among a large number of men? Are not our feelings to a large extent literary? The experiments of suggestion reveal the constraining power latent in ideas.

And, if we see in rites the main phenomenon, it is fruitless, in order to derive feelings and beliefs from them, to look for a supernatural virtue inherent in these observances: it is sufficient to invoke the natural influence of deed on thought, so powerfully indicated by Pascal in the famous saying: "Take holy water, and have masses said: quite naturally, that will enable you to believe, and will blunt your wit."

Lastly, the regular evolution manifested, throughout the ages, by the religious phenomenon (taking the

general effect of its development) is, in itself, proof
that we are not dealing here with the manifestation
of supernatural influences. The discovery of one
general law of evolution controlling the history of
nature, has led to the elimination of theological
doctrines concerning the creation and the preservation
of the universe. An analogous conclusion is inevitable
with respect to religion, if its development is such that,
conformably to a law, each new moment is necessarily
linked with the preceding. And this is just what we
gather from the outline of religious evolution that
the psychologists have already succeeded in giving.

To sum up, the hypothesis of a supernatural and
mysterious cause of religious phenomena, such as
religious beliefs seem to demand, would doubtless
have to be maintained, at least provisionally, if the
application of the psychological method to the interpretation of religious phenomena left an unexplained
residuum. But, though it be clear that we cannot,
in like manner, expect to know everything and to
understand everything, the inference to be drawn
from our knowledge of religious phenomena, as from
that of physical phenomena, is this : we know enough
about them to consider the scientific method as
sufficing to indicate the way in which the phenomena
have been produced. Reality will not offer us
anything that, by the help of our principles, cannot
be explained. There is for us an unknown—not an
unknowable ; an unexplained—not an inexplicable.
For we explain psychologically, *i.e.* by the help of the
human soul's general laws, the religious phenomenon
understood in its essence ; and this same essence will
be found necessarily in every religious fact whatsoever.

II

It is in this way that certain psychologists expect to find, in bare psychology based on physiology, the means requisite to explain, finally and exhaustively, all kinds of religious phenomena. Their success in this respect is generally contested by the representatives of an allied science, equally devoted to the positive study of human facts, but envisaging these facts under another aspect, viz. the sociologists.

According to the latter, psychology only incorporates religion through impoverishing and mutilating it, through suppressing that which is its peculiar and essential element. Psychologists fasten on the subjective side of the religious phenomenon, and are fond of seeing in mysticism the religious manifestation *par excellence*. But inward religion is, according to distinguished representatives of sociology,[1] only a more or less vague and delusive echo of social religion as it appears in the individual consciousness. The mystic is an impassioned or meditative man, who adapts religion to life and to philosophy in his own special way. It is not in its derivative, perverted, subjective and doubtful forms that we ought to consider religion ; if we are really desirous of expressing it scientifically, we should have regard to its reality as concrete, primary, general and objective. It is not the dreamers, the exceptional beings, the diseased, the philosophers, or the heretics that we must consult : it is the orthodox, the representatives

[1] *L'Année sociologique*, published under the editorship of E. Durkheim.

of living, efficacious religion—of that religion which has been, which still remains an essential and important factor in the destiny of nations and of individuals.

Now, if we study, in this way, not the religious sentiment, but religions, we find that one of the essential notions belonging to them is that of the obligatory, of the forbidden, of the holy. Every religion is a moral power which imposes an obligation on the individual, which rules him, which thrusts upon him deeds or abstentions that are foreign to his nature. How is it possible for psychology to understand religious phenomena, seeing that she has only individual life at her disposal? The representatives of existing official religions—the men who form a true estimate of what religion is—are right in protesting against the feigned explanations of the psychologists. These explanations are nothing else than the sophisms natural to ignorance of the question. They emphasise in religion that which is not religion in the true sense, they pass by that which needs to be explained. Thus persist, in reality, after the psychologist has finished his task, those characteristics of religion which cause it to be regarded as a supernatural institution, irreducible to the data of science. And the philosophers are right in maintaining, against psychology, the principle of obligation and of prohibition — Kant's Categorical Imperative, with its transcendental origin. For the Kantian doctrine, on its negative side, very properly condemns the mistake made in believing that the idea of duty ought to be explained, as an illusion, by the mere operation of the laws relating to the individual conscience.

The reduction of religion to science, which the

physical sciences fail to realise, is beyond the special powers of psychology; and we should have to give up all hope in this matter, if, above psychology, there did not exist a supreme science in the light of which the mystery of things is entirely dispelled: this science is sociology.

.   .   .   .   .   .

In order to make ready for the elimination of transcendental causes, and to explain all phenomena by purely natural laws, psychology has wrought the necessary change. For subjective observation, which offers only phenomena to be explained, she has substituted an observation that is objective. She has set herself to study psychical phenomena from without, just as the physicist studies physical phenomena.

But this undertaking is easier to state than to carry out, especially when religious phenomena are in question. We are aware that the mystic raises his voice strongly against the employment of this method, which, according to him, is strictly debarred from the religious province. The mystical phenomenon is an experience, and an experience that is inexpressible by concepts and words. Nobody understands this experience unless he has undergone it himself. Such an experience cannot be studied from without. All the external signs through which we claim to form an idea of it, are of no avail for its interpretation.

Whatever may be the value of the mystic's objection, it is certain that the idea of a purely external observation, in psychology, is far from being clear, especially seeing that the psychologists have substituted, as primary datum of consciousness, the

synthetic psychical activity for the phenomena or
states of consciousness—external to one another—
that the associationist school assumes.   In that very
way, the application to psychology of the scientific
determinism, by virtue of which the associationist
theory had been conceived, became again arbitrary,
vague and uncertain.

Sociology avoids these difficulties.   She considers
the facts with a bent which makes possible the
application of a rigorously objective and deterministic
method.   Indeed, in social phenomena, the conspicuous
and objectively cognisable element is no longer a
simple concomitant, a more or less accurate symbol
of the reality which it is sought to reach : it is itself
that reality, or else it is connected with it in an
exactly assignable manner.   What is called the soul
of an individual is a reality, which differs, undeniably,
from the phenomena which manifest it.   But the
soul of a community is merely a metaphor, of which
the meaning does not go beyond the totality of those
social facts which are external and visible.   Having
to deal with realities which are absolutely at one with
their phenomenal manifestations, sociology admits of
a precise and rigorous objectivity, which, for a long
time perhaps, will be unattainable by psychology.

At the same time, it is evident that the sphere
wherein she moves is much more extensive.   Doubtless, all the characteristics that humanity exhibits in
social life, ought to be found beforehand, actually or
potentially, in the individual.   But that which can
only be an indeterminate and indiscernible possibility
for the individual, is unfolded in communities, operates,
evolves, and is expressed through noteworthy phenomena.   The incredible richness of human nature, its

marvellous power of adaptation, its fecundity in every sense, is only visible—only exists properly in external and collective life.

Seeing that she has such an exact object under her consideration, sociology ought to be able, in much greater measure than psychology, to submit human facts to scientific determination. Not without purpose did the metaphysicians, seeking the means of grouping facts under the idea of law, imagine behind these facts certain entities which regulated them. What guarantee have we that facts hold together, are driven into one another, form into systems, if there is no common principle underlying them? Ontology was nothing but a fictitious interpretation of this reducibleness of phenomena to one another that science postulates. It expressed by a hierarchy of concepts the supposed moments of the reduction. Ontology ought not to be set aside purely and simply ; it should be replaced by a method which realises, through experience, the systematisation that it constructed more or less *a priori*. Now, psychology lacks that principle of cohesion and of systematisation, which is requisite for the sure determination of phenomena. In the soul, the *ego*, conscious or subconscious, we are presented with confused notions which can do no more than base the vague relation of substance on accident. On the other hand, a given community is a distinct fact, and the determinism which links with this community all the facts of which it is composed (as the unconditioned with its conditions), is not less scientific than that which links together the phenomena of a given system in the material world, such as the solar system. A science of observation, sociology makes ready to outstrip observation. It occupies—between History, on which it is grounded, and Ontology which supplies it with a *raison d'être*—an intermediate position, resembling in this respect every complete science which, besides the facts that, in themselves, only serve as materials, possesses a principle fitted to uphold and guide the systematisation of those facts.

It is, then, to sociology that we must look for the full explanation or scientific determination of religious facts, as of every human fact.

. . . . . .

It follows from the very definition of sociology as a science that it does not undertake to study religion, but religious phenomena, and not even the indefinite totality of these phenomena, but the different class-manifestations into which they can be distributed. Like every science, it proceeds from the parts to the whole, from analysis to synthesis. Still hardly established, it is stronger in its studies of detail, its monographs, its historical investigations, than in its theories and generalisations. Having, meanwhile, analysed as completely as possible some of the most characteristic elements of religion—such as the notion of the sacred, of sacrifice, of rite, of dogma, of myth— sociology is now ready to point out the direction in which we ought to move if we wish to obtain really valuable scientific results.

And, in the first place, through her far-reaching inquiries, her historical studies, her comparative tests and analyses, sociology believes herself capable of determining with precision the real essence of religious phenomena. This essence is that which is found in all religious manifestations, what analysis distinguishes therein as the primary element to which all the others owe their existence and their character.

Now it is clear, in view of the labours of eminent sociologists, that this primary element is not what we call the religious sentiment; this latter is often at fault, and, where it actually exists, has the appearance of a very complex and contingent *ensemble* of derivative phenomena. Further, it is not belief, considered with respect to its object. Neither God nor the supernatural, conceived as substantial realities, is an essential element of religion, for they are often absent just where the religious phenomenon undoubtedly exists.

Invariably and pre-eminently, in all religious manifestations we find dogmas and rites; dogmas signify the sacred obligation of professing certain fixed beliefs, while rites are an accumulation of practices, similarly obligatory, having reference to the objects of these beliefs.

What we have to regard as essential here is that notion of the sacred, which is applied to certain objects, and which entails certain prohibitions or precepts. The thing regarded as sacred is a power which operates inevitably in an adverse or salutary sense, according as it is violated or reverenced. From this notion spring dogmas and myths, or theories and narrations relating to the nature and properties of sacred things. Out of this same notion proceed rites, or practices intended to overcome the hostile powers and to conciliate the beneficent powers.

These dogmas and these rites are the cause of the feelings and beliefs which are generated in souls. The sacred character of the object, together with the authority which it implies, is an argument for belief before which the intellect naturally bows. And the sum-total of emotions, of inclinations, of acts and of ideas, that instigates the relation with the sacred thing, develops and determines that sentiment—so intense and apparently special—which we call the religious sentiment.

In reality, there is no specifically religious sentiment, any more than a specifically religious belief. Sentiment and belief are, in themselves, identical, whether in religious life or in ordinary life. They are simply determined after another manner. In the religious life they assume a particular form, viz. obligation, resulting from the sacred character which is attributed to the object. This idea entirely pervades the creed and sentiment of the believer. It is his duty to believe ; and the object of his belief is just the obligation of offering to the sacred thing the worship which is due to it. His sentiment is a combination of fear or of love with the idea of something inviolable, and with the impressions that determine in the soul the practice of obligatory rites. It consists in piety, in reverence, in scrupulosity, in adoration ; it is either possession, or rapture. In all these psychical phenomena, we find merely the form, and not the substance of religion. Religious feelings and beliefs are ordinary beliefs and feelings, modified from without by the idea of the sacred or the obligatory.

That being so, we see clearly why psychology is unable to find, in the general laws of the psychical life, the unequivocal explanation of all the elements of religion.

Take, for example, the concept of obligation, the preponderating importance of which proceeds from the analyses of sociology. According to the psychologist, this concept is traced back : (1) to an abstraction, through which the natural and necessary bent of human activity towards certain objects is considered in its form only, being isolated as much from the acting subject as from the object pursued ; (2) to an elaboration of this abstraction effected by the understanding, through its categories, with a view to practice. Thence it follows that obligation is merely an illusion.

But Kant has very properly restored the special character and supra-psychological origin of moral obligation. Therein we find a reality which, inexplicable by psychology, is not on that account illusory, but ought to be referred to an order of things superior to the individual conscience. What Kant demonstrated through his analysis of concepts, sociology proves through the statement of facts. Not only is obligation the constant and fundamental phenomenon of all religion ; but everywhere, if we consider actual religions and not the artificial compromises or inventions of philosophers and dreamers, it appears as unrelated or even opposed to the natural leanings of the individual. It is no mere fancy which has been transformed into duty by the religions ; the noblest and most salutary among them do not allow the individual to be submitted to rules that he would not freely recognise, or impose upon him acts which more or less violate his nature.

Undoubtedly, the religious phenomenon, though produced in the soul of the individual, surpasses it, and cannot be explained by its faculties alone.

Does this mean that there is nothing for us but to accept the transcendental system that religions profess with regard to their own origin ? That system is, unquestionably, superior to the purely psychological explanations, since it takes into account, at any rate, the fact that has to be explained, instead of setting it aside *a priori* and in an arbitrary manner. And, for him who is not proficient in psychological studies, this system, to some extent, represents the truth provisionally. It is better, after all, to believe in some hypothetical or erroneous explanation of an existing law than to deny the law under pretext of not being able to explain it. Of what real moment is it that I see in duty a command of Jehovah, if, at least, I believe in duty and carry it into practice?

But the sociologist (and he alone) is not compelled to explain obligation as due to a transcendent cause; for he can furnish a natural equivalent of this transcendent cause—the ground, at once necessary and sufficient, of the phenomenon.

This equivalent is the action of the community upon its members.

A given community imposes naturally on its members certain obligations or certain prohibitions, the observance of which is regarded as the condition of its existence and its continuance. Doubtless, this society is only a collection of individuals. But, thus united, these individuals set before themselves certain ends that, as individuals, they ignore or reject. A collective will has no relation to the algebraical sum of individual wills. A community is a new entity; the expression "social soul" denotes, metaphorically, a positive truth. And, like everything that truly is, a given community tends to persevere in its being.

That is not all. Collective activity, once aroused, will not be confined to the particular object toward which it tends: it will exercise itself freely, without definite aim, according to the general law of activity which, of itself, pursues not only the necessary or even the useful, but the possible.

Hence, for individuals, many an obligation, the object of which will be found scarcely discernible, or even such as will have no other object than that of facilitating indeterminately the play of social activity.

Observation shows that religion is nothing else than the community itself, enjoining upon its members the beliefs and actions that its existence and development require. Religion is a social function.

The essentially social character of religious action explains, no less clearly than the Divine Transcendence of the theologians or than the universality of the Kantian Reason, the element of obligation inherent in every religious phenomenon; for the community is, moreover, outside and above the individual. Still further, the community is an observable and tangible reality; and so, it is through a fact, and not through a concept or an imaginary existence, that sociology explains the fact of obligation.

As to feeling and belief, they are, from the sociological standpoint, the echo, in the individual consciousness, of the compulsion exercised by the community on its members. This compulsion, the principle of which cannot be grasped by the individual as such, is for him—quite logically—an object of faith, of hope, or of love, and determines the infinite variety of his religious emotions. Even for him who would make clear to himself the social origin of religious phenomena, these phenomena, in becoming purely natural, lose nothing of their value; since it remains true, for the sociologist as for the average man, that the individual, by himself, can neither impose his will on the community, nor foretell the end and aim thereof. In proportion as he learns, through observation, to conjecture what is implied in the evolution of the social group wherein his lot is cast, he becomes, submissively and without any thought of self, the instrument of the preservation and well-being of that same group.

III

CRITICISM OF PSYCHOLOGY AND OF SOCIOLOGY

The importance of psychology and of sociology, if these systems are well founded, is considerable. They effect a radical change in the problem raised by the relations between science and religion. Instead of placing religion opposite science and inquiring if the latter is in harmony or in disagreement with the former, these systems actually bring religion within the special sphere of the sciences : they put the science of religions in the place of religion. Religion exists —it is a given fact. Why, in our treatment of this fact, should we isolate it from others ? How can we dispute this course, and why are we afraid of it ? The true scientific attitude does not consist in assuming *a priori* that some fact is strange—perhaps supernatural—and in seeking to get rid of it : it consists in analysing the fact as we do others, and in finding room for it within the general system of natural facts.

It is also to be noted that, in the religious sphere, this method, if it succeed, will lead, sooner or later, to the abolition of the fact itself, while the dogmatic criticism of religions has striven in vain, for centuries, to obtain this result. Indeed, in the religious fact is implied the idea of objects, of forces, of feelings, of states which cannot be reduced to ordinary phenomena, which cannot be explained according to the methods of science. It is in so far as they ignore or reject the scientific explicability of the elements of religion, that men are religious; and religion has only been able to exist owing to the non-existence of a science dealing with the natural causes of the religious phenomenon. Contrary, then, to the other sciences, which leave standing the things that they explain, the one just mentioned has this remarkable property of destroying its object in the act of describing it, and of substituting itself for the facts in proportion as it analyses them. Established in mind and conscience, the science of religions will no longer treat of the past.

Is it certain, however, that psychology or sociology furnishes the science of religions with all the data which would be needed, in order that it should be constituted a science properly so-called?

. . . . . .

We must distinguish between the scientific form and science. Scholasticism possessed the form—not the content of science. The ethical sciences, if we reduce them to statistics and calculations, would have the appearance, not the real value, of a mathematical science. In order that a science may exist in a true sense, the scientific form must be therein applied to a content which, drawn from reality, lends itself, unalterably, to receive that form. Is this the case with the systems that we have been considering?

The theory of genuine science has been framed by Descartes in terms which, in a general way, still harmonise with actual science. Science is a reduction of the unknown to the known, of the inexplicable to the explicable, of the obscure to the evident.

The first step to be taken by science is that of determining, somehow, the evident or the intelligible. Now, we gain the standard of evidence through distinguishing, in our representations, two elements—two poles as it were, viz. the subject and the object. On the side of the subject, nothing else than the intellectual activity which constructs science, but assumes as given the standard of scientific intelligibility, instead of furnishing it. It is on the side of the object, stripped of every subjective element, that we find our primary knowledge, with which all the later stages ought to be compared or connected if we wish them to be strictly scientific. This knowledge is that of extension or dimension, together with the various kinds of existence that are enchained therein, *i.e.* mathematical objects in general. Thus we find the first stage in knowledge, to which science has to refer and submit all the rest, if possible.

The task of science can be stated, yet again, as follows : to determine facts and laws. In order to be understood, this formula should be compared with the preceding. It is not facts and laws of any kind whatsoever that science seeks, it is scientific facts and laws, *i.e.* facts that are precise, measurable, objective, really intelligible—in other words mathematical, or reducible (whether directly or indirectly, and by degrees) to mathematical facts.

Are psychology and sociology, considered as dealing with religion, capable of exhibiting such facts and such laws ?

The psychological method here in question is that on which David Hume decided in his famous reduction of the principle of causality to a habit of the

imagination. Now, this method consists in regarding
the object as unintelligible, in so far as we consider it
in itself—setting aside the subject which imagines it.
It only becomes intelligible through being attributed
to an illusion of the subject in unconsciously projecting outside himself that which happens within. It
is of little consequence that the object is clearly
perceived. This clearness, which, moreover, is only
apparent, results from an artificial transformation
that the mind effects in its internal modifications for
the purpose of considering them from the outside—
this being the very condition of clear knowledge. In
short, Hume changes the meaning of the word to be
explained. It is no longer any question here of
referring the obscure to the clear, of comparing the
unknown with the known, but of seeking the origin
and real (*i.e.* immediately given) foundation of the
apparent and the derivative. The explanation is no
longer the reduction of the subjective to the objective :
it is the reduction of the objective to the subjective.

Notwithstanding what this involves, psychology,
when it wishes to be explanatory—*i.e.* when it is not
content with taking the inventory of the physical
and moral symptoms which are found in the religious
phenomenon—employs the method of Hume, refers
beliefs to states of consciousness, and dissolves objects
in order to leave standing the subject's modifications.
And so it turns its back on science properly so called.

If this psychology takes the name of science, it
must be pointed out that this word, as here used,
implies merely a very vague resemblance to the
physical and natural sciences. The task of psychology, since it succumbed to associationism, has
been to explain psychical phenomena by the special

qualities of consciousness, regarded in its living reality. But what is consciousness? Is it altogether in the present; or, charged with the past, has it, at the same time, an eye cast upon the future? Can we no longer hold that its function, *par excellence*, is to seek, for the individual, ends which pass beyond him; to ask, in view of what he is, what he may yet be, what he ought to be; to convince him that his existence and his action have a value, are able to assume one—admit of a rôle, a mission, a contribution to the progress of humanity and of the universe? But what is all this if not the admission of religious impressions; and, in thus taking consciousness for principle, is not the psychologist, perchance, finding room for religion itself at the heart of his system?

Sociology proceeds in a more genuinely objective manner. Is it certain, however, that she herself is concerned with facts and laws which are scientific in the strict sense? The physicist who has once found the means of expressing the scale of heat sensations by changes in the elevation of his liquid column, has no longer any need of consulting his subjective appreciation of heat. But the sociologist can make use of his objective documents only through considering them as mere symbols of the subjective realities with which he is ideally supplied by consciousness. In reality, the distinction that he sets up between sociology and psychology is delusive. Under all his formulæ, in all his explanations, a psychological element—irreducible and indispensable—is concealed. After all, it is men who form human communities, and what we call the collective soul has real existence in individuals alone. Are we, then, to regard these individuals as composed of two separable fragments—the individual *ego* on the one side, and a fraction of the social *ego* on the other ?

Human society is not an object, it is a subject. That which is therein real and living—which is the motive and the characteristic adapted for explaining the phenomena in so far as they are explicable—is found, in the last analysis, to be the wants, the beliefs, the passions, the aspirations, the illusions of the human consciousness. Not only is society a subject ; but, contrary to the individual consciousness, which is, in some measure, a given subject, the collective consciousness is an ideal subject. It is still further than the individual subject from realising the idea of scientific fact. Besides, it is not clear why the reduction of a religious fact to the conditions of existence and of improvement that underlie human communities, should necessarily have the consequence of naturalising religion.

Since religious precepts and rites have shaped human communities properly so called; since, as Protagoras taught, instruction concerning decency and righteousness has engendered politics and tightened the bonds of affection amongst men, the purely natural (*i.e.* mechanical and inevitable) origin of religious phenomena is not demonstrated in that way. If the community itself, once somehow established, gives instinctively and spontaneously to its institutions a religious character in order that they may have more prestige and more power, we may infer that the community pursues an ideal not easily realisable by the individual consciousness. May not, then, the conception, the pursuit of this ideal be, itself, the effect of a religious inspiration ?

Like consciousness, human society is a sphere revealing depths which it is difficult to fathom. There is nothing to prove that religion does not play therein the part of a principle instead of a mere instrument.

.   .   .   .   .   .

Why need we be troubled, some will object, as soon as psychology and sociology demonstrate that religious phenomena have nothing special in them, and that they are, in every respect, reducible to the fundamental phenomena of the psychological and social life ? Let us admit that something of what is called religion may be presupposed by consciousness and by society. This element no longer suggests anything extra-scientific, if it is equally present in all human phenomena. Regarded as immanent and universal, how does it differ from nature pure and simple ?

We meet, here, with the arguments through which psychology and sociology believe that they can deprive the religious phenomenon of every special characteristic. Of what value are these arguments ?

Psychology endeavours, first of all, to show that the religious phenomenon is, literally, nothing but a phenomenon, a state of consciousness. The transcendent entities that religion invokes are delusive : they are but the *ego* itself, externally projecting some one of its determinations with a view to contemplation, just as consciousness does in representing the outside world, and as the special constitution of the human *ego* demands. Whatever object it may have before it, the *ego* is only concerned with self ; and, if it takes the projection of its subjective states for independent realities, it is because the transformation of an internal modification into an external object occurs within it unconsciously.

Even if we allow this theory, does it hit the mark ? It brings to naught, assuredly, a material Olympus situated in some part of our terrestrial space, or a God regarded as the celestial inhabitant of unknown regions beyond the star-spangled vault. But the religious consciousness is no longer concerned with these material aspects of the divine.

If we understand by transcendence an existence outside of man, in the spatial sense of the word, the modern religious consciousness is foremost in declaring that a transcendent God, in this sense, is a factitious and purely imaginative concept. It is precisely with respect to God that the words transcendence, externality, objectivity require to be apprehended as simple metaphors. The progress of religion has consisted in transferring the Divine from the outside to the inside of things, from heaven to the human soul. " The Kingdom of God is within you," says the Gospel. Similarly Seneca has it : *Non sunt ad caelum elevandae manus . . . : prope est a te Deus, tecum est, intus est.*" [1] In other words, God is conceived, not as external to the religious phenomenon, as producing it or responding to it from without—all such representations making of him a corporal being similar to others; but as internally related to this phenomenon, and as distinguishing himself from the human being in a unique manner, without any natural analogy, at all events without any resemblance to the spatial distinction that the imagination sets forth under the word transcendence. This is what is meant by

[1] To raise the hands toward heaven is useless : God is nigh unto thee, he is with thee, he is within thee.

spirituality, which the higher religions consider as the special token of the Divine.

We have still to discover what the religious phenomenon is in itself. According to psychology, nothing is found therein which really distinguishes it from ordinary phenomena. The usual laws of psychology give a sufficient account of it. Psycho-physiological experimentation is able to illustrate religious phenomena, particularly by means of certain nervously affected subjects, just as it calls forth other psychical manifestations.

Numerous and important are the studies conceived after this method : it does not appear, however, that they succeed in elucidating the exact point which is here in question. It is not only that the determination of facts and of laws, in these matters, scarcely admits of precision and closeness. We must ask if the method followed is quite suitable for penetrating the essence and characteristic of the religious phenomenon.

This method is or intends to be objective ; it aims at being so to the utmost possible extent, in order to reach really scientific results. What is this but to say that it will only consider facts in those of their elements which are referable to general facts ? Objective means representable ; and, for the human mind, to represent a thing is to make it reappear in a familiar framework. That is why objective psychology sets herself to consider exclusively the materials, the manifestations, the groundwork or physiological circumstances — in a word, all the outside appearances of the religious phenomenon. These are, in fact, the elements which it has in common with other phenomena. But, in this very way, she will inevitably overlook what may well be taken as the special mark of the religious phenomenon.

And it is certain that the believer will fail to recognise what he experiences, what, for him, constitutes religion, in the descriptions of the religious phenomenon that are given from this standpoint. He will reply to the scientist who delusively expects, through objective examination, to comprehend the elements of the religious life, what the Earth-Spirit in Goethe's *Faust* replies to Faust himself:

> Du gleichst dem Geist, den du begreifst,
> Nicht mir.[1]

Indeed, religion is just that entirely inward, subjective content of consciousness, which scientific psychology thrusts aside in order to attend solely to the objective phenomena that are concomitant. Its distinguishing characteristic is to surpass these phenomena infinitely:

> Erfüll davon dein Herz, so gross es ist,
> Und wenn du ganz in dem Gefühle selig bist,
> Nenn es dann wie du willst,
> Nenn 's Glück! Herz! Liebe! Gott!
> Ich habe keinen Namen
> Dafür! Gefühl ist alles;
> Name ist Schall und Rauch,
> Umnebelnd Himmelsglut.[2]

But is there not illusion there, and may it not be that this subjective element is interpretable by an

[1] Thou art matched with the spirit that thou comprehendest—not with mine.

[2] Goethe, *Faust*: Fill thy heart with the invisible, great though it be. And, when thou art wholly blest in the feeling, call it then what thou wilt —Felicity! Heart! Love! God! I have no name for it. The feeling is everything: the name but sound and smoke, a mist obscuring the light of heaven.

objective phenomenon, as the sensation of heat is expressible by the rise of an alcoholic column ?

So far as the psycho-physiological conditions of the religious phenomenon are concerned, it is remarkable that not a few sociologists agree with the believer in denying that these can supply an exact account of the contents of the religious consciousness. The explanations that they furnish leave a residuum. Not that one can point out a phenomenon which remains independent and isolable in the depths of the religious consciousness, like a refractory substance at the bottom of a crucible. But the religious consciousness has a certain tinge, a distinctive mark, a special mould, that psychology overlooks, or that it regards merely as delusive and as calling for denial. It comprehends the idea of the sacred, of the obligatory, of something required by a Being who is greater than the individual, and on whom the latter depends. In truth, the religious element is shown in these things, and, as if from without, it bestows upon the concomitant phenomena a character that, by themselves, they would not acquire. If exaltation and melancholy assume, with particular subjects, the religious form, it is not because there is religious melancholy and exaltation : it is because there exist in the world religious ideas which the subject has realised, and which are impressed upon his imagination.

With a considerable number of persons, religion is simply imitation, it is not inwardly experienced in their feelings or in their beliefs. These persons reflect the sphere in which they live, the influences to which they submit. Placed amid other conditions, they could enjoy feelings and passions, psychologically similar—the same way of believing, of loving, of willing, and yet these phenomena would not have a religious character. Religion, within those souls which it really invades, is—one may say—a value that is unique and infinite : attributed, not by the imagination, but by consciousness properly so called, to certain ideas, to certain feelings, to certain actions, with a view to ends which surpass humanity. This form of consciousness goes beyond all objective psycho-physiological symbols. The individual, with an inward horizon limited to these symbols, could only consider the religious idea as a chimera and a nonentity.

Perhaps, however, there may be, even adopting the psychological standpoint, a way of attributing a genuine value to the religious idea : we can, for instance, regard consciousness as a communication (conscious at one extreme, vague and quasi-unconscious at the other) of the individual with universal life and being. The religious sentiment would, then, be the instinct or secret perception, so to speak, of the dependence of the part upon the whole.

But it is clear that such a doctrine would not only go beyond all objective psychology, but would be the rehabilitation and glorification of subjective psychology, seeing that to this latter would be conceded the power of probing, beyond the objectifiable part of the soul, to the depths of infinite being.

Objective psychology can see, in religious obligation, and in the train of ideas which accompany it, nothing else than illusions. But its arguments are not convincing, and all that they succeed in establishing is that, for the individual, the belief in obligation, in duty, in the sacred, is a faith, an adhesion that is contingent and disinterested. A faith, however, in

order to be approved by reason, should be founded
on intelligible motives. Where can the motives of
faith in duty be found? Sociology is prepared to
furnish them.

Social activity, which is a given reality, has certain
conditions of existence and of operation. We find
therein, contends the sociologist, necessities which
have their origin outside the individual, and which
are imposed upon him. The feeling of obligation is
nothing but the consciousness that the individual
gains in regard to these higher necessities. According to this conception, the individual is ruled, constrained, raised by religion as by a wholly external
power. The social and religious man is, in respect of
the natural man, like a higher kind of being who is
nearing the suppression of his former nature.

Is it right, however, to relegate, in this way, to
the lower plane (to consider, in short, as unimportant)
the subjective and individual element of religion?
Doubtless, the mysticism and inward life of the
believer do not offer, to the external observation of
the sociologist, suitable material, like political or
ecclesiastical institutions. Does it follow that they
are without importance? Perhaps, if we consider
the most rudimentary manifestations of religion, we
shall find this inward element, as seen therein, of
very little significance and importance. But is it
enough, in order to find out what religion is, to look
for its historical starting-point, and indifferently to
connect therewith the subsequent phenomena by a
continuity of fact? How, in matters of this kind,
can we argue from historical continuity to logical
identity? Such an element of religion, which was

first of all imperceptible, cannot have become considerable and essential. A consciousness which seeks self-apprehension, ends by discovering itself in ideas and feelings to which at first it only gave a wandering attention. An effect is able to detach itself from its material cause, and to develop itself at will.

Now, it is a fact of experience that religion, whatever its primitive form may have been, has become, among civilised nations, more and more personal and inward. Long ago the Greeks, with their profound feeling in regard to the value and power of man, transferred to the human consciousness the moral and religious struggles, which, according to the ancient legends, took place in a region beyond man, and determined his destiny without regard to his own effort.

The prophets of Israel and the teaching of Christ have, in this connection, brought out the preponderance of inward disposition; affirming that religious souls tend more and more to the belief that, just where these dispositions are lacking, there is no religion whatsoever. The difficult task, to-day, for religious authorities, is that of maintaining belief in the utility of religious externalities among minds for whom religion is, pre-eminently, an affair of the individual consciousness.

Far from implying the effacement of the individual, religion—as presented to us to-day—stands for its exaltation, at least if we have regard to that higher form of individuality which is properly called personality. The individual, through union with the object of his worship, i.e. with the source of all being, expects to become, in the truest sense, himself. Thus, in the Christian Trinity, the three hypostases

P

are veritable and distinct persons, on the very ground that, being inwardly united, they form but one single God. It is this special, and, as it were, supernatural relation that the ancient adage already indicated :

πῶς δέ μοι ἕν τι τὰ πάντα ἔσται καὶ χωρὶς ἕκαστον;

"How can all things form, at once, a single whole, and have, each, a separate existence?" Religion consists in believing that there is one being, God, who realises this miracle through the beings that live in him.

But, it will be said, nothing hinders the view that this very development of a higher individualism, revealing a natural trend towards the general well-being, has its origin, on close examination, in the necessities and in the activity of social life; that, if personality is apprehended by consciousness, not as an instrument, but as an end, we are then supplied with one case, among many others, of that transformation of means into ends which the human consciousness effects naturally.

Nothing can be more certain than the religious value and influence that is attributed by sociology, in this way, to the social bond. And it is remarkable that she finds herself, in this respect, at one with the very ideas of Christianity. Thus, we read in the First Epistle of St. John: "No man hath beheld God at any time: if we love one another, God abideth in us, and his love is perfected in us." The whole point lies in knowing of which community we are speaking when we explain by social influence the production, amongst men, of religious ideas and feelings.

Are we speaking of any community whatsoever, taken in its actual and observable reality? Is it sufficient that a community exist in order that its conditions of existence, of preservation and of development, be interpreted, in the consciousness of its members, by moral and religious obligations?

We can quite easily conceive that, in their ignorance and weakness, men allow certain necessities to be imposed upon them as categorically binding, which, in reality, are only hypothetical or problematical. But it is evident that, on the day when, instructed by the sociologists, they shall discover the mystification of which they are the object, they will cease to have, for social institutions, that superstitious reverence which previously possessed them. They will be able to continue their appreciation of these institutions as relatively stable and useful : they will no longer regard them as sacred.

Often, indeed, the idea that political institutions are derived, in a unique manner, from the conditions of existence belonging to given society, arouses in men the wish to modify them, much more than the desire for their maintenance. For these very conditions are not unalterable. They *have* changed, therefore they can still change. Now, man is so constituted that, for him to believe in the possibility of change, is next door to desiring it. And here is the remarkable thing : it is principally the religious spirit which disposes the individual to pass judgment upon institutions, to regard them as purely accidental or human, to rebel against them. The higher religious minds have assumed the attitude, with respect to the community, of representing, in themselves alone, right and truth, seeing that God was behind them ; whereas, behind given communities, they saw only man, nature, and circumstances. Far from the religious consciousness consenting to be merged in the social consciousness, it inclines man to put the claims of God in opposition to those of Cæsar— personal dignity in opposition to public constraint.

How could real society pretend to satisfy the consciousness of the believer? Does it, indeed, in its actual presentment, offer justice, love, goodness, knowledge, happiness, just as, for faith, these are realised in God?

Evidently, it is not of real and given society that we are speaking, when we explain, by the sole action of society, the religious attributes of the human soul; it is of ideal society, it is of society, in so far as it strives after that justice, that happiness, that truth, that superior harmony, of which religion is the expression. It is in so far as real communities already partake, in some measure, of that invisible community and tend to be conformed thereto, that they inspire reverence, that they justify the obligations which they lay upon individuals.

The ideal community has, in truth, an intimate connection with man's religious aspirations. The religious consciousness is, itself, considered as an instrument specially adapted for working towards its realisation. But the ideal community is no longer something definite and given which can be compared with a physical fact; to explain religion by the exigencies of this community, is no longer to resolve it into political or collective phenomena that can be observed empirically.

The ideal community is conceived and pictured by individuals—by the highest moral and religious minds of a nation. It tends to endow the individual (whom nature sacrifices) with his maximum of developmen-

and of value, at the same time forming, through the union of individuals, a whole more truly one, more harmonious, more beautiful than the combinations created by mechanical forces, or by instinct and tradition pure and simple. It tends to promote, to the highest degree that human nature allows, reverence for those spiritual things which are, one may say, of no actual service : justice, truth, beauty. These objects of thought, for which simple nature finds no place and with which she has no concern, it fashions into the supreme utility. In short, it assumes religion, is inspired by religion (being very far from fabricating it), and is, as it were, an appliance used for the purpose of bending the individual to ends which are repugnant to him.

At the root of all social progress is found an idea sprung from the depths of the human soul, and embraced as true, good, and realisable, while it represents a new thing, a chimera perhaps—a thing that is not already verified or recognised as capable of enduring. This idea is taken for object, because man sees therein, or thinks that he sees therein, an expression of the Ideal.

At the root of all social progress are found faith, hope and love.

Human consciousness and human society furnish science with the deepest principles that can be found for explaining religion, because it is in these two spheres that the religious principle is most clearly manifested.

PART II

THE SPIRITUALISTIC TENDENCY

CHAPTER I

RECOGNITION of the fact that religion must come to terms with science.

I. RITSCHLIANISM—Ritschl : religious feeling and religious history—Wilhelm Herrmann : distinction between the groundwork and the content of faith—Auguste Sabatier : distinction between faith and belief.

II. THE VALUE OF RITSCHLIANISM—The development of the specifically religious element—The danger of anti-intellectualism : a subjectivity without content—Chimerical pursuit of an internal world unrelated to the external world.

Besides the systems in which the idea of science predominates, and in which religion is only admitted to the extent and in the sense of being capable of union with science, the philosophical history of our time sets before us other systems in which, on the contrary, the idea of religion prevails, and for which the problem consists in maintaining, to the utmost, religion in her integrity, notwithstanding that the development of science cannot henceforth be ignored. According to these systems, religion is placed by herself, and based on principles which are peculiar to her. Now, recognising the claim of modern science to rule, not only things, but minds and souls, religion can no longer be satisfied with raising, between herself and

her rival, an insurmountable barrier.   The age in
which we live is one of general investigation and
comparison. It is, therefore, in seeking to reconcile
her claims with those of science which are exactly
determined, in (if need be) adapting herself, without
change of principle, to the admittedly lawful demands
of science, that religion will manifest her vitality and
her power of development.   Relying exclusively upon
her own formulæ, upon her certainty, and upon her
authority, without paying attention to current attacks,
she might delude herself for a time, but eventually
she would be condemned, in spite of all her efforts, to
wither away after the manner of plants deprived of
air.

Tendencies of this kind were already obvious
in a system, the historical beginnings of which can
be traced back to Kant and Schleiermacher ; but,
through the considerable influence which it possessed,
at the end of the last century, and which it still
enjoys to-day, this system re-enters the circle of contemporary ideas.   Its original framer was Albrecht
Ritschl,[1] the German theologian.

I

RITSCHLIANISM

The controlling idea of Ritschlianism, which we
may profitably consider here in its spirit and outline rather than in its special doctrines (palpably
diverse as set forth by various representatives), is
that religion, in order to be invulnerable and to be

[1] His principal work : *Die christliche Lehre von der Rechtfertigung und
Versoehnung* (3 vols.), appeared from 1870 to 1874.

realised in a genuine manner, ought to be thoroughly freed from everything that does not really belong to it; but that, on the other hand, it ought to comprise, integrally, everything that is needed to develop it positively, in all its originality and breadth.

As ordinarily professed, religion is mingled with elements which are foreign to it, and which pervert it. The first of these elements is philosophy, *i.e.* metaphysics and natural theology. We must, first of all, get rid of intellectualism, of scholasticism, which, after being expelled by Luther from the religious consciousness, was fraudulently reinstalled therein. Philosophy, having to do merely with the abstract, and only disposing of natural phenomena, cannot—as its very definition implies—reach the religious element which is life, being, supernatural activity. All theoretical knowledge whatsoever is powerless to grasp the object of religion; for the faculty of knowing, as it exists in man, is limited to comprehension of the laws relating to matter, and we are concerned here with purely spiritual things. Religion is made up of belief alone—not of knowledge: to blend with it philosophical or scientific elements is to corrupt it.

The second superfluous element that we must clear away from religion, is human authority, which brings it under the sway of Catholicism, and to which considerable importance is still attached in certain forms of Protestantism—Pietism in particular. The Christian has but one master, Jesus Christ.

Still, it is not sufficient to purify religion; we must realise it to the fullest extent. Schleiermacher enunciated a fundamental truth in declaring that piety is neither knowledge nor action, but a determination of feeling or immediate consciousness. We cannot, however, rest content with this very general principle, for it would be incapable of founding that systematic and specifically Christian theology, with which religion could not dispense without division into the various opinions of individuals. Feeling ought to be supplied with religious truths of a universal character. The special achievement of Ritschl lay in opposing to philosophical reason and authority, not religious feeling pure and simple, but religious history, *i.e.* Revelation, as the objective study of facts makes it known to us in the Gospel and in the general history of humanity.

The essential rôle of inward disposition is, moreover, by no means diminished under this view. It is, assuredly, in spiritual life and experience that religion is realised. Adopting the very theory of his disciple, Wilhelm Herrmann,[1] Ritschl ended by reducing the difference between metaphysical judgments and religious judgments to that between judgments of existence and judgments of value, and admitted that, if the Gospel is true, it is because, in the inmost recesses of consciousness, it is deemed worthy of being so : *wert, wahr zu sein.*

But, at the same time, in the Bible and in general history, feeling finds and recognises, according to Ritschl, the particular content with which it could not dispense, and which it would never succeed in discovering by itself alone. For example, the heart experiences the feeling of sin and the desire of blessedness. Now, to these sentiments correspond, in

---

[1] See *Wilhelm Herrmann et le problème religieux actuel*, by Maurice Goguel, Paris, 1905. On the notion of value is based the doctrine that Hoeffding maintains in his recent work : *Religionsphilosophie* ; religion (it is therein said) has to do, in its deepest essence, not with the content, but with the estimate of existence. Cf. Titius : *Religion und Naturwissenschaft*, 1904.

Revelation, on the one hand, a just and angry God, on the other hand, a merciful God. In this God, the religious consciousness finds the ground of impressions that natural objects fail to explain. Thus seeking in Holy Writ its meaning and its foundation, feeling becomes increasingly clear, satisfying and constant; it goes beyond the individual self, and can communicate with the feelings of others in a church; it actually realises the idea of religion.

Upon this principle, Ritschl constructed, as a single whole, his system of theology, which, while it upheld the teaching of Dogmatics in all its essential parts and in all its claims, separated it from all natural science, from all philosophy, from every purely human institution. This system was set forth expressly with a view to an exact and logically co-ordinated statement of all the ideas included in the primitive Christian Revelation; it was, essentially, the spiritual and eternal content of the Gospel.

.   .   .   .   .   .

The manner in which Ritschl secured, in the depths of the human soul, the development of the genuinely religious life, while sheltering this life from the attacks of science, satisfied the bent of many minds.

Kantianism had accustomed thinkers to supplement the world of science, or nature properly so called, by another world—that of freedom and of spiritual life, considered as not interfering to any extent with the world of the senses. And, accordingly, the progress of the positive sciences, the materialistic and deterministic tendencies evinced by several of their representatives, made thinking men wish to discover, for the objects of religious belief, a resting-place situated beyond the range of these sciences.

Moreover, history, to which Ritschl was attached, had become, during the nineteenth century, a science of the first rank, forming in some way an appendix to the sciences of nature ; and its special task, in conformity with the Romantic spirit which had furthered its progress, was that of seeking, no longer chiefly for what is ordinarily human and identical, at bottom, in the phenomena of different periods, but what, on the contrary, is distinctive, particular, characteristic and individual.

And this same Romanticism represented an exaltation of feeling and inward life ; expressed and developed a disposition of mind which was especially in harmony with the spiritual and mystical form of religion.

Already the inward Christianity of Alexandre Vinet, with its double and yet essentially single foundation—human consciousness and the person of Christ,—pointed in the direction that Ritschl was bound to follow; and the profound impression left by Vinet's teaching can be traced even to-day.

It is, therefore, natural that the Ritschlian tendency, in its general traits, should again attract many religious minds of our own day. In Germany, particularly, an entire school of theologians is grounded on the thought of Ritschl, which is maintained in principle while modified in its special determinations.

One of the most serious difficulties which Ritschlianism has raised is that evoked by Wilhelm Herrmann, the famous disciple of the master. According to Ritschl, the religious consciousness ought to recognise and apprehend itself in the formulæ of Holy Writ. But the theological formulæ that one finds in St. Paul, for instance, represent religious experiences which are peculiar to him, and which we ourselves, probably, have not enjoyed. How, then, can we adopt these formulæ? As repeated by us, they will constitute no longer an act of faith, but a mechanical or hypocritical performance.

It would appear that, beneath this objection, we again meet with the difficulty that the Reformation itself bequeathed to its disciples. The Reformation consisted, historically, in the contingent reconciliation of two phenomena : the exaltation of inward faith, following the development of mysticism in the Middle Ages ; and the return to ancient texts and monuments, regarded in their original purity, which occupied the humanists of the Renaissance. How from these two disparate principles, to frame a doctrine that should be one, has vexed the Protestant's soul.

The solution that Herrmann proposes, consists in separating two things which are, for Ritschl, closely united : the groundwork and the content of faith.

The groundwork, *i.e.* faith properly so called, is absolutely necessary, and is the same for all believers. It is this part of Revelation which has only to be accurately explained in order that every sincere soul may have an immediate experience of it.

But the special content of faith, the definite form of dogma, represents a more determinate experience, which may vary with individuals. This content, therefore, can be legitimately expressed in different ways, in accordance with the various experiences. For instance, the consideration of the inward life of Jesus produces such an impression in the human soul that, inevitably and by a moral necessity, it believes in Jesus. But the special idea of a substitutionary expiation realised by the death of Christ, is merely a contingent expression of the restorative action of Christ in us, and cannot be put on a level with the religious experience of all minds.

.   .   .   .   .   .

In France, a leading theologian, Auguste Sabatier, has adopted a standpoint which recalls that of Ritschl.

Intent on escaping from all interference of the physical sciences, and on securing the absolute independence and autonomy of religion, while careful not to ask for the least indulgence from science, Auguste Sabatier seeks for religion a sanctuary that is most familiar, and yet most remote from the visible and tangible things extolled by science. Religion has its origin, he thinks, in the feeling of anguish which invades the heart of man when he considers the two-fold nature—abject and sublime—which is in him, and the ascendency that the worst part of himself has over the best. From this anguish religion saves us, not by procuring new knowledge, but by bringing us into union, through an act of confidence or of faith, with the all-powerful and perfect Principle from which our being derives its existence.

What, then, is religion? It is the heart's prayer, it is redemption.

This redemption is a miracle, it is *the* miracle. How is it produced? The Christian can dispense with such knowledge. The laws of nature, in that very immutability which science reveals to us, become, for the Christian consciousness, the expression of the Divine Will. In order to be able to live the religious life, I need three things, and three only : the real and active presence of God within me, the granting of prayer, and the freedom of hope. These three

things are not affected by actual science—indeed,
it would appear that they could not be so by any
science.

If now I wish (and how, giving heed to the suggestions of my heart, can I refrain from wishing it?)
to develop these primary ideas, and to realise religion
in myself to the utmost possible extent, I cannot,
however much they urge me to it, invoke philosophy
or authority. Philosophy—a building of abstractions
—counts for nothing in comparison with the intense
feeling which has spontaneously sprung up within me.
She could only offer purely intellectual systems which
would not influence me, and which would, probably,
set me at variance with science. On the other hand,
the authority of any power whatsoever, were it that
of an imposing Church, would fail to create in my soul
that for which it asks—a conversion at once inward,
free and personal.

What is needed for the development of religion
within me, is the example and the influence of religion
already realised. Now, I find both these desiderata
in the person of Christ as put before me in the Gospel.
Jesus was conscious of a filial relationship in regard
to God. A man himself, he teaches us, he shows us
that men are sons of God, and capable of being united
with him. Through this consciousness of Jesus, we
are enabled to communicate with the Universal Father.
Christianity is thus the absolute and definitive religion
of humanity.

Must we go further, and determine, in a precise
and obligatory manner, the dogmas which shall interpret, for imagination and sense, these inexpressible
mysteries? Catholicism tries to do this, and academic
Protestantism follows suit. But these material addi-

Q

tions occasion the conflicts that we see raised every day between religion and science ; and, moreover, they are of no use to piety, seeing that there is even danger of their leading astray.

The Catholic religion comprehends three elements : faith, dogma and authority. Protestantism, seeking to restore Christianity in its original purity, has suppressed authority as a simply material and political principle, but has left dogma intact. It is quite time to let even dogma decay, in so far as it is an object of obligatory belief. Faith must be regarded as the religious element *par excellence*. Wheresoever faith exists, *there* is religion. What is called dogma is merely a symbolical interpretation—always inadequate and always modifiable—of the ineffable data of the religious consciousness.

All religious knowledge is necessarily and purely symbolical, seeing that mystery (as the word implies) can only be expressed through symbols.

It is between faith and its object that we are bound to distinguish. The first alone is essential, the second is a consequence and a contingent expression of the first.

II

THE VALUE OF RITSCHLIANISM

Whether under their precise form in the theological schools, or under their general aspect as a phase of religious thought, the ideas of Ritschl and of his disciples are very wide-spread even to-day. A large number of thinking men are disposed to place religion, exclusively or mainly, in feeling, in the inward life, in the spiritual communion of the soul

with God, and to put into the background, or even
to discard altogether, the doctrines which aim at
making it an object of theoretical knowledge, and
which, in that very way, risk bringing it into conflict
with knowledge of another order, *i.e.* with scientific
knowledge. The distinction between faith and creed,
similar to that between spirit and letter, between soul
and body, between thought and speech, between idea
and form, is widely approved at the present time.
It enables many intellectual people, who would set
aside religion if it were identified with dogmas that
were repulsive to them, to continue their adherence by
reason of what they regard as the principal religious
aspect.

And it cannot be denied that the standpoint of
Ritschl offers great advantages.

Setting aside *a priori* everything in the nature of
science, theory and knowledge, as foreign to religion,
the theologian no longer dreads that science will, at
some time, disturb his freedom. He has installed
himself in a domain which, by definition, has nothing
in common with the scientific domain : how could he
ever encounter science on the way of his choice ?
Science observes and links together the outward appearances of things : the pious man lives in God and
in the soul of his brethren. He feels the working of
God within him; in virtue of this very working he
prays, he loves, he hopes. Science has no hold upon
these phenomena; they are of an order other than
those which she studies. Science looks for theories,
and these phenomena are realities. How can theories
prevent realities from existing ?

If religion, understood in this rigorously spiritualistic sense, avoids all collision with science, it would be unjustifiable, according to the theologians of whom we are speaking, to maintain that this is effected through her diminishing and becoming utterly insignificant, so as to offer no resistance to her adversary. For the scientist, who has only to do with material realities, the purely spiritual may, perhaps, be a mere naught; but in this "naught" the religious man finds everything:

In deinem Nichts hoff' ich das All zu finden,[1]

said Faust to Mephistopheles.

And, firstly, he finds therein autonomy, independence, freedom. The Divine is but a word, if it is conditioned by nature and by science. If it is to be at all, it must indeed stand for origin, initiative, creation. The doctrine of free and, to all appearance, arbitrary grace, signifies in truth that the divine operation cannot be determined by things, since they only exist through it, but that it is dependent on itself alone, *i.e.* is perfectly free. It is not right to say that religion, banished from the world of sense, is confined within the heart—limited to those objects which are the heart's special concern. Established upon the very foundations of man's conscious and moral life, she is all-powerful, quickening and determining his entire existence.

And experience actually shows that the inward religious life—what is called Mysticism—is a singularly rich and potent reality. Communion with God is not only a source of emotions that are strong or tender, secret or expansive. It makes men of faith and of will, incapable of prostituting their convictions, ready

[1] In thy Naught I hope to find the All.

to brave everything in order to accomplish what God commands. Confidence in God involves confidence in self.

The mystic, for whom things, as they are given, represent merely scientific connection, sets his face resolutely towards practical life and towards the future. The falling back of the soul upon itself, the endeavour to find God within the *ego*, is only, indeed, the first moment of the mystical life. God is not an abstraction : he is the principle of things as of souls. He that is God-inspired will try to change the world, so as to bring it nearer to its principle ; and under the mystic will be revealed the man of action. Considering his resolution, his energy, his abnegation, his enthusiasm, his indomitable perseverance, who would wish to deny the reality of his feelings, and regard his inward life as a worthless dream ?

.   .   .   .   .   .

Thus religion, understood in the Ritschlian sense, will not only withstand the onslaughts of science, but will be able to develop in accordance with its own special genius, freely and effectually. Does this mean that the Ritschlian standpoint yields complete intellectual satisfaction ?

In the first place, it is impossible to ignore the modifications which the progress of knowledge and of reflection inevitably forced upon this standpoint even within the Ritschlian school. The principle assumed was, in reality, twofold. It was, on the one hand, feeling, inward experience, consciousness of man's relation with God ; on the other hand, it was history, the Bible, Revelation. Without doubt, revealed truth was not received in the sense of rational knowledge :

it was not and could not become knowledge, in the strict meaning of the word. If the truths of Revelation were able and, indeed, bound to be embodied in one system, that was from a purely formal standpoint, through an entirely logical method which defines, which arranges, but which, by itself alone, does not give actual proof. The reason for admitting the truths of Revelation remained wholly practical : it was the harmony of these truths with the needs of the religious consciousness, the value that they have for man, the strength and joy with which they endow the human soul. It continued not the less true that this Revelation was, and would necessarily remain, an objective principle, capable of guiding and reconciling individuals.

Now, thus understood, how was this position made good ? If, objects Herrmann, my personal experience ought to constitute for me the unique criterion of truth, can I be restricted to believing in the deeds which have been found possible by others (a St. Paul, a St. Augustine, a Luther), but which I myself have never experienced ?

That is not all. At the time of Ritschl's early speculation, the argument in favour of the Scriptural Canon was still tenable : it has since been demolished through the progress of criticism. The Scriptures no longer furnish faith with the sure foundation that we formerly expected to find in them. And Auguste Sabatier went so far as to say that, if an infallible authority is necessary, Protestants ought no longer to look for it in the uncertain and frigid letter of the Bible, but, after the Catholic method, in the supple and free intelligence of a living person.

Seeing that this solution clashed with the principle

of Ritschlianism, the school inclined to sacrifice, more and more, the objective element to the subjective element, revelation to faith. Herrmann no longer desired any other ground of faith than the impression felt by the individual in contemplating the inward life of Jesus. The angry God and the merciful God of the Bible, corresponding to the twofold feeling of sin and redemption, are no longer, for him, in any sense realities in themselves, originating our soul-states : our soul-states are the only certain realities, divine justice and pity being simply more or less subjective interpretations of them. Everything which is not individual faith pure and simple is merely a symbolical expression of that faith. The more dogmas, the more Churches, in the traditional meaning of these words. The individual can no longer get outside himself. He sees in dogmas metaphors that can be explained in accordance with his individual experience; a Church is, for him, an association of men united in the thought of rejecting every obligatory creed.

The weak point of this system is quite evident : it is a subjectivity without content.

Pfleiderer reproaches Herrmann with making the object of religion purely imaginary. To place God, says he, quite outside the sphere of knowledge, is to regard him as a mere object of aspiration. It is to maintain the existence of God solely on the ground that belief in God is salutary, comforting, inspiring, without asking if that belief is not contradicted by the teaching of science. Such a faith is incapable of proving that it is not a purely subjective delusion.

And it is certain that when we carry out, more and more, the refining method recommended by

Ritschl, when we make it our aim to abstract from the religious consciousness everything which does not spring immediately from the subject himself, we cannot help tending to deprive him of all that would justify belief according to his own view ; for a justification is a reason which goes beyond the subjective and crude fact in being characterised by universality and necessity, *i.e.* by objectivity.

What, at any rate, is this faith, which, rising in the face of dogmas and institutions, and scornfully rejecting their support, exclaims : " In self alone I find sufficiency " ? As its very definition indicates, it is faith considered as absolutely bare and as devoid of any assignable determination. Every expression of this faith falls away under intellectual definition, and language is, in this system, merely an effort of the individual to represent and explain to himself what he experiences in connecting it with the objects that exist outside him.

But how can we see in faith, thus separated from all intellectual content, anything else than an abstraction, an empty form, a word, a nonentity ? It is only too easy to declare that we can believe, with the same intensity and the same conviction, in things lovely and in things hateful, and that, if pure and simple faith sufficed to characterise religion, every fanatic would be a religious man to the same extent as a St. Paul or a St. Augustine. Moreover, are we actually satisfied with faith ? It is assumed, more or less tacitly, that this faith will be necessarily faith in Jesus Christ. Consciousness is invoked, but we are expected to add or to understand that Christian consciousness is here in question. Notwithstanding what may come of it, there is combined with faith an objective or intellectual element, with which, indeed, we cannot dispense if we wish to obtain a positive principle which shall have some meaning.

In fact, if we give full due to the religious consciousness, to faith, to love, without slipping into an abstract and empty subjectivism, we must not make it undergo a negative purification, a limitless mutilation and dissolution. On the contrary, we ought to enrich the subject, to enlarge it, to raise it as much as possible towards being and universality. The method to be followed, in order to get beyond the purely theoretical standpoint of the abstract understanding, consists in making use of all the resources of intellect combined with life, and not in seeking a standpoint beyond the intellect's reach. Rather than go, further and further, in search of a refuge against the attacks of science and of reason, we ought to be reconciled with this same science to the utmost extent possible, to ensure for reason all the development of which she is capable, and to create, by means of all these data, instruments for the realisation of ideal ends.

Is it really certain, moreover, that in confining themselves, as they do, within the inward tribunal of conscience, of the heart, of religious emotion, Ritschl and his disciples are sheltering themselves effectively from the incursions of science?

They argue on the hypothesis of a science which is only occupied with physical phenomena, and which would not dream of establishing a connection between these phenomena and moral phenomena. At least they admit that there are certain phenomena, emotions, impressions of the soul, which are not and cannot be

subverted by science. They speak freely about two
separate domains—the external world and the internal
world, things and consciousness. Herein we find,
definitely, the basis of their doctrines. They picture
consciousness as a sphere within which no natural
force can enter, and which science, confining her
attention to the outside of things, does not expect
to investigate any more than she possesses the means
thereto.

But the opposition of without and within, and the
conception of a soul-sphere impenetrable by science,
are simply metaphors, and metaphors which no longer
conform to the state of knowledge.

Science, it is true, for a long time claimed to
accommodate herself solely to the phenomena of the
material world. She left to metaphysics, or to literature, the phenomena of the moral order. But it is
quite another matter to-day. Having, since the time
of Descartes, more and more tested the efficiency of
order and method in scientific work, and the relations
between the different departments of knowledge,
science is henceforth prepared to begin the study of
all kinds of phenomena whatsoever. However far-off
an emotion of the soul may appear—however secret,
however hidden, however mysterious it may be for
the theologian—it is a real, given, observable thing :
therefore it is a phenomenon, connected necessarily,
according to law, with other phenomena. In vain
does the believer protest that his act of faith, his
prayer, and his sense of union with God, are to be
regarded as entirely spiritual, and as in no way
related to material things. Just because they fall
within consciousness, they are amenable to science ;
for the latter is, henceforward, specially concerned

in explaining, amongst other things, the genesis of states of consciousness, whatever they may be; and she possesses methods which enable her to bring nearer and nearer the internal and the external, the mysterious and the knowable, the subjective and the objective.

In a word, it is impossible to discover a retreat where we can feel sure of not being rejoined by science, unless, first of all, we ask ourselves what constitutes science, what is its range, and whether it has limits. Therein we encounter a problem which it is not sufficient to skim or to curtail by a few philosophical generalities, but which ought to be examined for its own sake, and from the standpoint of science herself.

CHAPTER II

RELIGION AND THE LIMITS OF SCIENCE

THE dogmatic conception of science and the critical conception.

I. APOLOGY OF RELIGION BASED ON THE LIMITS OF SCIENCE—
   Experience as the unique principle of scientific knowledge—
   Consequences : limits in the theoretical order, limits in the
   practical order—Scientific laws, simple methods of research—
   Limits and signification of the correspondence of scientific
   knowledge with fact—The latitude that science, so understood,
   leaves to religion for its development—Letter and spirit :
   contingent and relative character of religious formulæ.

II. THE DIFFICULTIES OF THE PRECEDING DOCTRINE—The polemic
   raised by a word : "the failure of science"—In what sense
   science confesses that she has limits—Precarious situation of
   religion in this system.

III. SCIENCE CONSIDERED AS PREDISPOSED TOWARDS RELIGION—
   Religious doctrines as outlined in science itself; the difficulty
   of maintaining this point of view—The nature of the limits
   imposed on science : they are not simply negative, but imply a
   supra-scientific "beyond" as condition of the very aim of
   science.

IV. REMAINING DIFFICULTIES—The autonomy of science and that of
   religion remain compromised—The insufficiency of a purely
   critical method.

Those who try to gain—in order to make of it the
sanctuary of religion—a nook infinitely removed from
visible realities, concealed in the innermost depths of

consciousness, give way particularly to the fear of meeting science on a common ground, where the latter, perhaps, would dispute their right to exist. They are disposed rather to steal away from the conflict than to risk being vanquished. Now, many thinking men, even among the scientists, have begun to ask if this fear is not exaggerated, if science, considered at close quarters and in its concrete form, is not really more favourable to freedom of religious development than certain theories—philosophically rather than scientifically inspired—declare.

We must, in this connection, have regard to the change which, during our own day, has been effected in the idea of science. Only a short time ago, science stood for absolute knowledge of the nature of things. She laid claim to sure and definite knowledge in contrast with variable and individual belief; and, emboldened by the conquests gained through the discovery of her true principles, she saw no limits to her range and power. It was, in short, the old-time metaphysic, with its ambition for perfect knowledge, transferred to the world of experience. But—unlike the æsthetico-rational systems of the Platos and of the Aristotles—it was a metaphysic which eliminated from the principle of things everything recalling human intelligence and freedom, so as to admit therein only material and mechanical elements.

Before such a science, it was natural that religion, if she desired to remain unassailable, should fall back upon a domain where all collision would be impossible.

But is it incorrect to say that this conception of science, as absolute and limitless knowledge, is not maintained, and that the science of to-day has become accustomed to quite another idea of her meaning?

Henceforward, is there no cause to ask anew how far science is really adverse to the existence of religion?

I

APOLOGY OF RELIGION BASED ON THE LIMITS OF SCIENCE

After feeling her way for a long time, science has at length determined her method by a kind of natural selection. She has chosen to rest upon experience, and upon experience alone. Doubtless, it is a question, after having verified the facts, of recapitulating them, of classifying them, of bringing them together and of systematising them. But this logical operation itself has need of experience to guide and to control it.

In adopting this mode of investigation, science has secured advantages that are infinitely precious. She can at length grasp the real, which she was never sure of reaching so long as she restricted herself to analysing and combining concepts which represent things in the mind of man. She obtains knowledge that is essentially useful in practice, experience furnishing man with the means of making nature repeat herself. She escapes from the endless uncertainty and the infinite variety of opinions; she forces herself upon every intellect, and all her acquisitions are, in a sense, definitive.

But these benefits, it may be remarked, have, as counterpart, a limitation of her range and of her philosophical value, which has very important consequences.

The famous speech of Dubois-Reymond, concluding with *Ignorabimus*, has never ceased, since 1880, to haunt people's minds. Of the seven enigmas that he specified, four at least—said he—were for ever insoluble : viz. the essence of matter and of force, the origin of movement, the origin of simple sensation, and the freedom of the will.

It is because these four problems are outside the range of experience. In fact, however great be the extension claimed for it, experience can reach neither first beginnings, nor final ends. Not only is it—and must always be—incapable of comprehending, in time, a first or a last phenomenon, which is undoubtedly nothing else than a fiction, but there is always the need of knowing to what extent the constant successions that it presents, suffice to explain the appearing óf phenomena. Existence only unfolds according to laws because there is in it a certain nature. What is this nature ? Is it unchangeable ? Why is it determined in one manner and not in another ? With what antecedent ought we to connect it in order to explain it experimentally ? These questions imply, for science, a vicious circle, and, in consequence, pass beyond it irresistibly. Through experience we verify laws, or relations that are relatively constant between phenomena ; but we cannot discover thereby if these laws are themselves merely facts, or if they proceed from some immutable nature which governs facts.

Limited in her compass, science is equally limited in depth. The phenomenon, as she apprehends it, cannot be identified with being. She only succeeds in stripping it of its subjective and individual elements through resolving it into relations, into dimensions, into laws. But, while the notion of law as the connection between two phenomena, however strange it may appear from the standpoint of reason, is at least clear for the imagination, which easily pictures two objects bound together by a thread, the hypothesis of relations pre-existent with regard to their terms is a non-representable conception, in which the human intellect can see merely the symbol of a thing that it does not understand. And if science tends, all the more, to gain the unanimous adhesion of thinking men through setting aside the notion of subject and of element in order to fasten on that of relation, the opinion is, at the same time, forced upon all minds, that this science is not the adequate representation of being, but a certain way of apprehending it, and that there must be some principle of reality in the very forms which she was obliged to discard, so as to reach the kind of objectivity that she had in view.

Manifest in the theoretical order, the limits of science are, in the practical order, still more evident.

The practical life of man, as a rational being, is conditioned by ends that he proposes to himself because they are deemed desirable, good, obligatory. Now, it is impossible for science to offer man, with reference to any end whatsoever, reasons that suffice to make him go in search of it. Science teaches how, through using such means, we are led to such a result. This only interests me if I have decided to pursue that result. Science informs me that many men consider such an end as desirable, good, or obligatory. Does it follow that I ought to think as they do? Have we never seen a man do well just in so far as his thought differed from that of other people? And do those whom we admire as superior, owe this superiority entirely to the acceptance of received opinions? Science establishes facts, presents as fact everything that she teaches us. But, in order that I may act according to my reason, I must represent an object to myself, not as a fact, but as an end, *i.e.* as a thing which may, conceivably, not be, but which ought to be. It is, therefore, characteristically human to suppose that science is not everything ; to give to the words—well-being, usefulness, longing, beauty, obligation—a practical meaning that science ignores.

Does some one urge that science explains these very concepts in reducing them to feelings, to habits, to traditions, and, finally, to delusions of the imagination? Such an explanation, if it is true, is nothing else than the destruction of what we call practical life in the rational and human sense. So long as human life shall continue, it will amount to the denial of this explanation. Practice, wherever found, oversteps the limits of science.

Social life, in particular, cannot be satisfied with the data of science. It needs, in order to reach a high level and to be fruitful, the devotion of the individual, his faith in human laws, in general well-being and in justice, his fidelity to the past and his zeal for the good of future generations. It claims his obedience, his self-denial, if need be his life. Now science, whatever may be said by those who confuse her with the scientist, could never furnish the individual with convincing reasons for self-surrender and self-sacrifice. Even the example of animals— on which many lay stress, but about which many also are disagreed—cannot carry full conviction to a reasoning man, because, thanks to his very intelligence, he discusses the legitimacy of the rule that is enjoined upon him, and succeeds only too well in preventing the wrong which he does to the community from rebounding upon himself. How will science, knowing only fact, persuade an individual in whom egoism prevails over self-sacrifice, that he ought to reverse the relation, and devote himself to a good that does not affect him? Will she try to show that the disposition towards self-sacrifice actually exists in the mind of each individual, as an unconscious echo of the influence of the community upon its members? But self-sacrifice, to be really genuine, must be spontaneous. And, as long as men devote themselves to the community, they will do it because they regard themselves as persons and not as mechanical products of the social organisation.

It is in this way that modern experimental science, just because it is based solely upon experience, appears as limited in its range, whether on the side of theory, or on the side of practice. Can science, at least in her own sphere of competency, offer the mind genuine certitude? Even that is contested; and many people believe that, within this same sphere, the value of science ought to be limited.

We ought to emphasise the change which has been produced of late years in the strictly scientific attitude. Science, until recently, was, or attempted to be, dogmatic. In her most rigorous investigations, she considered herself as definitely constituted; in others, she aimed at a like perfection. She sought, at every point, to appear under the form of a system, which, from universal principles, deduces the explanation of particular things. As regards form, Scholasticism was her ideal.

But no science at the present time—not even mathematics—is content with the scholastic pattern. Science, whatever form it may assume for the purpose of exposition or of teaching, is and remains, in itself, an endlessly perfectible induction. It is a question of knowing how this induction is effected.

We must be careful, here, to distinguish between laws and principles which are the result of induction, and the facts which underlie them.

According to the Baconian philosophy, which, for a long time, prevailed among scientists, the laws of nature imprinted themselves necessarily upon the human mind, provided that the latter got rid of its prejudices, and surrendered itself in a docile manner to the influence of things. No active participation of the subject in knowledge properly so called could be traced. The subject was only manifested as such in his feelings, which science was specially bent on disregarding.

The study of the history of the sciences, combined with the psychological analysis of the formation of scientific concepts in the human mind, has led to an entirely different theory.[1]

Scientific laws and principles have the appearance of being directly drawn from nature, owing to our formal way of stating them : "phosphorus melts at 44° C."; "action is equal to reaction." But this dogmatic form, however convenient it may be, only reflects the precise result of scientific study.

Science has, in reality, occupied herself with the search and discovery of hypothetical definitions which enable her to interrogate nature. The property of melting at 44° C. is part of the definition of phosphorus; the so-called principle that action is equal to reaction is part of the definition of force. Not one of the

---

[1] V. Duhem, *La Théorie physique*, 1906. E. Le Roy, *Un Positivisme nouveau.* Revue de métaph. et de mor., 1901.

elements embraced in these formulæ, is really given, nor can it be given in the exact sense. And, further, their combination is not given. But the mind, compelled to seek, and to know what it seeks, forms (through choosing and determining the data of experience in a suitable manner) certain definitions which enable it to put exact and methodical questions to nature.

These definitions, moreover, are not all on the same plane. Some of them are particular and derived, some are general and fundamental, as in the preceding instances. The most general definitions are, naturally, the most stable : hence the form of principles which they assume in our speech, and which easily causes them to be taken for absolute knowledge.

Lastly, there is a notion which appears more necessary than all, inasmuch as it is necessary to all, viz. the notion of science itself. This notion is still a definition, fabricated like all the rest. I call science the hypothesis of constant relations between phenomena. Scientific study consists in the interrogation of nature according to this hypothesis. Similarly, a judge forms a conjecture before questioning the accused.

The affirmations which these definitions imply being imagined in order to render interrogation possible and useful, are, and can only be, hypotheses, seeing that it is a question of examining, no longer a determinate individual, able to appear as a complete whole, but Nature—infinite in every direction—whose future manifestations, in particular, cannot be given us. But, so long as the critical study of their origin and their rôle has not been carried out, we confuse these hypotheses with absolute principles : first of all because, having given them the form of the latter, we are inclined to transfer the peculiarities of the form to the content itself; then because certain of these principles are presupposed by all the rest, and that which is essential to our systems, seems essential in itself.

This theory, which the study of the formation of scientific concepts suggests, is forced upon the mind, when we come to reflect that, experience being our sole way of communicating with nature, exact formulæ, on a level with our principles, would constitute an absurdity, if they had to be considered as drawn, just as they are, from nature. From experience alone, ever changing and unstable, we can but derive correspondingly shifting impressions. A systematic intervention of the mind can alone explain the transmutation that science makes experience undergo.

And the mind, in this operation, is so well aware of instituting, through its definitions and its theories, simple methods of research, that it does not hesitate to admit, equally, theories that are different and even contradictory in their fundamental hypotheses, when these theories furnish equivalent conclusions, and are all useful in studying various classes of phenomena.[1] It could not be so, if the mind had to see, in the ruling ideas of its theories, the absolute explanation of things.

But, it will be said, whatever may be the origin of science, it is a fact that she harmonises with things, and that she enables us to make use of them. To be able to act on things is to possess some of their own methods of action. Doubtless, our knowledge will

[1] See H. Poincaré, *La Science et l'Hypothèse* ; *La Valeur de la science.*

probably never succeed in being even with things ;
but it grips reality more and more closely ; even its
contrivances, its conventions and its fictions have no
other aim than to be adapted to it ; and the approxi-
mation, always increasing moreover, which it attains,
cannot be confused with a radical incapacity to reach
the truth.   Besides, we must come to an understanding over the word truth.   Science no longer expects
to endow the mind with a close copy of external
things, which apparently, just as we suppose them,
do not exist.   She discovers relations that experience
verifies through the senses.   It is enough that she
may and must be called true, in the human meaning
of the word.

Our authors reply : What does this verifiability
prove ?   It is natural that scientific laws should
succeed in experience, seeing that they have been
invented for the very purpose of enabling us to
anticipate the natural course of things.   We have,
moreover, a convenient trick of conceiving them as
successful, even when, in point of fact, they do not
succeed.   We imagine, in that case, other laws as
contradicting the action of those which are admitted.
And thus we multiply additions and corrections in
order to save the principle to which we are accustomed,
until at length, our theory becoming inextricably
complicated, we abandon a principle which is no more
than an occasion of difficulties, in order to make trial
of some other, for which, undoubtedly, the future has
a like fate in store.

The fact is, the alleged correspondence between our
concepts and experience is, somehow, wrongly defined.
We confuse the correspondence of mathematical or
scientific concepts among themselves (one that can be

very precise) with the correspondence of those concepts to experience. Now experience, if we isolate it from the scientific concepts that are mingled with it, is no more than a very vague perception. After all, we only know a thing in so far as the theory concerning it is borne out obviously in practice. But how are we to determine the degree of truth that a hypothesis ought to possess in order to be practically useful? It is a fact recognised in logic, that from false premisses one can deduce a right conclusion. We experience every day that a method may succeed perfectly without having any intrinsic connection with reality. Mnemotechnic processes may be instanced. Therein we have what are called empirical receipts. Who can prove that our science, with its empirical starting-point, does not remain empirical in its results? As it is given us, scientific attainment implies, between science and things, a certain correspondence—not an identity; and a correspondence which, indeed, is only in the end a practical notion.

How, precisely, do our scientific theories present this ill-defined correspondence which is to demonstrate their truth? Through experience, through facts. It is admitted that facts are there, outside the mind, and that the latter discovers the means of shaping its conceptions in accordance with them; and science is called true because we believe that she represents, more and more exactly, this external reality which does not depend upon her.

But the whole of this imaginative construction is artificial. In reality, the fact with which the scientist is reconciled, is not something raw and independent of the mind: it is the scientific fact; and this latter, if we look carefully into its formation, appears as having been fashioned already, arranged, constructed in some way, so as to be capable of corresponding with the hypothetical laws that science has introduced into her definitions.

We must distinguish scientific fact from raw fact. The latter, whatever its origin, is only the stuff out of which science carves, in her own way, what she will call facts. A scientific fact is, indeed, the reply in a book of questions; and this question-book is nothing else than the series of laws or hypotheses already imagined by the mind in order to give an account of phenomena that are similar. It is by means of our theories, of our definitions, of an already existent science, that we enunciate, that we determine, that we perceive the facts which are to take the name of science. These facts are no less handled with a view to their being adapted to theories than the theories are formed with a view to being adapted to facts. The agreement of the theories with the facts is, to an extent that it is impossible to fix, the agreement of those theories with themselves.

This means, after all, that the human mind can only operate according to intellectual rule. And its mode of operation consists (being given certain forms and categories) in finding out if it can be brought into connection with the things which are laid before it. It only knows, it only perceives, on condition of possessing, previously, certain moulds of knowledge, of perception. What is the primary origin of such anterior knowledge? How is it to be described? What is its value? Even in being stated, the problem passes beyond the domain of scientific facts. We are merely aware of this—that our knowledge, our perception, can never be other than a rendering, in our speech, of the realities which are given us. This holds good equally of facts and of laws ; and, also, it must certainly be stated that facts are offered us solely under the operation of certain laws, since they can be perceived only through being related by consciousness to types that pre-exist in it.

From this general condition of knowledge, science cannot escape. Even scientific knowledge is and can be no more than a language, by means of which the mind grasps as relatively intelligible, *i.e.* as recognisable and pliable, the greatest possible number of the objects which are set before it. How has this language been formed ? What portion of reality is it capable of expressing ? With what degree of fidelity ? These questions are clearly embarrassing, seeing that the mind can only approach them with the aid and in the name of the very prejudices that we desire to control. At all events, they carry us beyond the domain of scientific experience no less than that of common experience.

From these considerations it may be inferred that science is not an impression stamped by things upon a passive intelligence, but an *ensemble* of symbols imagined by the mind in order to interpret things by means of pre-existent notions (inexplicable as regards their primary origin), and to gain, by such means, the power of making them serve the realisation of its purposes.

.   .   .   .

Such a doctrine is, it would seem, much more likely than Ritschlian dualism, to solve, in a rational manner, the problem of the relations between science and religion.

Indeed, according to this doctrine, the living part

of science, the sum of positive knowledge symbolised by its formulæ, does not differ at bottom from the kind of beliefs upon which our practical life rests. Science could not, *a priori*, decree that simple belief ought to be banished from the human mind, since she herself admits it, and retains it in her fundamental notions. Religious belief, *i.e.* faith, cannot therefore be set aside on the mere ground that it is a belief. Enough for us to realise that it may coexist with science in the same intelligence, that it does not run counter to the beliefs which have actually been adopted on the authority of science.

But, in this respect, modern science allows religion great latitude. She does not claim to bear sway over all forms of being. She confines herself to those sides of it which are amenable to the scientific category, showing no inclination to deny that quite other categories may conceivably encounter (in the real or in the possible) a theme which corresponds to them. The scientist asks : Do we find in things constant relations ? Must we infer thence that the wants of the religious consciousness are forbidden ? Does there exist any power capable of making the world better ?

Not that religion can, henceforward, ignore the teaching of science. Every appeal to science is a pledge of knowing and of reverencing her. It cannot be denied that she subsists to-day upon a certain number of ideas which interest religion, at least as they are presented to us in their concrete reality. The most important, perhaps, is the notion of evolution.

It is very difficult, and raises, doubtless, a metaphysical rather than a scientific problem, to know what, precisely, this evolution is, what it implies and signifies in its origin and in its nature. But it has a phenomenal and scientific meaning about which everybody is agreed, viz. that living creatures—and, perhaps, things generally — change, or can change, not only in certain of their manifestations, but in the totality of their ways of being, and that we cannot, *a priori*, limit the extent of this change. Possibly transmutations take place in the germ, possibly they result from the influence of environment, possibly these two causes co-operate ; but it is invariably maintained that there is no longer a fixed difference between the nature of a being and its modifications, and that what are called the essential peculiarities of a species may, henceforward, be conceived as a mere phase of evolution, become relatively stable.

Now there actually exists a whole school of theologians who make it their special aim to bring the external history of religion into agreement with these theories.

They start from a distinction which every thinking man is led to make at all times, and which is, in truth, the basis of life and action as a whole : the distinction between principle and application, between idea and its realisation. We desire with our thought, we realise with things. It follows that there is in any action, in any realisation whatsoever, something besides thought, viz. a material form, which, if external conditions happen to be modified, will necessarily have to be modified correspondingly, under pain of a change in meaning, and of no longer expressing the same thought. Why is it that our writers of the sixteenth century require explanation at the present time, unless it be that the language has changed ? In order to say, nowadays, the same thing that they intended to

say, we are often obliged to use other words. All
action, all life implies this distinction, for life consists
in being established by means of the environment in
which we find ourselves ; and, when this environment
changes considerably, the living individual is offered
a choice of two things—either to evolve or to disappear.

Religion cannot escape from this law. She aims
necessarily at being effectual, and she can only be so
through speaking to man in his own words. She
only offers the mind a comprehensible meaning, if
she, in some way, conforms to the categories which
pre-exist in that mind and which constitute its
standard of intelligibility. There are, therefore, in
all genuine religion two parts, although the point at
which the one ends and at which the other begins
cannot be indicated exactly : there is religion properly
so called—life, will, action ; and there is the visible
realisation of religion, or the combination of religion
in the strict sense with the conditions of existence
inherent in a given community. The first element
is immutable, in the symbolical sense which this
word assumes when applied to a spiritual principle
that is essentially living. The second is, inevitably,
bound up with the evolution of things.

Not only, then, does the theologian of whom we
speak respect the data of science, and refrain from
insisting upon the maintenance of such and such a
belief under a form which to-day seems impossible ;
but he incorporates into theology itself the principles
that science has definitely established, in particular
the principle of evolution.

The creative and regulative conception, as originally
presented, remains ; but the interpretations which it
receives, the formulæ through which it is made out-

wardly communicable, the institutions which develop its action in the world, are subject to evolution. On the one hand, the causal link which connects the succession of these forms with the primary conception, and the close resemblance which they cannot help retaining (seeing that they are the expressions of one and the same original), guarantee their spiritual unity; on the other hand, the manifestations of religion share the law relating to all living things, in following, as regards their evolution, the world of which they form part.

Henceforward, these expressions which could, originally, be understood in their literal and material meaning, ought to-day, if we would have them preserved, to be understood in a metaphorical sense—thus rendering them compatible, in the only way possible, with the progress of knowledge. For instance, the statements—" He descended into hell, he ascended into heaven "—can only retain their value, if, setting aside a material localisation that is inconceivable to-day, we get behind the imaginary picture to the spiritual meaning: the idea of the union of Christ's soul with the righteous men of the ancient Law, and the final glorification of his humanity.

Moreover, we could not regard this use of allegorical interpretation as futile and chimerical, on the ground that, at all times, threatened doctrines have had recourse to it, and have misused it to a childish extent. Metaphor is the language even of the full-grown man ; and, if we look carefully into the matter, we hardly ever use any word in its strict meaning. What is called the life of words is nothing else than the necessity whereby we come to evolve the meaning of words in compliance with the change of ideas, if we would preserve them, through this same change, as social life requires.   An idea cannot, immediately, create its form; for, in that case, it would not be understood by anybody.   It necessarily adopts—at least for a time—the given form which constitutes for existing society the standard of intelligibility; and, by means of this form which was not made for it, it is expressed, through adding to the literal, or substituting for it, a metaphorical meaning.

The existence and the development of religion are then, according to what may be called the Progressive School, nowise disturbed by modern science.

In the groundwork of religion are found the fundamental religious truths which, owing to their essentially metaphysical character, escape from contact with a science whose sole object is the phenomenal.

Religion contains, in addition, several quasi-immediate expressions of these fundamental truths : dogmas and rites which, spiritual in a sense and lived rather than formulated, scarcely admit of conflict with science.   Thus it is that Christianity calls God, father; men, sons of God and, as such, brethren one with another; in like manner it teaches the kingdom of God, sin, salvation, redemption, the communion of saints.

There remain particular dogmas and rites.   In so far as these contain elements borrowed from the knowledge and from the institutions of a determinate period, they may chance to be at variance with the ideas and institutions of another period.   That is of no consequence, unless the science and the institutions of yesterday contradict, in some measure, those of to-day.   Religion is not responsible for these variations : she cannot be affected by them.   She remains identical, while undergoing an external evolution.

Moreover, two modes of evolution are conceivable. Either religion will retain her formulæ as the legacy of a bygone science and civilisation, while disengaging, from their literal and material meaning, any spiritual meaning that can be recovered therefrom. Or, resuming the proud tradition of St. Paul, of St. Athanasius, of St. Augustine, of St. Thomas, of the great organisers of Dogmatic Theology, she will not be afraid of converting to her own use the philosophical and scientific notions of the present age, in order to make of them the symbol—always contingent, doubtless, but directly intelligible for the actual generations—of that religious life which is eternal and inexpressible.

II

THE DIFFICULTIES OF THE PRECEDING DOCTRINE

The system which grounds religion on criticism of science, embraced by some with an ardour that is occasionally combative, has raised, for others, strong objections. Some years ago much angry discussion raged around a formula which summed up this system from a controversial standpoint : " the failure of science."

From the eloquent protests which this war-cry called forth, it is sometimes difficult to derive conclusive arguments. Thus, enthusiasm was shown in enumerating the great discoveries of modern science, and especially the marvellous applications of these discoveries. But our precise endeavour is to know if these advances, which have reference chiefly to the material side of life, fully realise the promises which the science of yesterday often made with respect, not only to the material, but to the political and moral life of humanity.

Others said : Science has not failed, since no reasonable and genuine science has ever been able to promise what you charge science with not having bestowed. This reply contains the implication that science is not the be-all and end-all of man.

Through these apologies of the modern scientist, there runs, nevertheless, a leading idea, which science, indeed, impresses more and more upon the mind : that of the impossibility of assigning any limit to her progress. No doubt there are immense differences between the physical order and the moral order, between animal communities and human communities. But are we bound to infer that the distance which separates inorganic matter from living matter, or real movement from abstract mechanics, is insurmountable ? And, besides, continuity is shown, more and more, between these apparently separate realms. Why should we debar the future from thoroughly establishing the coincidence of science with being, under all its forms ?

It is urged that, of all the inventions which science has given us, not one satisfies the moral needs of human nature, and that the science of the future will not prove more adequate in this respect, seeing that such needs are extra-scientific.

But it is a mistake to lay too much stress on this objection. The acquisition of certain truths has created in the mind of the scientist a distinct feeling of assurance and of competency. To this standard, henceforward, he refers every intellectual activity :

and, consequently, he regards as vain and illegitimate those inquiries which do not conform to it. It is true that he no longer ventures, as formerly, to enunciate absolute results, unrelated to our means of knowing; he declares, indeed, that all science is relative. But this expression must be taken in its true sense. It does not mean that, outside the domain in which science moves, there is another domain—that of the absolute, in which it would be allowable for other disciplines to have full play: on the contrary, it warns human intelligence against venturing into any region that would be inaccessible to science. For, if a thing is unknowable for science, such an object is, *a fortiori*, unknowable for every other discipline. And, strong in the sense of a competency which belongs to her alone, where she says—I know, science means: here is knowledge for the human mind; and where she says—I do not know, she would have us understand: here let no one claim to possess knowledge!

It is, therefore, by no means clear that modern science, notwithstanding her diffident mien, is more favourable than dogmatic science to the free development of religion. From the standpoint of science, religion is merely a collection of arbitrary conceptions; for she can only assume the form of science, and—even then—not without risking her integrity, as the example of Scholasticism shows. As to the inward principle of religion, it cannot, obviously, be compared with the truths of objective experience, to which alone science gives heed. And it is not enough to urge that what we wish to maintain, beyond the limits of science, is not another science, but a belief. A belief, from the scientific standpoint, has value

s

only if it is, at one and the same time, based on the observation of facts and adjusted to a meaning that science can accept.

Restricted to the domain that, apparently, science has given up to it, religious belief cannot, even within these limits, make sure of its independence and its freedom of development. Every scientific advance threatens it. The believer follows anxiously the vicissitudes of the scientific explanation of things, expecting to see, here a fissure disclosed, there a gap filled up. He provokes, through his intemperate zeal for adaptation and accommodation, a comparison that is unfavourable to his own cause. For, in contrast with the resolute and triumphant advance of science, he can but offer the suspense and timidity of belief; and religion seems no longer to exist save as an honoured name, which once had a great deal behind it, but which is to-day a mere remembrance that the piety and imagination of the faithful strive to embellish, still, with the colours of reality.

Such are the dangers which threaten religion, if she is limited to the search for those advantages which may accrue to her through scientific gaps. According to several philosophers and scientists, however, these dangers are unreal. We threaten religion with them because we persist in considering science as hostile ; but, in this way, we yield to prejudice. Instead of arguing so freely on science and her conditions, let us examine some of her most important results ; and we shall find that, even within her own limits, science shows a religious tendency. We must examine this way of looking at the matter.

III

SCIENCE CONSIDERED AS PREDISPOSED TOWARDS RELIGION

Notwithstanding the reputation for Materialism and Naturalism which often clings to science, there are not a few philosophers and scientists by profession who persist in denying that the methods and contents of science are opposed to the principles of religion. Some of them—not among the least influential—deem it possible to maintain the Scholastic view of the two ways, different with regard to their beginning, convergent with regard to their direction, and find, in modern scientific doctrines themselves, the rudiments of religious dogmas.

It is thus that certain scientists discern, in actual evolutionism, the indication of the religious dogmas of the Divine Personality, of the Creation, of the Fall, of the efficiency of Prayer and of the soul's Immortality.[1]   A like eminent physicist[2] gives, as the outcome of modern science, the Lord's Prayer and the essential points in the Creed of Christendom.

As a rule, however, it is in a less direct manner that men of to-day seek in science an introduction to religion. The point over which discussion prevails, is the character and the exact significance of the limits of science. Do these limits represent a pure negation, an absolute negation, so that, beyond her own special province, science forbids us, emphatically, to look for anything, to imagine anything? Or do they merely offer a relative negation—what Aristotle calls a

---

[1] Armand Sabatier, *La Philosophie de l'effort.*
[2] Sir Oliver Lodge, *The Substance of Faith.*

privation, the want of a thing which is demanded, required, implied by the very fact of our being aware of it ?

According to the thinkers with whom we are now dealing, the limits of science represent, strictly, for the human mind, the privation of a knowledge which would be necessary in order to convert our science into complete knowledge. Science knows enough to realise that she is not self-sufficing. Her principles are negative concepts, indeterminate as regards their content. Now, it is impossible for the human mind not to wonder what a thing is, when taught simply that it is neither this nor that. It is, therefore, quite clear that science herself (not some psychical activity external to science) involves the possibility of a knowledge superior to scientific knowledge. "Reason's final move," said Pascal, "consists in recognising that there are an infinity of things which go beyond her."

And, in the first place, as regards her meaning and general methods, why need we say that science wages war against religion ? Science endeavours to submit phenomena to laws, *i.e.* to regularity, to persistence in change, to order, to logic, to correspondence. She seeks simple and universal laws, to which she may reduce the diversity and intricacy of the laws of detail. In this very way she is disposed to see in the world a process that is one and harmonious, *i.e.* beautiful. And, certainly, a single space—our Euclidean space—appears sufficient to explain all the properties of real extension ; a sole law, that of Newton, governs the phenomena of the astronomical world. In physics we may, perhaps, be satisfied with two fundamental laws : the conservation of energy and the principle of least action. Science tends toward unity, discovers unity : do we, then, make an arbitrary use of words in saying that she leads Godward ?

But, at the same time, she admits that her aim is unattainable. In fact, her principles are only hypotheses obviously tolerated by experience. She can say : no other hypothesis has, hitherto, so successfully endured the verification of facts. She cannot say : this hypothesis is the truth. The very mode of her knowledge—the interrogation of Nature by means of an hypothesis—allows her to find actually sufficient explanations, but not to convert her sufficient explanations into necessary explanations. And, nevertheless, the positive and absolute explanation cannot fail to exist. Science convinces us of it, even while she declares her inability to furnish it.

According to that philosophy which is named mechanical,[1] the properties of bodies are explained by a clear and positive principle—that of Matter and Motion. It must be noted that to-day, even among those who maintain the legitimacy of employing the mechanical standard to explain all phenomena, very few presume to say that with sufficiently powerful instruments it would be possible to perceive the movements that they imagine. They make use of motion as the most convenient symbol for the purpose of discovering and expounding the laws of phenomena.

But many physicists consider this very symbol useless, or, at all events, liable to be discarded as a

---

[1] *Vide* Lucien Poincaré, *La Physique moderne.*

mere auxiliary, with which science has nothing more
to do when its rôle is fulfilled. According to them,
the attempt to reduce to movement the whole of
observable phenomena has failed, in spite of the
increasingly cunning and intricate contrivances of
modern mechanists. The method of real unification
has been set forth in Thermo-dynamics, become
Energetics. Now, this science is constituted through
setting aside the proper nature of things, in order to
consider simply their measurable manifestations. Is
what we measure extension or movement, or something quite different? That is of little consequence.
By means of these measurements we can discover
laws, construct theories, elicit principles which enable
us to classify known phenomena, and, by way of
inference, to put fresh questions to Nature. What
more is wanted? Energetics, in gathering all that
science contains of the strictly experimental and
scientific, and in rejecting every metaphysical and
unverifiable residuum, has realised the most perfect
form that physical science has yet known.

What, now, is the *energy* which this particular
science takes for her sole aim? It is only a negative
idea. It is neither movement, nor any of the concrete
realities that we observe. It points to a knowledge
which we lack.

It appears possible to embrace, in Energetics, every
variety of the modes of change—not only local movement, but physical movements properly so called,
i.e. changes of property and of composition: all that
Aristotle termed alteration, generation, and corruption. But this possibility can only be applied to
the form of phenomena. And this form, not having
in itself any physical property, the formulæ which

represent it would be useless, if phenomena were not, in addition, classed according to their strictly physical resemblances and differences, *i.e.* according to their qualities. Thus the qualitative distinction subsists for the mind of the scientist under the unity and the identity of mathematical treatment.[1] What is this notion of quality? Clearly it is, from the scientific standpoint, a mere negative notion : it is the idea of a condition—irreducible to magnitude— of the magnitudes that observation commits to analysis. But it is, at the same time, the idea of a reality, and is, therefore, not a pure negation. It is the indication, given by science herself, of an aspect of being which outstrips the experience of the senses and the methods of science.

Analogous conclusions are to be drawn from Biology. It is to-day the well-nigh general opinion that, if life, in its maintenance, consumes no energy which is peculiar to it, yet it cannot be referred, purely and simply, to physico-chemical forces. This thesis is even, at times, set forth in such precise and positive terms that the domain of Biology would seem to be less limited, as regards the knowledge of being, than that of Physics. In fact, not only are we assured that life exists, and is no simple mechanism, but its definition is given : it is a consensus, a hierarchy, a solidarity of the parts and of the whole; the unification of heterogeneous elements ; a creative and controlling idea ; the effort to maintain a definite organisation through making use of the resources and combating the obstacles that the environment presents. All

---

[1] See Duhem : *La Théorie physique*, 1906. *L'Évolution des théories physiques*. Rev. des quest. scientifiques, Louvain, October 1896.

these definitions have a positive as well as a supra-mechanical meaning; and, when they are taken as really scientific, it is easy to conclude that science, of herself, introduces us into a world other than that of properly external phenomena.

But we are deceived if we regard these formulæ, in so far as they are positive, as genuinely scientific data. On this understanding, they are metaphors, derived from the feelings which are bound up, in our consciousness, with the exposition of life. They serve the biologist as a sign, an indication, a formula for specifying a certain class of phenomena, which he calls vital, just as the words—force, mass, attraction, inertia, serve the physicist for specifying the phenomena that he calls physical. But, while psychic symbols were capable, with the physicist, of being exactly converted into mathematical symbols, the terms which define life have preserved, for the biologist, a subjective meaning. That is why, from the strictly scientific standpoint, their signification is only negative. They indicate that the characteristic phenomena of life are not reducible to physical mechanism, are not mechanical under any aspect.

And yet, even the scientific idea of life is not a negation pure and simple: it is the affirmation of an unknown, comprehensible as regards its manifestations, but incapable, itself, of objective investigation. It constitutes the reverse of a thing which necessarily has an obverse. This negative concept which, scientifically, is very efficacious, would disappear, and, with it, the relative explanations that it furnishes, if we considered the positive unknown, of which it is the duplicate, as having no real existence.

The study of the problem relating to the origin of

living species determined the development of a theory which, to-day, seems to dominate science entirely, viz. that of Evolution. The differences which distinguished this theory from so-called orthodox beliefs, caused people, first of all, to think that it was in every way inconsistent with those beliefs, and that, since religion implied Providence, Creation, Mind and Freedom, the word evolution could only mean mechanism, brute necessity, materialism.

Meanwhile, the criticism that science herself offered with regard to this theory was not long in showing that the idea of evolution was far from being simple, clear and precise, as could be imagined in the first stage; that it admitted of various meanings; and, at all events, that it was by no means the pure and simple negation of the ideas of Creation, Freedom and Mind, which people had supposed. And, pointing out that the theory of evolution introduced into the world a unity, a continuity, a life, a fecundity, a harmony, a common trend, which the theory relating to fixity of species hardly corroborated, certain scientists and philosophers arrived at the opinion that, far from being opposed to religious ideas, Evolutionism presented, with respect to the world and its development, a conception far nobler and more worthy of a Divine Creator than the traditional dogma of the immutable multiplicity of fundamental forms. This interpretation, sooth to say, goes beyond the scientific meaning of the theory. But it is no exaggeration to assert that the scientist's idea of evolution—to an even greater extent than his ideas of life and of energy—is, in itself, incomplete, and, properly speaking, a negation which implies an affirmation.

At the present time it appears to be established that the form of existence to which we give the name of species, is not immutable and enduring. The chief objection which used to be urged against Darwin, viz. that we see species disappear, but do not see them appear, has now been removed. The experimentalist, through quite sudden transmutation, creates species. From one species may be produced several, more or less divergent. Nothing, therefore, any longer prevents us, in principle, from regarding the totality of existing species as the outcome of evolution.

What is the significance of this hypothesis?

Evolutionism necessarily raises the question of the origin of variations. It has not been able, so far, to reach, with regard to that origin, solutions that are universally admitted. It wavers between two opinions, which are alike based upon a number of facts and experiences, and which, for this reason, certain scientists seek to reconcile and to combine. According to one of these standpoints (recalling that of Darwin) the initial transmutation takes place in the germ. Certain of these transmutations are preserved, increase and become stable types. According to the other standpoint (actually that of Lamarck) the influence of the environment, and the struggle of creatures to adapt themselves thereto, are the essential causes of the transmutations. And the blending of these two standpoints is quite conceivable. For the idea of modification in the germ does not exclude that of influence of the environment, any more than the idea of influence of the environment excludes that of modification in the germ. Adaptation to the environment can be reflected in the process of the reproductive cells, as certain experiments show,[1] and a transmutation in the germ can be combined with adaptation to the conditions of existence.

Can we say that the concepts employed in these explanations are, in the scientific sense, positive concepts?

The doctrine of variations in the germ explains these variations, either by a kind of spontaneous creation, or by the development, under the influence of some circumstance, of latent pre-existing characteristics. Either creation, or innateness—such are the suggested hypotheses.

The doctrine of reaction on the influence of environment implies, in the living being, either the property of acquiring and of displaying a determinate tendency under the influence of the uniform action put forth by an external cause, or the property of modifying itself, so as to comply with external conditions.

As to the relative fixity of the modifications, it is likened to a habit that the being contracts, whether of itself, or under the influence of a relatively constant environment.

In spite of appearances, the concepts of creation, of adaptation, of preservation, are far from having, here, a positive sense—at least from the scientific point of view. For, whatever is positive in the content of these concepts is subjective, indefinable, incapable of scientific exposition. These concepts mean that we cannot compare the formation of living species with the production of a chemical compound. Indeed, they are much more remote from scientific language than were the concepts implied in the

[1] Bonnier, *Le Monde végétal*, p. 332.

theory of immutable species. In the latter, the living world, like the inorganic world, was made up of definite and unchanging elements, finite in number: the sundry combinations of these elements constituted the hierarchy of classes. On the other hand, living and evolving, no longer merely in each of the individuals which compose it, but in its totality, the vegetable or animal world resembles in appearance only, a material collection—a finite number of fixed and homogeneous unities. The change is therein conceived as radical; and the definite, the stable, on which science is based, are no more than contingent and provisional.

These concepts are, for science, only negations and problem-statements, for they transcend the mechanical standpoint. They suggest the idea of an explanation analogous to that which consciousness takes in regard to its own acts. The living being, according to the adopted formulæ, seeks to maintain and unfold its life; and, in order to accomplish this, it determines itself and modifies itself in harmony with the circumstances which surround it.

Such explanations are usually called teleological. According to an acute philosopher,[1] in order to bring them into conformity with the facts, it would be necessary to conceive them as superior, not only to mechanism, but to teleology. Teleology leads to our ranking the vegetable world beneath the animal world, instinct beneath intelligence, when we ought, really, to see therein different developments of one and the same activity. The rich and widely varied process corresponds to the idea of spontaneous creation

---

[1] Bergson, *L'Évolution créatrice.* Cf. Rudolf Otto, *Naturalistische und religiöse Weltansicht*, pp. 214-15.

far better than to the idea of an end conceived in advance and determining the story of the realisation.

Although these views may recall, in some measure, the Spinozistic doctrine of life, it seems indisputable that the positive content of fundamental biological concepts is extra-scientific, and, consequently, that these concepts are, scientifically speaking, merely negative concepts.

It does not follow that science can set aside their positive and subjective signification as useless, chimerical and purely verbal. For, in becoming simply quantitative, exact and objective, these concepts would lose all that characterises them, and renders them helpful to the scientist in his researches and in his syntheses. Kant used to say that, though devoid of substantial value, in the sense that they do not bring us any real knowledge, certain principles have a regulative value, in so far as they enable us to class phenomena and to organise experiences, as if they truly represented the real methods of Nature. This doctrine appears applicable to Biology even to-day. But it shows us science suspended in a reality that goes beyond her means of investigation.

After all, the moral sciences, are, in this respect, especially significant.

These sciences are understood in two ways : either as normative sciences, or as purely positive sciences.

Understood as normative sciences, they furnish directly, by their special content, the guiding principles of human life which we should vainly seek in the physical sciences. They offer or prescribe for man certain ends to be pursued : *e.g.* the development of personality, duty, happiness, harmony between the individual and the community, justice, general benefit, solidarity, union of sentiment. Now it is clear that such aims are not, in themselves, ultimate principles adequately conceived, but that they represent problems of a particular nature—problems which cannot be solved by the aid of experience alone.

According to some people, these aims are nothing else than a vista opening towards the Infinite, towards the Perfect, towards the Divine. If it were so, the moral sciences, through their controlling ideas, would indeed be a true introduction to religion.

Thinkers of another school affirm a much closer analogy between the moral sciences and other sciences. They aim at representing them as just the natural science of man, considered in its moral and sociological manifestations. The moral sciences study the actions of men in their modes and in their causes, as the biological sciences study animal functions and forms of existence. As to practical rules, they are, under this conception, applications of science, but are not part of it. All science, in fact, by virtue of being science, is theoretical : practice precedes it or follows it, but does not, in any way, interfere with it.

So understood, the moral sciences would have a sure way of breaking off every connection with religion : viz. through becoming purely narrative. They would be limited to showing that men have, through the ages, spoken, in such and such sense, of justice, of happiness, of duty, of right, of personality, of solidarity, or of collective conscience, without having to inquire into the origin and philosophical significance of these notions—without considering their value. But a science which is merely narrative, is not, properly speaking, a science. In order to resemble the physical sciences, the science of moral phenomena must become explanatory.

Moral science, at the present time, no longer proposes, in general, to explain conscious life and social life by purely physical causes. Psychology, Ethics and Sociology, without breaking the bonds which connect them with the material sciences, claim their own special principles. We shall, therefore, explain moral phenomena, not only by the physiological and physical conditions of human life, but also by strictly moral causes, such as : the conditions of consciousness; the properties of intelligence and of will; the influence of feelings, of inclinations, of ideas; the peculiar rôle of such ideas as those of individuality, of happiness, of duty, of equality, of liberty, of tradition, of collective conscience, of solidarity, of humanity, of justice, of harmony, of progress, of reason, etc.

What are these principles? Regarded scientifically, they are only negations. They are subjective phantoms, taking the place of objective causes, which our intellect ignores and cannot apprehend in themselves. All that is precise in the explanations drawn from such principles, amounts to this: the phenomena in question are not explained by the efficient causes which we have at our disposal. By a logical trick—having brought in ideas, ends, conscious life under its intelligible aspect—we clothe these fluid things with formulæ, we treat them as beings and as mechanical forces of a kind, and we make use of them as efficient causes. We then imagine that we have given a scientific explanation. But how are we to determine scientifically the meaning and value of such explanations? Whence comes the moral life, the longing after progress, the wish to create anew and to improve Nature?

What is it that we want? Whither are we tending? To reduce all this possibility to necessity, all this ideality to reality, all this contingent future to actual data, is obviously to see in human consciousness nothing but a mystifying power. And, in that case, what becomes of the explanations furnished by it? They are no more than illusory explanations of phenomena that are themselves illusory.

From the strictly scientific standpoint, these ideas are merely negations—the denial that a mechanical explanation is possible. But here again, and here especially, it must be said that we have to do with imperfect negations which are wrapped up with corresponding affirmations. What use could the scientist make of these concepts, if he were obliged (like the mathematician) to be indifferent as regards their subjective and practical meaning? He gives so little heed thereto that it is this very subjective meaning which he decks with the name of scientific notion. When the astronomer, following appearances, argues on the assumption that the sun revolves round the earth, he knows that he can argue also—and even much more easily—on the hypothesis that it is the earth which revolves round the sun. But the moralist or the sociologist who should endeavour to interpret the subjective appearances with which he is concerned, in objective terms, would find himself transported to the antipodes of the reality which interests him, and would no longer be able to argue about it at all. In order to speak of men, of their individuality, of their personality, of their solidarity, of their individual or collective conscience, we are obliged to assume that these terms mean something—an assumption which, from the standpoint of an objective science, is very debatable. The explanations of the phenomena by moral and sociological concepts are nothing else than an ill-disguised appeal to explanations which go beyond the compass of a morality and a sociology that claim to be scientific in the strict sense.

To sum up, according to the philosophers whom we are now considering, the limits of science are not negations pure and simple. Much rather are they the indication of a reality, for us transcendent, without which these very limits would be incomprehensible, and which the scientist ought, more or less, to bear in mind if he would succeed in giving to his concepts a concrete meaning that renders them available. Science, therefore, is not absolutely neutral. She reveals a bent; and, if this bent remains very general, it is at least directed towards the same ends that the religious consciousness postulates.

Religion, henceforward, must no longer be presented as an arbitrary conception, tolerated theoretically, perhaps, by science, but unconnected with her: science even seeks her, without knowing it. And thus, while she freely develops in accordance with her own principles, religion knows that her affirmations, in their general principles, correspond to the postulates of science. She is only too anxious to incorporate, from science, all that can help forward her own work; and it is an observable fact that the thinkers of whom we speak, far from dismissing science as an alien or a rival, invoke her aid with the utmost vehemence, in order to gain, on the historical and natural side, an idea of religion that shall be the truest, most enduring and most complete possible—therefore the most worthy and the most efficacious.

T

IV

REMAINING DIFFICULTIES

And assuredly, this way of understanding, and of contriving the reconciliation of religion with science, is one of the strongest and most conclusive that can be imagined. It is not certain, however, that it thoroughly satisfies the convictions of the scientist any more than the convictions of the religious man.

In spite of all his efforts to accept unconditionally the teachings of science, without deferring to them in any way, the spiritualistic thinker runs the risk of being disavowed by the scientist, when he interprets the limits of science in a sense that is favourable to religion. If there is one contention upon which science insists as fundamental, it is that she knows not whither she is going. While acknowledging her limits, she does not profess to know anything beyond them ; and every attempt to interpret her ignorance, as well as her certainty, arouses her suspicion. Science is essentially jealous of her independence, of her autonomy, of her right to ignore.

On her side, religion continues to wonder at being obliged to ask science for permission to exist. She has, indeed, no intention of raising her voice against the results of scientific demonstration. She has no difficulty in understanding that, between her and science, there ought to be agreement, and that radical heterogeneity is impossible ; since, if God exists, he is the cause of the world which, by reason of its laws, is the object of scientific study, and, between cause and effect, there cannot fail to be some relation. But she, on her side, claims autonomy and free development. Like every living thing, she wishes to be herself, and to unfold from within all her powers. But she is in danger of being restricted in a system which, when all has been said, seems to subordinate to scientific conceptions, religion's right to assert herself.

Neither science, then, nor religion feels herself—in this system based on the limits of science—fully in possession of the autonomy which both alike demand.

It is true that the problem appears to defy the keenest intellect. For it is necessary to discover a way of conceiving religion, at one and the same time, as free to develop herself according to her own principles, and as connected with science through certain intelligible relations. But, if this difficulty appears disconcerting, may it not be because we still picture religion and science as existing side by side in space, and as contending for it after the manner of material things? We try to find out what room science gives up to religion, and wonder if the spatial area occupied by science implies, or does not imply, another space which extends beyond. All these expressions are only metaphors, transcripts of reality in the language of spatial imagination. Can the relation between religion and science be so simple, so closely analogous to material relations? Must it not be, on the contrary, very difficult to grasp and to define? Is it not bound to be, in some way, unique in kind?

But, if this is so, we must, in order to discover it, employ another method—more metaphysical than that which we have just been considering. The latter is strictly critical. It consists in reflecting upon science and upon religion, as they are given us; in asking what are the conditions of existence enjoined on both, and how, being subject to these conditions, they can be reconciled. This method can only, in the end, place religion and philosophy opposite one another, like two powerful rivals who aim at mutual extermination. Perhaps we should be able to discover a relation of a more intimate and more supple kind, if, instead of restricting ourselves to the consideration of religion and science from without, and to the criticism of principles, we sought to understand both of them in their genesis—to give some account of their origin and of the internal principle of their development. For this purpose we should have to make our appeal, no longer only to philosophical criticism, but to philosophy properly so called, to a theory of the first principles of intellectual life and of moral life. This is what a certain number of very acute thinkers have tried to do—thinkers who are as careful to respect the freedom of science as they are jealous for the liberty of religion.

CHAPTER III

THE PHILOSOPHY OF ACTION

I. Pragmatism—The scientific concept as hypothetical imperative ;
the pragmatistic notion of truth.

II. The Idea of a Philosophy of Human Action—Science, the
creation of man's activity — Religion, the realisation of the
human soul's deepest want — Dogmas as purely practical
truths — Religion and Science correspond to the distinction
between the source and the means of action.

III. Critical Remarks — Difficulties inherent in the concept of pure
activity — Necessity of a strictly intellectual principle for
science and for religion itself.

To constitute a theory of the first principles of intellectual and of moral life, had been the aim of
Descartes, and he believed that he could find in
reason the common source of all truths—not only
those relating to science, but those of a practical and
even religious nature. If his rationalism has been
shown inadequate, can we not, nevertheless, recover
his intention through substituting, for reason properly
so called (*i.e.* the specifically intellectual faculty),
activity, which philosophy since the time of Descartes
has, more and more, presented in its originality and
value ? Would not the Philosophy of Action enable
us to see religion and science derived, in the human
mind, from a common source ?

I

PRAGMATISM

It is an idea now grown familiar to scientists, that the mind takes an active part in the production of science.   But, in saying this, they usually mean that the discovery of truth calls upon the mind for effort and inventiveness, for the intelligent use of all the resources at its disposal.   They are not prepared to assert that science *per se*, science as constituted once for all, is merely a mode of human activity.   Justified by facts, an hypothesis becomes law.   The way in which the mind discovered this law has, henceforward, no more than an historical interest.

For the philosophers with whom we are now dealing, on the contrary, the mind considered in its activity is not only the agent of science : it is veritably the subject and the substance thereof.

This point of view is found to-day—maintained in an original manner—among the adherents of a famous philosophical school styling itself Pragmatistic.

According to the Pragmatists,[1] not only does science assume an incessant contribution by the active mind which looks at things from its own standpoint and creates symbols adapted to its use; but she is predisposed to action, and has no other aim than to promote action.   Go back to the origin of scientific concepts : always you will find that they denote methods to be followed in order to lead up to the

[1] See William James, *Pragmatism*, New York, 1907 ; F. C. S. Schiller, " The Definition of Pragmatism and Humanism," *Mind*, 1905 ; " Axioms as Postulates," in *Personal Idealism*, edited by H. Sturt, London, 1902 ; *Studies in Humanism*, 1907 ; The Review *Leonardo*, Florence, editor, G. Papini.

appearance of such or such phenomenon, in order to obtain such or such result. They are rules with regard to action, hypothetical imperatives : outside this signification, they have no real content. A proposition which does not engender practical consequences has no meaning. Two propositions which do not lead to a difference in the way of acting, present nothing but a verbal difference.

To say that the signification of scientific formulæ is purely practical, is to say that these formulæ refer, not to the past, but to the future. Science considers the past merely with a view to the future. She tells us what we must expect if we perform such or such act; what sensations will be produced within us, if, actually, we experience such or such sensation.

In this way is reached the pragmatistic idea of truth. Truth is not the agreement of our conceptions with such or such part of a whole, given to us ready-made, and answering to the name of world : it is, purely and simply, the service that a conception can render us, if we purpose such and such result. Truth stands for verifiability, and verifiability means aptness in guiding us through experience.

The truth of a conception, then, is never certain till after the event. And a demonstrated truth can only, even when it is direct, have unerring reference to the past, not to the future.

That is not all. Science not only aims at action, but is herself action, efficacious and creative power. Is this future, the goal of her inductions, predetermined ? Is it our ignorance alone which hinders us from predicting it infallibly ? The rationalists affirm this. For them, "reality is ready-made and complete from all eternity." According to a well-known formula, the present is charged with the past and big with the future. Quite different is the standpoint of the pragmatists. They believe that reality is, in fact, "still in the making," and that the future is not predetermined in the present. And, among the causes which create the future, they put in the first rank science herself, seeing that, free and human, she enjoins on Nature effects which the latter, by herself, would not produce.

Still further, the belief which, in our consciousness, accompanies ideas, the faith in the realisation of an event, is, itself, according to the pragmatists, a factor in that realisation. Faith can create its own experimental verification, and become true through its very action.

And faith is not, in the human soul, a state that is superadded from without, and withdrawn from the influence of the will. Doubtless, it is not in our power to adopt any belief whatsoever. But life lays before us alternatives in which the choice, so far from being prescribed by the intellect, would be impossible if we were tied down to purely intellectual reasons. Religious problems, taken in their essential and practical meaning, illustrate this. Are human society, the world, the universe something foreign to me of which I speak as *That*; or, are they so nearly related that I can address them as *Thou*? My conduct will differ entirely, according as I shall decide in the one or in the other sense; and the decision clearly depends upon my will. It rests with me to believe or not to believe in my duty towards others and towards the world, and, consequently, to modify, or leave just as it is, the course of events.

Truth itself is, therefore, in a measure, something

that cannot be defined—a human product, not only because it is man who has created knowledge, but because the very object of knowledge, viz. existence (of which knowledge is, seemingly, only an effect or a representation), far from being a thing ready-made from all eternity, is constantly being made by the action of the concrete beings which are its substance, and, in particular, by human action, which is grounded precisely on knowledge and on belief.

II

THE IDEA OF A PHILOSOPHY OF HUMAN ACTION

It would be difficult to arrive at a more penetrating and a more ingenious exposition as regards the part of action in science, than that which the representatives of pragmatism have given. But we must ask if the character and significance of this same action do not remain in this doctrine (at least when it is considered apart) somewhat indeterminate : such an inference would seem, already, to follow from the great variety of thinkers who range themselves, or are ranged by critics generally, under the name of pragmatists.

An idea, a true belief, we are told, is a belief at once verifiable, beneficial, efficacious—a belief which pays. But the meaning of the word "pay" varies to an unlimited extent. One man accepts payment in hard cash alone. A Newton desires to be paid in generalisations which shall reduce to unity the laws of the universe. The former demands of science material enjoyment. The latter expects from her the pride of knowing and the supreme joy of penetrating the structure of things. Another man calls beneficial that which favours peace of mind, or moral power, or harmony of ideas, or the expansion and development of existence, or the realisation of a society, at once united and free, cherishing the ideal aims of humanity. Not one of these views is excluded by pragmatism: not one is logically enjoined by it. It is a method rather than a doctrine; a determination as regards the relation of theory to practice, rather than a theory of practice itself. Hence pragmatism, as such, does not exhaust the idea of the Philosophy of Action.

Anxious to arrive at a more complete realisation, a certain number of thinkers endeavour to show, lying at the root of science, not only a general predisposition towards efficacy and practice, but action in the full sense of the word—action with the positive marks which distinguish it from simple intervention in the course of phenomena, and which alone constitute it veritable action.

The doctrines which spring from this thought are, it must be confessed, very divergent, and, in order to understand them in their precision, we must study them separately. They have, at least, one common tendency which it is not impossible to make clear.

. . . .

So far as it relates to science, this tendency is as follows:

When we argue, say the representatives of a philosophy widely circulated in recent years,[1] that the postulates, principles and definitions of science are mere agreements, the outcome of an arbitrary choice, we mean that—occasioned, suggested perhaps

[1] See Poincaré, Milhaud, Duhem, Le Roy, Hoeffding, etc.

by experience—they neither are nor can be prescribed by it. Between experience and the concepts that we employ with a view to its scientific interpretation, there is solution of continuity. But it does not follow that these concepts are artificial inventions. The determination which is only furnished very incompletely by things, has its final reason in the mind itself which imagines hypotheses, which constructs definitions. It is not chance, it is not any casual activity, which effects scientific method : it is a definite activity, capable of being specified.

In the first place, the ideas by means of which science is framed, are genuine inventions. They are not merely contingent : they are well founded, they are fruitful, they have that intrinsic value which distinguishes the creations of genius from the caprices of imagination. And these inventions are produced throughout with a richness, a variety, an inexhaustible novelty. Each of them struggles for continuance, becomes modified, is adapted to the progress of knowledge, and only succumbs in order to call forth new inventions. Through such indications we recognise the action of a real being which strives to establish itself, to subsist, to develop itself, to obtrude itself. What is the nature of this being ? It is shown in the end, with respect to which all these creations are conceived.

The endeavour of the mind to adapt its ideas to the facts yielded by experience, is set forth with insistence, and rightly so. Modern science aims at taking possession of the real world, being dissatisfied with the sterile contemplation of an imaginary world. But we should deceive ourselves if, adopting this standpoint, we believed that we could eliminate the human philosophy of the Platos and of the Aristotles which seeks to fashion the sensible world, wherein our intellect cannot recognise itself, into a world that shall be intelligible.

Scientific hypotheses tend, in a general way, to put into the world unity, or simplicity, or continuity. These distinctive marks are not facts of observation : they appear, at first, as the opposite of reality. They are even difficult to reconcile among themselves. For, since we are given the infinite multiplicity of the parts composing our world, the search for unity implies that all these parts act and react upon one another : such an assumption seems, of necessity, to involve an inextricable complexity. Similarly, in seeking continuity, we find ourselves discarding a simplicity that is far better ensured by a plurality of categories radically distinct from one another.

What, then, are these ends which science pursues, if not laws that the mind enjoins on things, because, being moulded in a certain way, it cannot assimilate them as they are presented by brute experience ?

But unity, simplicity, continuity, constitute what we term intelligibility. It is not, therefore, any chance life of mentality which is manifested in scientific invention : it is the special life of an intelligence, of a reason, which has in it a certain standard of intelligibility.

Is this all that can be said ; and is reason merely the drudge of science ? Has the labour that she accomplishes, any aim external to herself ? Is she solely bent on practice, using the word in its utilitarian sense ?

It would seem difficult to deny the existence, in humanity, of a disinterested science, or — if the statement be preferred—of a science whose supreme interest lies in scientific research. Numerous, even to-day, are the scientists (inheritors of Greek thought) who would say, with Aristotle, science for the sake of science : " All occupations are more necessary than that of the scientist, but not one of them is better."

It will be objected that these thinkers convert the means into an end. That may be so. But this transposition, which is regarded as erroneous, is a great law of nature, and one of the sources of its fecundity. Although matter may be means with reference to life, nature displays it as if it were an end in itself. Animal instinct, which serves man as means only, is, for the animal, an end. The richness of human development is due to the fact that each individual, through a peculiar estimate of his métier, believes that this métier is the highest and noblest end of all. What is beauty, save certain aspects of things, set aside and developed for their own sake? What is play, save the pure and simple exercise of our faculties, considered as an end in itself? What does it matter, after all, if we consider a thing, in origin and according to historical evolution, as end or as means? The appreciation of the value attaching to things does not depend upon their teleological rôle. If man intends to place science above what is useful, or to decree that science is, itself, the supreme utility, how can we show him that he is wrong? In considering the practical judgments of men, we must admit that they love to unsettle, in this way, the given order of means and of ends, and to establish as the supreme thing that which, originally, was only a secondary and inferior object. And nearly everything that is new and great begins thus.

Science, moreover, detached from utility properly so called, is not, by virtue of that alone, transformed into an absolute end.   It furnishes the means requisite for the development of reason ; and reason—as Descartes taught—in order to exist, to develop and to be determined according to its nature, must be fed on truths.   Like everything that exists, reason is to be found only as operating, as growing through her own method even ; and it is by the aid of science (her most perfect intellectual method) that she puts forth the intellectual powers which lie within her.

Accordingly, science is not a work of nature, merely providing a field for consciousness ; it is not, further, a simple provision of receipts, indicating utility as the sole ground of existence.   It is a determinate activity —the specifically human activity in so far as it is reasonable and intelligent.   And what has been said about science applies equally to languages.   As M. Bréal[1] has ingeniously demonstrated, languages do not exist in the sense of having their principle of existence and of evolution outside the human mind. We recognise in the human mind, in the intelligence and the will, the only true cause of language ; and language cannot be detached therefrom, because there is no life in it other than that which it derives from this same mind.

.   .   .   .   .   .

While certain scientists thus exhibit science as immanent in the intelligent activity of man, a corresponding doctrine has been put forward in regard to religion.[2]

Religion is often presented as a system of beliefs

[1] *Essai sur la sémantique*, Paris, 1897.
[2] *Vide* Maurice Blondel, *L'Action*, Paris, 1893.

and of precepts imposed on man from without. It is shown, more or less rationally, that such an authority has genuine grounds, that it enjoins the profession of a particular creed, and the fulfilment of particular practices ; moreover, religion is made to consist entirely in obedience to this authority.

But—say the philosophers with whom we are here concerned—while admitting that these demonstrations are forcible, and that the articles of faith, thus imposed, offer the mind a sufficiently clear meaning, seeing that belief has to do with ideas rather than with words, how can we be sure that these beliefs and these rites will constitute for man a religion, in the sense given by conscience (Christian conscience and tradition in particular) to that word ? Religion abides within the soul : it is a supernatural life. There are not two existences—the one beside the other, and independent of one another—for that would mean two distinct persons : it is the individual himself, preserving his identity when the manner of his life is infinitely raised. How could beliefs have such an effect, if they had no intrinsic connection with the nature of the subject ? It is not inconceivable that a belief of this kind—even logically based—concerns man's heart and conscience as little as belief in the principle of Archimedes, or in universal gravitation. If religious beliefs were only logical beliefs, the acts that we term religious would be, for man, merely external movements in which his soul would have no share.

But, we may contend, man is finite, fallible, inclined to evil ; and religion ought to be the action of God working within him for his transformation. How are we to find in Nature herself a religious tendency ? For the finite being there is only one fitting attitude in the presence of the Infinite, viz. obedience. Or, forsooth, do we desire that the finite, of itself, should comprehend and include the Infinite ? That would only be rendered possible through identity. In maintaining such a view, we fall into the abyss of Pantheism.

This way of reasoning, reply the philosophers of action, would be plausible if man were nothing but understanding. For the understanding, indeed, the relations of things are replaced by those of their concepts ; and it is very true that, after all, concepts only admit relations of inclusion or of exclusion. From the intellectualist's standpoint, if God and man are not identical, they must necessarily be external to one another. And on this supposition, the moment that Pantheism is set aside, religion can only be, for man, a compulsion imposed from without.

But man is not only understanding : he is yet again—and more immediately—activity, or rather action, *i.e.* constant movement towards an object which he desires to possess as calculated to support and enlarge his being. Now, does it not seem that we could find, in the conditions of properly human action, this special immanence of the supernatural in the natural—union without absorption—which religion claims, and which the understanding is unable to prove ?

The action which is here in question is, properly speaking, the action of the will, or action *par excellence.*

According to the new Philosophy of Action, if only man wills explicitly that which he wills implicitly, *i.e.* if he gets a clear idea of the end whither his will naturally tends, and if he is seriously determined to realise that end, he will understand that he has need of God, of the Supernatural, in order to accomplish his own will.

What is action? Shall we say that a man acts, that he acts in his capacity as man, just in so far as he displays vigour, and seeks to convert external objects to his own use?   For action an end is needful ; and this end, in order to exist, in order to lead to a veritable action, must be something else than what Nature is able to realise with her mechanical laws. He who acts, looks forward and upward. The laws and the knowledge of given conditions he regards as merely instruments for the realisation of something new and better than what Nature would effect.

What does man really wish? What is the initial will that gives the impetus to his entire moral and intellectual being?   It is in the determination of this initial will that lies the main problem of human life.

Action aims at the realisation of a purpose. Perfect action will be that wherein the power shall appear as equal to the wish. But let us consider the various modes of human—purely human—action : scientific activity, individual action, social action, action that is purely and simply moral. Not one of them admits of that equality which we are seeking.

Science implies a determinism which only conceives itself as posited freely by a mind which dominates it. Self, society, humanity, certainly offer man aims which respond to the leanings of his will. But it is impossible for him to pursue these aims reflectively without wishing to transcend them, without declaring that they lead him, whatever may come of it, to seek something beyond.

And thus action reveals to man the presence within

him of an initial will, superior to every will that is limited to the things of this world.

Thenceforward an alternative is laid down for his conscience. If he merely acquiesces in willing that which is given him by experience, his will necessarily remains unsatisfied and impotent. But if, disengaging his actual will from objects which cannot satisfy, he regulates it by that ideal will which surpasses it no less than the whole of nature, we then perceive that he may be able to obtain that equilibrium of will and power which is the utmost limit of his aspiration. Either will without power, or power through renouncing, in a sense, his will: such is the alternative. It raises in his mind the idea of a being at once transcendent and immanent in regard to man: immanent, seeing that it is his will and his first impulse; transcendent, seeing that it is not given, and cannot be given, in the objective world wherein his understanding confines him. Here is to be found the veritable supernatural: life, power, being, required by human action — something, moreover, that human action, by itself, is incapable of realising.

Between the two terms of this alternative, choice is necessary, inevitable. All action, indeed, implies it. And this choice, the terms of the problem being given, can only be an act of faith, of hope and of love, i.e. the very act which forms the basis of religious life.

In this manner the strictly religious need is referred to the essential conditions of human action. It is no longer a mere subjective datum, which analysis, perhaps, may be able to dissolve and to deprive of its prestige: it is, besides being the condition of human action, the condition of all knowledge, of all consciousness—therefore, in the long run, of all facts, in so far as we relate them to existence and apprehend them as realities.

But religions do not consist solely in this secret revelation of the self: they are presented under the form of dogmas, which set before the mind precise and special objects of belief, whence proceed determinate rites. What is the origin and significance of these dogmas? [1]

If they had to be considered as knowledge, in the full and scientific meaning of the word, they would not take precedence of reason, in particular of modern science and thought.

A dogma, in the strictly theoretical sense, is a proposition which gives itself out as undemonstrable. Now, the theoretical reason only allows that which is demonstrated or demonstrable to some extent. Shall we say that dogmas are demonstrated according to the method of authority? But does not modern science make a special point of repudiating the method of authority?

A dogma is, in the second place, a proposition that is incapable, even as regards statement, of being placed on a level with clear and distinct conception. Certainly, its titles and definitions are determinate, settled, fixed; and it is this which presents to the mind the illusion of knowledge. But who can express, in really intelligible terms, what he means by the Divine Personality, by the action of grace within the human soul? Who can say, so as to satisfy his own intelligence, what he means by God?

[1] *Vide* Edouard Le Roy, *Dogme et critique*, Paris, 1907. Cf. George Tyrrell, Fogazzaro.

Magst Priester oder Weise fragen,
Und ihre Antwort scheint nur Spott
Über den Frager zu sein.[1]

Lastly, if we must accept dogmas literally, why shut our eyes to evidence? They are, taken thus, formally irreconcilable with science.

For all these reasons, the question henceforward resolves itself into these terms : either dogmas will decay, or they will be understood in a sense other than the strictly theoretical sense.

Does the search for a dogmatic significance which may not be essentially theoretical, constitute a daring enterprise—the substitution of a new standpoint for that which tradition has bequeathed?

According to our authors, it is proved by the actual analysis of dogmas, and by the study of their history, that they do not give themselves out as knowledge, above all as positive and adequate knowledge. Their signification is, pre-eminently, negative: "*Non hoc a me, Fratres, expectatis,*" says St. Augustine, "*ut explicem vobis quomodo cognoscat Deus. Hoc solum dico : Non sic cognoscit ut homo.*"

How are we to take, as positive, clear and distinct, the concept of the Divine Personality? The combination of these two words throws the mind into an abyss of difficulties. This dogma says clearly that God cannot be conceived as a thing, as analogous to those objects which we know through the senses. Adopting the statement of St. Thomas—whose faith, after all, was cramped within Scholastic formalism—dogmas describe divine things negatively, *via remotionis* : setting aside those determinations which are unfitting.

---

[1] Goethe, *Faust* : Thou canst ask priest and sage : their answer seems but a mockery to the questioner.

Does this mean that being is therein simply conceived as tantamount to nothingness—a conception which would only give rise to an abstract affirmation, devoid of real import ? The vague and the indefinable, taught Leibnitz, do not signify nullity ; and it is perfectly legitimate to suppose that we have some effective idea of a thing, although we may not be able to grasp it distinctly in thought—especially when we have to do with objects which, in essence, exceed the framework of our concepts. We live, in fact, by concepts that we only understand dimly. They precede and guide both action and scientific investigation itself ; the latter, after all, is nothing else than an endeavour to reduce them to distinct ideas.

Considered from the practical and moral standpoint, dogmas become, once again, clear and positive. What is the Divine Personality ? Having regard to the understanding, I can make no answer. But I can grasp immediately such a precept as this : Behave in your relations with God as in your relations with a person.[1]

If a dogma is, before all else, a practical precept, it does not follow that the theoretical forms under which dogmas are usually presented to men, are contemptible or indifferent.

These forms are necessary : human action is not cut off from thought, any more than true thought is separable from action. The action which is the cause of dogma is thought-action, *i.e.* action united to an idea which, by reason of being vague (as it inevitably must be, through the disproportion of its object to our understanding), is no less an outline of intellectual intuition, an incentive to thought, a source of con-

---

[1] Le Roy, *Dogme et critique*, p. 25.

ceptions and representations. Dogma is not, therefore, an exclusively practical proposition : it contains a theoretical element. Even within man's spirit, the letter has power.

Now, it is natural and expedient that the letter be brought out and developed.

Pure intuition, stripped of all representation, is imperceptible for consciousness, and incommunicable. Language with its infinite efflorescence, science with its system of symbols, our external world itself with the various relations of which it is composed, are only signs adopted by man for the purpose of noting his impressions and communicating them to his fellows. And all thought leads to expression, all activity is productive of forms.

Thus, from dogma itself radiate forms calculated to fix it before the mind, and to furnish man with the means of making it a subject of discussion.

And, in accordance with the fundamental law of knowledge, these forms, in order to realise the intelligibility and communicability of which they ought to be the instruments, are adapted to the categories actually present in the minds which receive them. We may say of the mind what we say of the body : it is fed only upon substances which can become its own substance.

That is why, in the speculative theories with which dogmas are enveloped in order to become imaginable and intelligible, one recognises, from age to age, the scientific and philosophical ideas which represent the successive states of human wisdom. How can we reproach man with consecrating to the service of God the choicest productions of which his intelligence is capable ?

The history of dogmas, nevertheless, serves to remind him that the divine law is essentially practical, and that the meaning concealed within it transcends absolutely all the illustrations and explanations that man may attempt to offer. Intellectual study which, in its very essence, is relative to the conditions of intelligibility in a given society, can do no more, with respect to religious dogmas, than furnish symbols, *i.e.* a language always useful, always perfectible and provisional.

. . . .

In this manner have been constituted, in our day, by parallel paths rather than by common consent, a philosophy of science and a philosophy of religion—both of them founded upon the conditions of human action. If we compare these two philosophies, we find that their agreement is sufficient to admit of their being combined into one whole under the title of the Philosophy of Action.

On two sides the notion of life is considered as fundamental. On two sides life, becoming conscious of itself, is expressed through symbols which the understanding creates—forms at once stable and variable, analogous to the provisionally fixed types which mark the stages of evolution in Nature.

It is, moreover, a single life, human life in so far as it is special and superior, which is, on either side, the end to be realised. The Philosophy of Action is thus, as it were, the common stem from which branch off science and religion. Their distinction is explained, accordingly, as well as their connection. For human activity properly so called has two essential forms : the activity of the intellect and the activity of the will. Science is the expansion of the first ; religion, the full realisation of the second. However incommensurable may be the world (the object of science) and God (the object of religion), they are reunited in man, whose nature, in its unity, partakes of both.

This philosophy—so its representatives think—enables us to conceive the relation between religion and science in a more inward and spiritual way than was possible for the adherents of intellectualism.

Science furnishes man with the means of external action. Through her, he can translate his will into movements more and more adapted to impose it upon the material world.

But it is natural that human activity, endowed with such a power, should inquire into its own principle and end. It is through the raising of this question that a way is opened into the religious sphere. Religion is that higher wisdom which offers an end worthy of such an activity, and which communicates to it the secret power requisite for willing this end adequately and efficaciously.

In developing the idea of science and the idea of religion, the mind sees them, thereby, come together.

The last word of science is the reduction of Nature to intelligible symbols, which place her at man's disposal. But, however exalted be the objects through which the universe is explained, they are conceived by man—they do not embrace man. Man, if he reflects, asks himself what they are worth—whether he ought to be absorbed in them or to make use of them. Man, particularly modern man, who has become keenly aware of the immensity of life, and, especially, of the splendours of moral and religious life, uses his intellect to examine the claims of the intellect itself. In the name of that secret

import of truth which constitutes the ultimate ground
of reason, he asks if the intellect, as it is realised in
science, is sufficient in itself and satisfies his human
sentiment. Now, to put such a question, is already
to imagine the possibility of religion.

On her side, religion would have man be a co-
worker with God. She does not, therefore, despise
human faculties. She expects the human mind to
apply its own language—the whole of the signs and
forms at its disposal—to the expression, as profound,
true and adequate as possible, of that which, in itself,
altogether surpasses human language. More than
this : religion has, evidently, not the sole intention
of urging upon individuals a confined and solitary
life. God has not withdrawn from the world : he
carries on his work therein. Religion, therefore, calls
upon man, by means of that science which brings
him material power, to do his share in labouring for
the coming of the Kingdom of God.

Thus understood, the relation between religion
and science combines, according to the thinkers with
whom we are dealing, two conditions which, contrary
in appearance, are no less equally necessary : fundamental unity and respective independence.

That which constitutes the unity of science and
of religion is human action, from which they both
spring, and which finds in them the means of realising
itself in all its fulness.

That which guarantees their independence is the
general property, inherent in life, of allowing, simul-
taneously, different developments, which would appear
incompatible if we judged them solely by the concepts
which represent them. The contradictions which
the analyst finds in the human heart, seem to him

inexplicable. They are only contradictions from the logician's abstract point of view. In reality they are different manifestations of life. Life is bounteous, and tends to bring into existence all that is capable of being. It would even appear that she delights in presenting the coexistence of extremes—what we call opposites.

Science and religion are two moments of human life. The one is that life in its expansion towards the external world; the other is that same life, turned, on the contrary, towards its own principle—towards the principle of all life, and drawing thence the power of reaching infinitely beyond itself. The difference between these two developments is such that they cannot in any way contradict one another. Each of them can, practically, be conceived as independent and autonomous.

Science and religion, it is true, necessarily meet on a common ground—that of the forms and concepts which correspond to natural facts. But, according to the Philosophy of Action, neither for religion nor yet for science, do these concepts constitute adequate expressions of the truth. Two systems with more or less different symbols are not an offence for the human mind, which accommodates itself to them, up to a certain point, even in science; and inquiry into the agreement of the symbols of religion with those of science can, in imitation of bygone times, be prosecuted again nowadays without religion having to sacrifice anything; just as the thought of an ancient author need not be modified in order to be given us translated into present speech, when the current translations have become unintelligible.

III

CRITICAL REMARKS

The Philosophy of Action is an effort well worthy of attention.   It is an endeavour to find in consciousness, in being, as it is immediately given us, a principle more profound than the intellect, capable of removing the contrasts which the intellect leaves standing, and of procuring, in this way, the fundamental unity of the soul's various powers with their free and full development.   This philosophy, still in its infancy, though it may have germinated under cover of the great classical systems, is destined, perhaps, to make much further progress.   And, maybe, it will increasingly bring satisfaction to minds eager for knowledge as well as for wide, overflowing and generous life. Under its present form, it would seem to be only partially successful in solving the difficulties which have to be faced.

And, we may begin by asking, is the agreement which it establishes between science and religion, as real, as clearly defined, as would appear at first sight?

Activity, we are told, is the common origin of both.   What activity is here in question?

Is it a bare and indeterminate activity?   Then several questions are involved.   Of what value is an indeterminate activity?   How is such an activity to be distinguished from a mere power of change, or even from mechanical forces which produce aimless movements?   The fact that a movement is accompanied by consciousness, does not suffice to constitute it a thing of supreme worth, capable of establishing both science and religion. If consciousness is, with respect to this activity, only a passive sensation and an epiphenomenon, its presence has a merely speculative interest.

We may, indeed, shun this difficulty through taking as our principle, no longer an indeterminate activity, but human activity as such, *i.e.* the determinate action that man ought to accomplish in order to be truly man, in order to carry out his human métier to the fullest extent. But then it would seem that we are only avoiding one obstacle to encounter another.

Human activity, we are told, has two determinations, two directions, viz. intellect and will. Through its development as intellect it produces science ; through its realisation as will it leads to religion. The relation between religion and science is thus reduced to the relation between intellect and will. But, in that case, the difficulty is only changed. For the question of the relations between intellect and will—even when we consider both, not as ready-made faculties, but as real spiritual activities—remains obscure and subject to various solutions. And the dualism that we expected to surmount through transferring the problem from the sphere of concepts to that of action, may reappear with all its difficulties.

Whatever be the way in which the Philosophy of Action reconciles religion and science, can we say that this philosophy furnishes, henceforward, a true theory of each of them, taken apart ?

The Philosophy of Action multiplies, in vain, analyses and clever arguments : it finds difficulty in persuading the scientists that science not only invents all the concepts, all the standards by which she encompasses phenomena, but fabricates phenomena themselves. Desirous, henceforth, of showing that all our knowledge is and must continue insuperably relative, science, on her part, readily multiplies the proofs of man's contingent intervention in all scientific achievement. But if the attempt is made to carry this demonstration to its furthest limit, and to infer that fact itself exists through human invention, she protests. It is just because fact, in some way, is within us, while, at the same time, incommensurable with our definite standards, that we are compelled to put forth so much mental effort to determine it, and that the results obtained by us are never more than approximations, imperfect and provisional acquisitions.

On the other hand, as regards the work accomplished by the mind for the purpose of creating scientific symbols, the scientist is bound to admit that we have only to do, here, with purely arbitrary operations which, in the end, are merely conventional. These operations are determined by certain intellectual principles ; they tend to bring within our knowledge things that are intelligible ; they correspond to an ideal that we set before ourselves. They imply, in short, what we call reason, the sense of being, of order, of harmony.

That is why scientific pragmatism, when it comes to be developed, has ill success in maintaining its initial statements, but returns more or less to the affirmation of being, of reason, which formed the basis of the classic theory of science.

Still, it may be urged, who knows if objective reality itself may not be pure action, may not be fluid and essentially unstable continuity ?

Modern evolutionary science is ready to face a

reality of this kind. She will not, by way of discipline, renounce her idea of being, of fact and of objectivity. But she will strive, continuously, to verify and note the given state of things, then to bind together these successive states, according to laws. Unquestionably, experimental success is the sole criterion. But the scientist does not conclude thence that the future is partly indeterminate, and that he can himself, in reality, create the fact which will verify his conceptions. On the very ground of faith in the number of antecedents requisite for the production of the phenomenon, he maintains his deterministic standpoint, because he considers this faith, itself, as the outcome of laws.

What is this but to say that science, in proportion as she becomes more aware of her own conditions and activity, deviates from radical pragmatism and from the philosophy which places action before intellect instead of making it end there?

At all events, does religion, as the Philosophy of Action develops it, remain unchanged in essence?

It is assumed, at the outset, that everything which appeals to the understanding is an expression, a symbol, a vehicle of religion, but is not religion itself. According to this view, the religious sphere would be composed exclusively of practice, of life.

But, in reality, all feeling, all religious action involves ideas, concepts, theoretical knowledge. What will be left, when, from religion as it is given us, we shall have, actually, eliminated every intellectual element?

This argument is overlooked, however, and pragmatists demonstrate the existence, within the mind, of a principle distinct from thought, even as Diogenes demonstrated movement by the fact. Man acts, and action is irreducible to concept.

But what is this same action? For we must certainly have some idea of it, in order that we may discover therein the foundation of religion.

It is, acute philosophers tell us, human action in its widest meaning. It is not the particular operation of such or such faculty: it is man in his entirety, uniting all his powers in order to reach out towards his end. Truths that we have begun by making, in a sense, our life, through aiming at full self-realisation, become—discerned and elaborated by the understanding—doctrines and objects of belief.

Assuredly, it is the task of man to bring together and combine, in this way, all the powers which he has at command, in order to labour towards the fulfilment of his destiny. But the intellect, in this total operation, has no less share than the other faculties; and its rôle will necessarily consist in checking, by means of its concepts, the operation of the other faculties. We are no longer obliged, under this view, to regard practice as independent of theory.

Are we to infer, then, that the special operation of the will is meant? But the will requires an end; and can it be said that an intelligible formula is offered the mind in the suggestion of a will which takes itself for end—which has no object other than its own principle?

Throughout these ingenious theories, search is made for action as self-sufficing, and as not dependent upon any of the concepts by which we may endeavour to explain it or to justify it; pure action, action in itself—that is the aim.

What is this but to maintain that, whether we will or no, an indeterminate pragmatism again confronts us? We can speak of human pragmatism, if human action, taken in itself, be the supreme rule; of divine pragmatism, if divine action, conceived as outside all intellectual determination, is to be made the basis of human action.

Action existing solely for and through action; pure practice producing, maybe, concepts, but not depending, itself, upon any concept,—does such an abstract pragmatism still deserve the name of religion? And are we not involving ourselves in an endless process, when we try to find in practice, apart from theory, the essence and the only true principle of religious life?

Is it not when we connect a deed with a particular belief that we use the phrase: religious deed? Surely, what we call a symbol and a vehicle is, in some way, an integral part of religion?

CHAPTER IV

WILLIAM JAMES AND RELIGIOUS EXPERIENCE

WHILE theologians, scientists and philosophers— eager for definitions, for arguments, for proofs— wasted their energies in trying to establish the logical possibility of religion, of science, and of their harmony, there have always been found men for whom all this subtle investigation was superfluous, inasmuch as they lived by a conviction grounded on a principle that outweighs in value all argument, viz. experience.

X

Such souls are called mystics. For them the objects of religion are given, and quite as immediately certain as are, for the scientist, the facts which he seeks to conform to laws.

The spirit of the mystical method is to be found once again in certain contemporary doctrines, exempt from ecclesiastical prejudice, but especially constituted so as to agree with living reality. The finest illustration of this tendency may be seen in the doctrine of Religious Experience as expounded by the psychological specialist, William James—that profound and delicate thinker whose literary style is so captivating.[1]

I

THE DOCTRINE OF W. JAMES ON RELIGION

What standpoint ought we to adopt, if we would realise that which, in religion, is characteristic and essential? According to William James, of the two aspects under which religion is presented, the external aspect and the internal aspect, the second is the superior. It is of no consequence that, chronologically, the various religions may have appeared as institutions before being displayed as personal life : at bottom, they are the creations of those religious geniuses who founded the institutions. At all events, personal religion has, in the course of ages, repelled institutions, and, henceforward, they will only continue if they are upheld by believing and pious souls.

It is not, therefore, simply because psychology is his special study, it is because he sees in personal

----

[1] William James, *The Will to Believe*, 1897 ; *The Varieties of Religious Experience*, 1902.

religion the groundwork of religion, that William
James sets himself to examine religious phenomena
from the single standpoint of psychology.

The method employed by him is that which he
regards as in conformity with psychology properly
so called : what may be named radical empiricism.
This phrase, ordinarily used to designate a system,
can be retained, even by those who reject the system,
for the purpose of characterising a method. Imputing
to psychology the atomic hypothesis, we have sought
too long—in the data of consciousness—so-called
simple facts or psychical atoms, in order to establish
between them connections analogous to those which
are formulated by physical laws. Such elements
neither are, nor can be, given. They are inventions
of the systematic mind. That which is given, in
psychology, is always a certain field of consciousness,
embracing a multiplicity and a diversity shifting and
incessant. It is under this figure, the only true one,
that we may hope to understand religious phenomena.

We must, in the first place, consider the psycho-
physiological totality of which they form part ;
then gradually distinguish concomitant and kindred
phenomena, and push forward, in this way, to the
determination of the strictly religious element.

This task accomplished, another is enjoined : that
of determining the value of the fact thus revealed by
analysis.

(a) The Nature of Religious Experience

It was formerly possible to imagine that religious
facts were unique of their kind, and for a long time
they were treated as such. But absolutely singular

facts would be doubtful facts, the progress of knowledge leading us generally to discover continuity just where superficial observation has made us believe in unbridgeable gaps. To this law of continuity religious phenomena offer no exception. They belong to a class of phenomena ever more clearly defined, that of the modifications of personality.

The study of these phenomena among the subjects in whom they are produced with most intensity—such as those who suffer from nervous disorder or are temperamentally disposed towards mysticism—makes us recognise, as belonging to human nature in general, the characteristics which are, so to speak, the soil from which the religious consciousness springs.

The hallucinations of certain subjects, for instance, are specially remarkable : instead of attaining their full development, which is made manifest by the appearance, in the imagination of the subject, of a concrete object similar to those that carry meaning for us, they stop at a stage wherein the subject has a sense of presence and of reality, without any definite image (or even any image whatsoever) appearing to him. And this bare presence produces faith, and this faith determines action. In like manner, the moral imperatives of Kant, without being, in any way, objects of sensible representation or of theoretical knowledge, determine in the soul a practical and efficacious faith.

Now, certain mystics experience analogous states. An object which they conceive as the Divine Being, but of which they have no representation, is given them as real, and affects their heart and their will ; and the sense of this reality and of this action is, for them, all the stronger in that they conceive the object as pure reality, stripped of every sensible image.

This sense of presence, apart from every object of perception, has never, says William James, been properly explained by Rationalism. It outlives, for the subject who experiences it, all arguments which are given him with a view to proving it illusory : belief in the reality of sense-objects, for example. But pathological cases only differ, apparently, in degree from the phenomena of normal life. There is, therefore, every reason for allowing that man possesses a sense of reality other than that which is comprised in the working of his ordinary senses.

Another indication of the religious consciousness is inherent optimism or pessimism, and a remarkable development of this is seen in certain neuropaths.

We may divide men into two categories : those who, in order to be happy, have only to be born once, and those who, congenitally unhappy, need a new birth : " *once-born* " and " *twice-born* " characters.

The first are naturally and instinctively optimists. They see the world governed by beneficent powers, who are bent on deriving good from evil itself. And this optimistic faith is wonderfully effective in overcoming evil and in obtaining happiness.

Opposite the born optimists Nature sets the pessimistic temperaments. The latter are haunted by the sense of an irremediable misery. All performance, all existence, seems to them to end in failure. They cannot reflect upon the objects of our desire without seeing futility in them—upon the causes of our joy without piercing through them to emptiness. But chiefly, reflection upon their own deeds, upon their

thoughts, upon their inmost wants, afflicts them
throughout with a cruel malady: scrupulosity. Worry,
anxiety, persistency in fretting—this secret ill follows
them everywhere. How can they be freed from it?
The melancholiac has a distinct feeling that the charm
of life is a free gift, that the elect alone are entitled
to taste it. If healing is possible, it can only come
through a supernatural intervention.

Certain neuropaths present a remarkable particularity—what may be called the divided self. There
are within them two selves: the one pessimistic,
the other optimistic; the one mediocre, the other
well endowed. And they are impotent to reconcile these two characters. We are reminded of the
duality which St. Paul found within him, and which
he expressed in the familiar passage: "What I would,
that do I not; but what I hate, that do I."

Lastly, the conversions—sometimes instantaneous
—of individuals, the *revivals* which take sudden
possession of an entire multitude, are connected with
a phenomenon classed among neuro-psychical affections: the substitution, more or less abrupt and
complete, of one personality for another within the
same consciousness.

Thus religious manifestations are not, for man,
adventitious and foreign expressions: they form part
of a group of manifestations which result from human
nature itself.

This is not tantamount to saying that religious
phenomena may be identified with the pathological
states which resemble them. Even genius, in an
altogether superior way, has for condition a rupture
of equilibrium in the organism, and is accompanied

by abnormal manifestations. Concentration of energy
upon one faculty means the withdrawal of that faculty
from others: superiority in a particular domain involves almost feebleness and insufficiency in others.
Religion, in proportion as it is the more mingled with
enthusiasm, must therefore be a rupture of equilibrium,
a frenzy.

It cannot be defined through organic conditions
which, so far as we are able to judge, may be sensibly
identical for phenomena that are absolutely different
as regards their rôle in our life. It ought to be
considered in itself, according to the immediate feeling
of consciousness.

This feeling is indescribable. Viewed from without,
it enters—like all that is viewed from without—into
such or such category of the understanding: to see
from without is to assimilate. But, for the subject,
it is unique—possessing originality, richness, fulness
in the highest degree; no one can speak about it,
except he who has experienced it.

As far as it is possible to suggest the idea through
words, it is a feeling of intimate and perfect harmony,
of peace, of joy; it is the feeling that all is well without us and within us. It is not a passive and inert
feeling. It is the consciousness of sharing in a power
greater than our own, and the longing to coöperate,
with that power, in works of love, of concord and of
peace. It is, in short, the exaltation of life—of life
as creative energy, and of life as harmoniousness
and joy.

Sometimes, as with those whom we have called
the once-born men, this feeling is, from the start,
installed within the soul: religion is then a constant
impression of order, of love, of power, of confidence,

of security ; it is a spontaneous and unalterable optimism. With those, on the contrary, who, in order to be at peace with themselves, need to be regenerated, the desire for religion is made manifest by anxiety, dissatisfaction with self and with things ; and the second birth is signalised by what is felt to be a shifting of the seat of personal energy. Instead of saying *no!* to everything that happens to him, the regenerate man will say *yes!* Instead of falling back upon himself, he will seek out others with affection and with devotion, urged by a sense of genuine brotherhood. Henceforward he looks at everything in a new light, he reacts, after another manner, in response to all actions that affect him. And those who, in this way, obtain good through overcoming evil, have probably a wider career before them, and can reach a higher perfection than those who, from birth, find their lot an easy one. Every victory is, for the twice-born man—for the man who strives and who knows the cost of the struggle,—the prelude of a fresh victory.

From these observations it follows that religion is essentially a matter of personal concern. In reality there are as many forms of religious experience as there are religious individuals. Religion is bound up with life ; and everybody lives according to his own temperament and bent of genius.

Several traits of the religious consciousness are brought out in strong relief through the consideration of certain phenomena or of certain subjects.

Prayer, that religious act *par excellence*, implies the conviction that, thanks to the action of a Being who transcends our self and our world in their finitude, events can be realised, either within us or without us, which this world could not have brought about.

Conversion is accompanied by the sense of a supernatural action which, abruptly or progressively, transforms our being in a profound and definitive fashion.

In mystical states, the subject recognises his union with God, as well as the shifting of his centre of personal energy which results from this union. Mystical states could otherwise be mistaken for aberrations of the religious sentiment: they are the extreme form of that consciousness of the individual's exaltation through fusion with a greater than self, which is inherent in religious life, *i.e.* in religion.

The study of such phenomena as prayer and the mystical state makes clear this fact—that, although religion may be at first mere feeling, intellectual elements, beliefs, ideas, are always more or less involved therein. Prayer makes prominent the faith or initial belief which appears inseparable from religious emotion. The religious man considers himself as related to a superior being, with whom he can come into the closest union, and who will grant him a self-harmony, a joy, a power, that, of himself alone, he could never secure.

This belief comprises all the intellectualism that can be found in elementary religious experience. But human imagination and intellect, eager to fashion models of things and to arrive at an explanation of them, formulate additional beliefs and theories which are increasingly determinate and intellectual, and which, by degrees, transform religion properly so called into theology and philosophy: an efflorescence in some degree natural, seeing that it follows from the tendencies of human nature; yet adventitious, for it

does not form part of the simple development of
religious experience, but exists as the combination of
that experience with the various acquisitions of the
intellect.

(b) *The Value of Religious Experience*

Such are religious facts, regarded from a purely
descriptive standpoint. It would not be permissible
to rest content with this study, and to set aside, as
out of date, the question of estimating the religious
consciousness, and of learning to what extent its
beliefs are rationally justifiable.

William James approaches this second task from
the Pragmatistical standpoint.

There are, says he, two kinds of judgments :
existential judgments concerning origin, and spiritual
judgments relating to value. The second kind of
judgment has nothing to do with the first. Whence-
soever an idea or a feeling may come, if the idea is
verified by fact, if the feeling is fruitful and beneficial, this idea, this feeling, have all the perfection
that the word value can represent.

The determination of value ought, moreover, to be
made, as well as the determination of the fact itself,
according to an entirely empirical method. An idea,
a belief, a feeling, possess value if experience confirms
them, *i.e.* if the event corresponds to the expectation
that they contain.

This being so, for him who would know the value
of religion, consideration of its existential conditions,
of its origins, of its genesis, is beside the mark. It is
valuable in so far as it is productive.

It is, therefore, exclusively by its fruits (adopting

the Gospel phrase) that William James will judge the tree. He will try to discover what, in truth, are the effects of religious emotion—if these effects are good and desirable, and if they can be obtained in any other way than that of religion.

. . . . . .

The fruits of the religious life are to be found in Saintliness. It is possible that the manifestations of saintliness : devotion, charity, strength of soul, purity, austerity, obedience, poverty, humility, may sometimes be exaggerated and of doubtful value. It is no less certain that, where it is inspired by the religious principle properly so called, saintliness increases, in the world, the sum of moral energy, of kindness, of harmony and of happiness. Doubtless, the ascetic does not always make the best use of his strength of soul : he readily attributes an excessive importance to the life of the body. But he manifests the capabilities of will. He creates energy and power. Now, it is a mistake to suppose that man can exist without struggle, and that heroism, henceforward, must be regarded as a thing of the past. Nature has not formed man, he obtrudes himself upon her. He only lives and grows through maintaining and increasing human energy. His very existence depends on continual self-renewal and re-creation. The saints, with their ideal of love and peace, may be ill adapted to the community wherein they live. What are we to infer from this ? Does the saint, does the mendicant, personify the human ideal ? If the saint is at variance with his time, it is because, in advance, he strives to fit himself for a more perfect society ; and, in thinking of it as already existing, he contributes towards its realisation.

The efficacy of religion is not only moral. The Gospel tells us that Jesus came to heal the sick, without distinguishing between sickness of body and sickness of soul. His word gave health of soul to fishermen, sight to the blind, hearing to the deaf, life to the dead. In other words, purity of heart and faith in the beneficent almightiness of the Creator, influence even man's physical condition to an extent that we cannot measure.

Das Wunder ist des Glaubens liebstes Kind.[1]

That is not all : among the effects that faith produces there are some for which it is a condition, not only sufficient, but necessary. Neither individuals nor communities have yet discovered elsewhere an equal source of disinterestedness, of energy and of perseverance. Just where man believes that he can act through material means, he adds thereto, knowingly or unknowingly, what is to-day called "suggestion"; and frequently it is suggestion that proves effective rather than the material means. In this way are cures wrought by the doctor, who, indeed, frankly allows that all treatment of disease is partially suggestive. Now, whether for the patient, or for the doctor, the suggestion that is here in question implies faith in the healing power of nature and in the efficacy of faith itself; such a belief is analogous to religious belief.

Religion is useful, and, in certain cases, irreplaceable : what more do we need in order to call it true ? If truth is, in the last analysis, that which is, that which continues, and that which engenders, religion

---

[1] Goethe, *Faust* : Miracle is the beloved child of faith.

is quite as true as our belief in natural beings and forces.

In given religions, however, are involved special beliefs which cannot be connected directly with observable facts. Of what value are these beliefs?

Two ways of proving their legitimacy have been attempted, viz. that of Mysticism, and that of Philosophy.

According to the mystics, there should be— particularly in certain subjects—a perception of God and divine things, similar to perception of the material world. Not that the subject can define and describe that which appears to him. But he has, in certain privileged moments, the irresistible impression that his feeling is knowledge, that he sees with the heart. And, although our concepts and our words may be insufficient for interpreting this singular intuition, the imagination seems able to combine them so as to cause, in the soul that has had the experience, a reawakening of these supernatural states. Perhaps music also has at command similar accents, direct and spiritual in a sense, which our spatial and traditional language fails to express.

It is, no doubt, true that mystics are powerless to prove the truth of their intuitions and the value of their experiences. Still, it has to be allowed that mysticism, through the suprasensible significance which it adds to the ordinary data of consciousness, strengthens and makes more efficacious the religious sentiment. If it does not furnish the knowledge that we are led to expect, it brings, at least, fresh arguments for maintaining, against Rationalism, the original reality and power of religious emotion.

For their part, certain thinkers believe that they are on the way to prove, in a rational manner, the objective truth of religious conceptions : they are philosophers proper. According to William James, all the philosophico-theological arguments which have in view the demonstration of God's existence, and the determination of his attributes, are illusory. In fact, only those notions have a real content which are interpreted by the differences in practical conduct. But all these speculative constructions have no bearing upon life.

Does this mean that every attempt to connect the religious sentiment with the nature of things, and to determine its objective significance, is necessarily barren ?

As a matter of fact, in the religious sentiment itself, however strictly we limit it, there is implied a faith which claims to be objective in its range : faith in the existence of a Being, greater and better than ourselves, who, in communicating with our consciousness, shifts the centre of our personality.

Can we regard this faith as legitimate, or is it, indeed, merely the metaphorical expression of a subjective somewhat that we cannot hope to understand in the least ?

On this fundamental question William James thinks that new light has been cast through a discovery which only dates from 1886, but which appears destined to have a brilliant future—that of subconscious psychical states, or (following the terminology which Myers [1] has made current) of the Subliminal Self.

Long ago Leibnitz loved to repeat that there are far more things in the soul than those which consciousness perceives; that innumerable lesser perceptions are to be found therein, exerting an influence greater than we imagine; that, through these subconscious perceptions, man is brought into communication with the Universe, so that nothing happens in it without some echo being produced in each one of us. These lesser perceptions were, for Leibnitz, the very substance of feelings. And if, from the standpoint of knowledge, feeling was very inferior to thought, from the standpoint of being, it realised a participation of the individual in the life and in the harmony of the Whole, infinitely greater than that which our distinct perception could claim.

The theory set forth by Myers is an experimental transposition of these views of Leibnitz.

According to Myers, we may consider human personality as composed of three concentric circles: (1) the seat or central part; (2) the margin, which extends round the centre to a limit marked by the disappearance (at least seemingly) of consciousness; but (3), beyond the very limit of this marginal self, Myers believes that he has demonstrated experimentally the existence of another self, in comparison with which the preceding two—differing only in degree—make but one: the self situated beneath the threshold of consciousness, the subconscious or subliminal self. We encounter here a kind of second consciousness, which, in ordinary life, is unknown to consciousness properly so called. For certain subjects,

---

[1] Myers, *Human Personality and its Survival of Bodily Death*, 1903.

in certain circumstances, the existence and efficacy of this subconsciousness are made manifest in a direct and sure fashion. This is what Myers tries to prove in his account of various more or less exceptional observations.

Even in man as normally constituted we find many facts which seem inexplicable ; now this theory accounts for them very well. Thus, man verifies within him the presence of faculties which do not conduce to the preservation of the species, and which, consequently, cannot be developed under the sole influence of the law of natural selection. The productions of genius are like revelations of a world other than our own. In a general way, man's ideal aspirations are disproportionate to his actual condition.

These facts are explained if we admit that, on the side of his being which transcends his conscious self, man is related to another world than that which comes within the reach of his senses—to beings whom, for this reason, we may call spiritual. Accordingly, this theory gives a very satisfactory interpretation of the most characteristic religious phenomena.

Conversion, for instance, would be regarded as the more or less sudden introduction, in the field of normal consciousness, of dispositions which have been formed and accumulated secretly within the subliminal self.

In a similar manner, mystical states would be the consequence of an interpenetration—realisable by certain subjects—of the subliminal region and of the supraliminal region. The subliminal self communicating, in fact, with a world inaccessible to the ordinary self, the latter, confronted by realities exceeding its power of apprehension and of expression, would remain dumfounded, or would endeavour to obtain some representation of the supernatural visitant proportioned to its normal condition.

Lastly, prayer would be nothing else than an appeal from the ordinary self to powers with whom the subconscious self, underlying the ordinary self, is able to enter into communion.

And thus the doctrine of the subliminal self would secure an objective foundation and a scientific value for the elementary belief immediately involved in religious fact. That belief consists in affirming the existence of an external power whose action the religious man experiences. Now, according to the doctrine of the divided self, the determinations of the subliminal self which enter into the ordinary self are not explained by the history of that self; they take objective form, following the general law of its perceptions, and give the subject the impression that he is dominated by a foreign influence. As, moreover, the subliminal self contains faculties higher and more powerful than those of the ordinary self, the latter is justified in connecting the inspirations derived therefrom with a Being, not only external, but superior to it.

It may, therefore, be said that, in affirming its relation to a greater-than-self whence proceed salvation, power and joy, the religious consciousness expresses a genuine fact, and that, in this way, the reality of the object of religious experience is given in that same experience.

It is otherwise with the special beliefs relating to the exact nature of the mysterious realities with which our subliminal self communicates. These are

Y

undemonstrable for the theory of the subliminal self, as well as for mysticism and for philosophy. They are over-beliefs, *i.e.* beliefs added by the imagination, by the intellectual and moral temperament of communities and of individuals.

Undemonstrable, they are not, on that account, to be deemed valueless. We must remember that religion is an essentially personal matter. It ought, in its effect upon the individual, to shift the centre of his personality, to transport him from the region of egoistic and material emotions into that of spiritual emotions. Now, if this phenomenon implies, before all else, an action originating beyond the conscious self and producing a change in it, the explanations, ideas and beliefs which the understanding intercalates between the cause and the effect, are themselves capable of exercising an influence upon the dispositions of the conscious self, upon its readiness to receive the inspirations of the higher self. And the conditions of the religious impression necessarily vary with periods and circumstances, with the knowledge and growth of individuals. It is, therefore, not only tolerable, it is desirable that every one shall view the religious phenomenon in the way which is, for him, the most efficacious.

William James, for his part, without pretending to attribute to his own over-beliefs the same value as to the fundamental belief immediately involved in the religious phenomenon, adopts, with regard to several important points, the affirmations of positive religion.

The invisible world, he holds, is not merely ideal : it produces effects in our world. It is, accordingly, very natural to conceive it as a reality corresponding to what religion calls God. Similarly, it is well to believe that "we and God have business with each other," and that, "in opening ourselves to his influence, our deepest destiny is fulfilled."

Besides, as man's destiny is clearly linked with that of other beings, the religious person, in order to gain confidence in things and the inward peace for which he longs, must needs believe that the same God to whom he is related, supports and governs the entire world, in such a way as to be not only our God, but the God of the Universe.

Lastly — and here William James, without any dissimulation, deserts the camp of the scientists to range himself on the side of popular opinion—since every fact is, after all, particular, since universals are but Scholastic abstractions without reality, we must attribute to God no mere general and transcendent providence : he is not the God of the religious consciousness if he is incapable of giving ear to our prayers, and of attending to our individual wants. The practical God in whom we believe has then the power of intervening directly in the course of phenomena, and of working what are called miracles.

As to belief in immortality, there is really nothing to show that it is unfounded : it has not been proved, and it seems unprovable, that the actual body is the adequate cause, and not a purely contingent condition, of our spiritual life. But this question is, indeed, secondary. If we are convinced that the pursuit of those ideal ends which are dear to us is guaranteed in eternity, I do not see, says William James, why we should not be willing, after having accomplished our task, to leave the care of furthering the divine work in other hands than ours.

II

THE DOCTRINE OF WILLIAM JAMES ON THE RELATION BETWEEN RELIGION AND SCIENCE

In this way, taking religious experience as the starting-point, is developed the theory of religion. William James does not fail to inquire into the position of this theory with reference to science.

Experimental like science, why should not religion claim our adhesion to an equal extent?

According to certain critics, such an assimilation would be impossible. For religion does not mean experience in the same sense as science : she means it in an anti-scientific sense. Experience, as science conceives it, is the depersonalisation of phenomena, *i.e.* the elimination of all that which, in given phenomena, is relative to the particular subject who observes them. Everything in the nature of final cause, prepossession of utility, of value—in a word everything that expresses a feeling of the subject, is outside scientific fact ; or, if these elements become, themselves, objects of science, that will be through our success in considering them, not *per se*, but in some special condition or observable substitute for internal feeling. Religion, on the contrary, rests upon facts taken in their subjective and individual elements. She has to do with man in so far as he is a person, and she personalises all that affects him. She cares little for the necessary universality and unity of natural laws : the salvation of an individual is more important, in her eyes, than the entire order of Nature. That is why there is fundamental incompatibility between the standpoint of religion and that of science. The relative persistence of religion amounts to no more than a survivial, destined to disappear before real experience—before impersonal and scientific experience.

These objections, in William James's opinion, are not conclusive. It is not clear why the circumstance that a succession of states seems purely subjective, should suffice to prevent these states from constituting an experience. Let the subjects be deluded in believing themselves sick, in believing themselves healed, and in attributing their healing to a supernatural intervention : what matter, if we have to admit in all this a series of facts which follow one another in accordance with a law ? Now, it is a fact that certain painful and injurious feelings are cancelled by certain beliefs, and do not seem curable by other means. Are you going to refuse religious aids to the miserable whom they can save, on the plea that to heal by means of religion is to heal against rule ? The production, by faith, of the object of faith, is not only an experience for the subject, it is an experience.

Why should there be merely one way of handling Nature and of modifying the course of her phenomena? Is it not conceivable that, vast and multifarious as she is, she ought to be approached and treated after various methods, if we would make the largest possible use of her resources ?

Science fastens upon a particular element of Nature, such as mechanical movement, and, in this way, arrives at the phenomena which are dependent thereon. Religion, through other means which equally affect our world, realises both similar phenomena, and phenomena of another kind.

"Science gives to all of us telegraphy, electric lighting, and diagnosis, and succeeds in preventing and curing a certain amount of disease. Religion in the shape of mind-cure gives to some of us serenity, moral poise and happiness, and prevents certain forms of disease as well as science does, or even better in a certain class of persons. Evidently, then, the science and the religion are both of them genuine keys for unlocking the world's treasure-house to him who can use either of them practically. Just as evidently neither is exhaustive or exclusive of the other's simultaneous use. And why, after all, may not the world be so complex as to consist of many interpenetrating spheres of reality, which we can thus approach in alternation by using different conceptions and assuming different attitudes, just as mathematicians handle the same numerical and spatial facts by geometry, by analytical geometry, by algebra, by the calculus, or by quaternions, and each time come out right? On this view religion and science, each verified in its own way from hour to hour and from life to life, would be coeternal."[1]

But, it may be said, all these considerations are exclusively practical, and the scientific point of view consists properly in distinguishing between Practice, which is quite other than knowledge—is, indeed, one of the very objects that Nature offers for our investigation, and Theory, or the determination of the elements and relations of things, according as they are capable of being proved and acknowledged real by every intellect. That is why science, in regarding those experiences which the religious apologist

[1] William James, *The Varieties*, etc. pp. 122-3.

invokes, separates them into two parts : the one subjective and foreign to science, the other objective and scientific, but destitute of all religious significance.

We know that this radical distinction between theory and practice is expressly rejected by William James, whose pragmatism reduces to purely practical criteria the very principles on which rationalism relies.

As regards the relation between religion and science, William James brings forward considerations which outstrip mere pragmatism.

All our knowledge, says he, starts from consciousness. That is, henceforward, an established truth. Now, a revolution was made in psychology, and consequently in the philosophy of science, on the day when it came to be understood that the psychological datum is not, as Locke believed, a certain number of simple elements : sensations, images, ideas, feelings, comparable with letters or with atoms, which we should have to relate externally in order to make of them the representation of a distinct and transcendent reality ; such a datum was found to be, in truth, what is now termed the "field of consciousness," *i.e.* the state of total consciousness which, at any particular time, exists in a thinking subject.

The distinctive character of this new datum lies in this : instead of being clearly defined and circumscribed, like a collection of atomic elements, it has a range to which we cannot assign exact limits, or, rather, in which limits are undiscoverable. The state of consciousness, in fact, involves both a centre and a margin, but the periphery is more or less floating and indeterminate.

We may now learn that this margin itself is connected, in a continuous fashion, with a third

region, which, unsuspected by our consciousness—even
hidden—cannot, in any degree, be measured by us
with respect to its range and to its depth. Hence,
that which is really given, that which is the necessary
starting-point of all speculation as of all practice, is
not the imaginary sum of our states of consciousness,
but this illimitable field, wherein the seat of clear
knowledge — already so complex, and undoubtedly
irreducible to a determinate number of conceptual
elements—is only a point, ceaselessly modified, moreover, through its relations with the media to which
it is bound.

If such are the primordial data over which the
activity of the human mind is exercised, what use do
religion and science respectively make of them ?

Religion is the fullest possible realisation of the
human self. It is the human person, marvellously
raised through his close communion with other persons.
It is, in some measure, an apprehension of being as it
is constituted before having been limited, arranged,
distributed in categories by our understanding, so as
to comply with the conditions of our physical existence
and of our knowledge.

Science, on the contrary, is the selection and the
classification of all that which, at any time and for
any mind, can be the object of clear and distinct
knowledge. The sum total of these elements is what
we call the objective world. So long as we consider
them apart, as happens in the clearly conscious perception from which scientific knowledge proceeds, we
do not find within us their ground of existence, and,
therefore, we represent them to ourselves as pictures
of things that exist independently of us. We shape
these images, we label them, we observe the order of

their usual presentment, we create formulas which help us to anticipate their return ; and by means of these formulas we obtain any states of consciousness that we may desire.

If such is the respective origin of religion and of science, how could the latter ever take the place of the former ? Religion takes as her starting-point a concrete bit of experience, a *full* fact, comprising thought, feeling, and, perhaps, the faint sense of participation in the life of the universe. The starting-point of science is an abstraction, *i.e.* an element extracted from the given fact and considered separately. We cannot expect man to be satisfied with the abstract, when the concrete is at his disposal. That would be " something like offering a printed bill of fare as the equivalent for a solid meal." Man uses science, but he lives religion. The part cannot replace the whole ; the symbol cannot suppress reality.

Not only is science unable to replace religion, but she cannot dispense with the subjective reality upon which the latter is grounded. It is pure Scholastic realism to imagine that the objective and the impersonal can suffice, apart from the subjective, in our experience. Between the subjective and the objective no demarcation is given which justifies, from the philosophical standpoint, the divisions which science imagines. for her own convenience. Continuity is the irreducible law of Nature. And our so-called impersonal concepts need to be constantly revivified through contact with reality, *i.e.* with the subjective, in order that they may not degenerate into inert dogmas, at variance with scientific progress. Personality is not, compared with impersonality, a kind of initial disorder of which nothing would remain, once everything were put straight. It is the wondrously rich and ever-renewed source from which science must borrow without intermission, if she would not sink into unprofitable routine.

The relation between religion and science has this appearance when we bring them into opposition. But such an opposition is the result of our defining both science and religion in an artificial manner. On the one hand, we identify science with the physical sciences. On the other hand, we make religion consist in dogmas which symbolise it. But if science is, above all, knowledge of facts, of data, there exists a psychological science as legitimate as physical science, and there is no reason why the characteristics of the latter should be imposed upon the former. And, if religion is essentially an experience—something felt and lived—it need not, *a priori*, be contrary to a science which, itself, only leads up to a certain interpretation of experience.

Now, it is found that a like fact, the continuous extension of the conscious self into a subconscious self, on the one hand is recognised by psychologists, while, on the other hand, it offers a satisfactory account of what is essential in religious experience. The relation between the conscious self and the unconscious self serves, therefore, to connect religion with science. It is, in short, the common starting-point of scientific activity and of religious activity : the latter tending to enrich consciousness by means of subconsciousness, the former to reduce invasions from the subconscious region to the forms and to the laws of consciousness.

The fundamental affirmations of the theologian, and his general method in the establishment of

religious beliefs find, moreover, a justification even
in science, so regarded.

The theologian would have man brought into
relationship with One greater than himself, distinct
from himself. Now, the subconscious is distinguished
from the conscious in consciousness; and the psychologist has every reason to suppose that, in the subconscious region, the human soul communicates with
beings that are—some of them at least—greater than
itself.

The theologian affirms the reality of the beings
which appear to be given in religious experience.
This belief is like that of the scientist, who imagines
a permanent world of forms and of laws as the pledge
of a universal and never-ceasing possibility of uniform
perception.

Last of all, we come to the great religious conceptions around which crystallise the systems of theology.
These conceptions are not formed otherwise than are
the principles on which scientists base their theories.
They are hypotheses, arranged so as to group facts and
to represent their connections in a manner agreeable
to the intellect and to the imagination. Science
could not find fault with theology for imitating her
method.

One reservation only is enjoined on the theologian.
Imaginative theories and symbols are not the essence
of religion; they aim at expressing religion in human
language. Now, it is clear that the actual sciences
share, to an ever-increasing extent, in this language.
Doctrines ought, therefore, to be unceasingly reconciled, as regards their formulas, with the essential
results of science, just as these latter, in their broad
hypotheses, evolve with the whole of human experi-

ence, and with reason which is the living witness of that experience.

To sum up, according to William James, religious experience is as useful and real as scientific experience. It is even more immediate, concrete, expansive and profound. Further still, it is presupposed by scientific experience. It can, moreover, from this time forward—thanks to the psychological theory of the subconscious—look to science herself for support.

It is developed in the same way as science, and is in harmony therewith. There is, then, no ground for believing that it is only a survival of the past, and no longer an essential element of human nature.

III

CRITICAL REMARKS

This doctrine is not a logical construction which is made up of materials taken here and there, shaped so as to fit into one another, and collected from without according to a plan. Much rather would it appear to be the religious life itself, understood, as far as possible, in its given complexity, and elucidated by sympathetic and penetrating reflection. Hence the special character of William James's works, wherein, expecting to see an author, we find a man.

Rich and varied as it is, this doctrine has a central point—a focus from which light is shed upon the whole. This centre is the theory of the field of consciousness, regarded as the basis of psychology. To apply this theory to religion, and, thereby, to bring religious phenomena within the normal life of

man : that is the task which William James has
given himself.

From this standpoint he maintains that religion is
essentially an experience—something that we feel and
live : it is the sense of spontaneous and re-established
harmony of man with himself, *i.e.* of the actual man
with the ideal man ; it is, at the same time, the sense
of man's communion with a Being greater than
himself—a Being who produces this harmony and is
revealed as an inexhaustible source of energy and of
power. This twofold sense becomes, in the religious
person, the very mainspring of conscious life.

Furthermore, and still adopting this same standpoint, religion is an essentially real and personal
affair. Religion in itself, one and immutable, is but
a shadowy Scholastic entity. We must look only for
religious persons, for religious lives, and we shall then
find that there are as many religions as individuals.
It is not without purpose that William James entitles
his work : *The Varieties of Religious Experience.*

These views are of the greatest interest.

They actually eliminate from the essence of religion
all that is chiefly objective, intellectual, or practical
in the material sense, and that can be transferred,
indifferently, from individual to individual : for
instance, dogmas, rites, traditions. They put in the
foreground the emotional and volitional element,
which is embedded in personality and cannot be
separated from it.

Consequently, they find the religious type *par
excellence* in Mysticism, disengaged from visions and
ecstasies which are not essential to it, and referred
to its principle—the intensity and widening of the
inward life. And they set up, as examples of the

religious life, the great originators for whom religion was primarily a life, a personal experimentation, an extension of human nobility and power : men like St. Paul, St. Augustine, Luther, Pascal.

Such a religion is no organised affair; we cannot enumerate and class its elements, observe and describe its evolution, or foretell its destiny. It is a living thing, creating and re-creating itself continuously, which would only cease to exist if the energy and will of its representatives died away.

Such a religion is not, moreover, a passive mysticism ingulfed in contemplation : it is an enlargement of activity, pursuing ever loftier ends, and appropriating to itself the forms necessary for their realisation. At the same time, far from being a plea in favour of ruling men and of enjoining upon them uniform beliefs, it is, for every one, the duty, not only of reverencing, but of cherishing what, in another's religion, is peculiar and personal; since only that which is connected with the person exists and is efficacious, and persons are and ought to be different from one another.

And, while preserving its own character, viz. relation to that which is, for us, supernatural, religion —as William James interprets it—is expressly reinstated in human nature. Just as he linked mystical experience with normal religious experience through exhibiting, in the former, faith become intuition, so he makes religious experience re-enter ordinary experience through seeing therein the development, conformable to general psychological laws, of elements which are present, though usually unperceived, in every working of immediate consciousness.

Religion, then, forms part of man's normal life ;

and since, besides, it contributes to the preservation, to the integrity and to the prosperity of that life, even reason combines with instinct and tradition in favouring its continuance.

Not less strong is the position that William James's doctrine secures for religion, in comparing it with science. No conflict is conceivable between them, seeing that religion lies altogether in changes of the feeling which forms the centre of our personality, while science has to do only with represented phenomena, and is limited to observing and noting their usual course.

On the other hand, science and religion are interconnected. They have one and the same end—the happiness and power of man ; one and the same method—experience, induction and hypothesis ; one and the same field—human consciousness, of which religion is the whole, science a part.

. . . .

However brilliant and clever may be this doctrine, is it proof against every objection that can be urged either by scientists or by religious men ?

As regards the scientists, their opposition was only to be expected. They deny that the mode of knowledge invoked by William James corresponds to what they call experience.

Scientific experience ends in affirming—not only does such a thing appear to me, but it is. And the statement that it *is*, means this : it is capable of being perceived by everybody endowed with normal sense and intellect, who observes the phenomenon in those conditions wherein it is offered to me now.

But the descriptions that William James puts

forward, usually borrowing them from the subjects themselves, reveal to us merely subjective impressions. They tell us that some person, more or less abnormal, had the feeling of an objective presence, either of the unreal, or of communion with supernatural beings. They make known to us the circumstances, the changes of this feeling. They carry us back, apparently, to the subjective descriptions of hallucination and of psychical disturbance. And William James himself, from the very first, hardly seems to attribute to them any other significance. By degrees, however, in proportion as he studies the higher forms of the feeling of possession, and particularly the emotions of the great mystics, he comes, almost, to regard this feeling as denoting, by itself, the real and objective existence of a spiritual being, distinct from man, with whom his consciousness may enter into communication.

Doubtless, William James confidently sets aside, as pure fictions of the imagination and of the understanding, all detailed and precise descriptions concerning the nature of these myterious beings, and their relations with our world. But of the intellectual element which is usually associated with the emotions, he retains something in the end : viz. the affirmation of a higher intervention that is given, in some way, with feeling itself. Similarly it would seem, the metaphysical psychologist Maine de Biran taught that a special feeling — the feeling of effort — contained within it and revealed to us the action of an external force, operating conjointly with our will. But Biran could not successfully establish his point; and it is not clear how William James can show that the proposition—"I feel within me the divine action," is identical with this other proposition—"The divine action is exerted upon me."

Must we, with certain writers,[1] interpret the doctrine in a strictly idealistic sense, and maintain that, from beginning to end, it is merely concerned with feelings, with emotions, with beliefs, considered from the purely subjective standpoint? After all, that which saves us, is not a God separated from our belief, but our belief in God.

It is certain that William James adopts the standpoint of radical empiricism, and that, in the objects existing outside us, he can only see fictions of the imagination and artificial contractions of the understanding. Between hallucination and perception, he clearly allows only a difference of degree, and, consequently, he is able to begin his analyses with the study of cases which evidently illustrate nothing but a morbid hallucination.

But it does not seem that this recourse to a universal subjectivism suffices to remove the difficulty. In order that even a subjective experience may be called experience, in the philosophical as well as in the practical meaning of the word, we must be able to distinguish—at least ideally—between the given subject who feels certain emotions, and a knowing subject, who verifies impersonally the existence of these emotions. Otherwise, it is a question of being, of reality — not of knowledge. A tree is not an experience.

Now, the state of the subject, in the religious phenomenon, appears to be especially incompatible with the duplication here necessary. The subject, wholly absorbed in the feeling of communion with the

---

[1] Cf. Flournoy, *Rev. Philos.*, Sept. 1902.

Infinite, no longer distinguishes between the real and the imaginary. Are his very emotions true, under such conditions; or are they only those simulated factitious emotions (objectively insincere in spite of their intensity and of their evidence) which are described in the forcible English phrase : *sham emotions*? Far from a mystical state being able to constitute an experience, it is necessary to ask, further, if it is a state of consciousness, since mystical absorption actually tends to annul consciousness.

Here we encounter the real problem which is at the heart of this discussion : is there no other experience than that which the duality of a subject and an object implies ? May not this experience, belonging to distinct consciousness and to science, be derivative and artificial, in comparison with that primary and genuine experience which is truly one with life and reality ? Such a doctrine, in fact, appears to follow from the substitution of the field of consciousness for states of consciousness in William James's psychology.[1] The primary datum, according to this doctrine, is an infinite continuity of impression and living experience, from which our clear perceptions only emerge in an elaborated and altered shape, calculated to assist us in the pursuit of certain practical ends.

Upon this matter opinion is divided. Some are inclined to see in the subliminal self an enlargement, an enrichment of consciousness, while others declare that they can only see therein an impoverishment, a contraction, a vestige, a residuum. In regarding it closely, say these latter, we find nothing in this so-called higher consciousness which was not previously

---

[1] Cf. the theory, similar in certain respects, of H. Bergson : *Introduction à la métaphysique.* Rev. de Mét. et de Mor., 1903.

in the ordinary perceptive consciousness. The supernatural aspirations of the mystics are reminiscences; such purely spiritual creations are forgotten states of consciousness which, according to ordinary psychological laws, have been mechanically combined with other states of consciousness, thus engendering a psychical organism which consciousness does not recognise. This "unknown" cannot escape the fate of all mysteries that have been opposed to science: the progress of observation and of analysis will bring it into the region of the known and the natural.

However evident such a refutation may appear, it must be noted that it admits and takes for granted the said psychology of states of consciousness, *i.e.* atomic psychology: in other words, it adopts the very standpoint that William James considers factitious and inadmissible. It may be, therefore, that this refutation is merely a *petitio principii*.

Most certainly, science assimilates an increasing variety of phenomena. But it is not through preserving, purely and simply, her ancient forms—after the manner of shallow minds, of William James's *old fogies*—that she obtains this result: it is through enlarging them, through adapting them, and, in case of need, through transforming them. In fact, none of her forms—not even those which support all the rest, viz. mathematical and logical forms—are really immutable. When it can be shown that there exist phenomena irreducible to the classic psychological types, psychology will do what physics and chemistry do in a like case: she will seek other principles.

In truth, how is it possible, in the present state of our knowledge, to prove that everything presented to the mind—inventions, contrivances, ideas, objects to be defined, ends to be sought and to be realised—is only what we have already observed? Did not the already-observed itself begin by being observed in some way? Do we know precisely what is meant by observing, and where the limit of our observation is reached?

The possibility of an experience, wider than, and even different from, that of the five senses which we have actually at command, seems, indeed, scarcely contestable. But, in order that he may claim to have in view a genuine experience, and not a mere feeling, there must assuredly be, in the notion conceived by the subject, something which corresponds to what is called objectivity. To believe in God is, in some way, to believe that God exists independently of our belief in him. Now, no subjective particularity of experience—not even a sense of overplus, of beyond, of illimitableness—can, by itself, guarantee the objectivity, the reality of that experience. William James himself appears to admit this fully, when, analysing the immediate data of the religious consciousness, he tries to discover therein, not an indication or a testimony, but the very reality—immediately given —of a relation between the soul and some higher being.

How are we to understand this transition from the subjective to the objective?

Even the theory of the subconscious is insufficient to justify it, for the subconscious itself only becomes real for consciousness through entering therein, *i.e.* through taking the subjective form.

The essential phenomenon is, here, the act of faith by which, experiencing certain emotions, consciousness declares that these emotions are real and come to it from God. Religious experience neither is nor can be, by itself and separated from the subject, objective. But the subject gives it an objective import by means of the belief which he inserts in it.

Thus mingled with faith, does religious experience cease, on that account, to be an experience? This can scarcely be the opinion of William James. For certainly, in his thought, the very idea of objectivity, characteristic of sensible experience and of scientific experience, contains necessarily a portion of irreducible belief. The category of positive existence, independent of every subjective element, is, after all, a belief. Belief or faith is at the heart of all knowledge.

Just as some have questioned if William James's religious experience is an experience in the scientific meaning of the word, so others have wondered how far it deserves to be called religious.

The subject, says William James, knows that the religious mystery is wrought within him, when—in response to his cry of distress: "Help!"—he hears a voice saying: "Take courage! Thy faith hath saved thee." The human self is naturally in a divided and failing state. If harmony is re-established, if strength beyond its own resources is given, it is through the assistance of a greater than itself.

But, according to Hœffding,[1] the truth of the matter would seem to be that these phenomena themselves are insufficient to characterise an experience as religious, if there is not combined therewith an appreciation of the value attaching to the harmony

---

[1] Hœffding, *Moderne Philosophie*, 1905. Cf. the same writer's *Religionsphilosophie*.

and to the power which the subject sees thus bestowed upon him. Conceived as purely analogous to natural things, this harmony and this power call for no divine intervention. But if the psychical phenomenon is interpreted by the subject as the restoration of union between God and man, between the ideal and the real, or—adopting Hœffding's precise doctrine—between values and reality, then the subject will attribute the appearance of this harmony and power to the action of God as the source of values; and experience will, in that way, present a religious character.

And, truly, it is concept or belief combined with feeling, which, alone, effects such a characterisation. In order that an emotion may be religious, it must be regarded as having in God—himself understood religiously—its principle and its end. It is, therefore, faith, involved in religious experience, which characterises it both as experience and as religious.

The importance of faith is, here, all the greater, because, according to William James himself, it does not only accompany emotion, but has a real influence upon it, and can, in certain cases, actually produce it. Religious faith, which, maybe, manifests God within it, is not an abstract idea: it heals, it consoles, it creates its object. Even in the midst of his painful search, Pascal hears the Saviour say : " Be comforted : thou wouldst not seek me, if thou hadst not found me ! "

But, if this is really so, religious experience is not that principle, completely independent of concepts, of doctrines, of rites, of traditions and of institutions, which the analysis of William James seemed to disengage and to indicate. For these external conditions are, in some way, elements of faith. As they assume it, so they react upon it, and determine its content. In the religious experience of a given individual, if we analyse it, we shall always find— incorporated in his faith—a multitude of ideas and of feelings bound up with the formulas and practices which are familiar to him. Of religious faith, indeed, it must be said that it is, in part, a translation of action into belief.

It appears, then, permissible to inquire, with Hœffding, if the very fact of religious experience would survive the disappearance of all the intellectual elements—external and traditional—of religion.

Have these elements, moreover, no other value than that which they derive from their connection with the religious consciousness of individuals? Is personal religion, by itself, the one essential of religion?

Doubtless the social rôle of religion, however considerable history shows it, does not suffice to prove that religion is, originally and essentially, a social phenomenon. It may be that religion was, indeed, born within the souls of individual enthusiasts, and that, spreading through imitation, through contagion, it took, by degrees, the form of doctrines and of institutions—as happens when beliefs are needed to secure the preservation and the power of a given society. But, even though the social aspect of religion were an effect, and not a cause, it would not follow that purely personal religion is, at the present day, the only important and deep-rooted form of religion.

The individual, in so far as he strives after religious perfection on his own account, already shows that he cannot confine himself to a solitary holiness. No one can work out his salvation quite alone. For human personality only develops, only realises itself, only exists, through the effort that men make to understand one another, to become united, to enjoy life together. And thus, common things, acts, beliefs, symbols, institutions, are an essential part of religion, even in its personal form.

But the individual person is not alone in having a religious value. A community, also, is a kind of person, capable of exhibiting its own virtues—justice, harmony, and humanity, which exceed the limits of individual life. In bygone days the control of the material and moral destinies of the community rested with religion. If to-day it no longer exercises political authority, can it not still claim to show the nations their ideal ends, and to develop in them the faith, the love, the enthusiasm, the spirit of brotherhood and of self-devotion, the ardour and the constancy, that are required in order to work for the carrying out of such ends?

A common task surpasses a purely personal religion. It implies, among the members of a given community, collective reverence for traditions, beliefs, and ideas, which tend to the fulfilment of its mission and to the realisation of its ideal.

If feeling is the soul of religion, beliefs and institutions are its body; and there is only life, in this world, for souls united with bodies.

CONCLUSION

CONCLUSION

THE inevitable encounter. The conflict is properly between the scientific spirit and the religious spirit.

I. RELATIONS BETWEEN THE SCIENTIFIC SPIRIT AND THE RELIGIOUS SPIRIT—(a) The scientific spirit—How are facts, laws, theories, established ?—Evolutionism—The experimental dogmatist—(b) The religious spirit—Is it compatible with the scientific spirit ?—Distinction between science and reason—Science and man : continuity between the two—The postulates of life they coincide with the principles of religion.

II. RELIGION—Morality and religion : what the second adds to the first—Vitality and flexibility of religion as a positive spiritual principle—The value of the intellectual and objective element—The rôle of vague ideas in human life—Dogmas—Rites—The transformation of tolerance into love.

The question of the relations between religion and science, considered historically, is one of those which provoke the utmost astonishment. Briefly, in spite of compromises again and again renewed, in spite of the determined efforts of the greatest thinkers to solve the problem in a rational manner, it appears that religion and science have always been on the war-path, and that they have never left off struggling, not only for the mastery, but for the destruction of one another.

For all that, the two principles are still standing. It was in vain that theology pretended to enslave science : the latter shook off the yoke of theology. Since then, it has been possible to imagine a reversal of rôles, and science has frequently announced the end of religion; but religion endures, and the very violence of the struggle attests her vitality.

When we consider the doctrines in which actual ideas concerning the relation of religion to science are embodied and defined, we see that they part into two divisions, representing what may be called the Naturalistic tendency and the Spiritualistic tendency respectively.

In the first of these divisions we found it possible to range as typical : the Positivism of Auguste Comte, or the Religion of Humanity; the Evolutionism of Herbert Spencer, with its theory of The Unknowable; the Monism of Haeckel, which leads to the Religion of Science; lastly, Psychology and Sociology, which reduce religious phenomena to the natural manifestations of psychical or social activity.

In the second division we decided to place : the Radical Dualism of Ritschl, ending in the distinction between Faith and Belief; the doctrine of the Limits of Science; the Philosophy of Action, connecting science and religion with one common principle; and the doctrine of Religious Experience, as it is expounded by William James.

To this list of doctrines a full survey would add many others. These examples, however, suffice to show with what strenuousness, perseverance, and resources on either side the struggle is conducted.

To foretell the result of this struggle in the name of logic alone would be a rash enterprise; for the champions of both causes have long been engaged in a dialectical onslaught without reaching any satisfying success. It is a question, here, not of two concepts, but of two actually existing things—each of them, according to the Spinozistic definition of existence, tending to persevere in its being. Between two living persons, victory does not always fall to him who can best arrange his arguments in syllogisms, but to him whose vitality is the stronger. Further, we are now considering the dispute between knowledge, under its most exact form, and something which is given, more or less, as dissimilar to knowledge. There is, necessarily, between these two terms a kind of logical incommensurability.

To settle the question through crowning, *a priori*, the empirical arch of evolution, which we trace or think that we trace in history, is likewise too simple a method. It is not always sufficient that a thing is old in order to reach its end. The life of ideas, of feelings, of morals, does not necessarily resemble the life of individuals. Moreover, when these things are dead they can be born anew—especially if they have been forgotten through the lapse of time. In this way are brought about revolutions, which are all the more effective in that they spring from the oldest principles. When Rousseau wished to renovate the world, he appealed to Nature as prior to all customs. Again, if history offers us evolutions of an apparently determinate type, it also shows us rhythmical movements, wherein the very development of one period leads to its opposite in another. The course of human affairs is too complicated to allow of our going back, from a given evolution, to the elementary mechanical causes which determine it, and which we must know before we can give any really scientific forecast whatsoever.

If it is true that religion and science can be likened to living things, how are we to measure their vitality, the reserves of power, the possibilities of renewal that they may conceal ?   Do we not see, even to-day, certain naturalists explaining the sudden transmutations that natural species occasionally present by qualities, hitherto latent, which some favourable circumstance unexpectedly brings to light ?

Instead of venturing, as regards the future of religion and of science, upon predictions that are easier to make than to verify, it may be interesting to consider the actual state of both, and to determine, in accordance with this study, the manner of conceiving their relations which, following Aristotle's formula, appears both possible and suitable.

Now, it would seem that the two powers which actually face one another may be, far less religion and science as doctrines, than the Religious Spirit and the Scientific Spirit.   It is of small consequence to the scientist, after all, that religion does not affirm anything in her dogmas which is in harmony with the results of science.   These propositions are presented by religion as dogmas, as objects of faith ; they unite intellect and conscience, they express, in short, man's connection with an order of things inaccessible to our natural knowledge : that suffices to make the scientist reject, not, perhaps, the actual propositions, but the mode of adhesion that the believer gives to them.   And the latter, in his turn, if he sees all his beliefs, all his feelings, all his practices explained and even justified by science, is farther than ever from being satisfied, since, thus explained, these phenomena lose the whole of their religious character.

We should, therefore, be committed to a rather immaterial task in seeking to discern a certain agreement between the doctrines of religion and the conclusions of science. Several thinkers on the scientific side are inclined to discard religion in principle and *a priori*, on account of that which is implied in her way of thinking, of feeling, of affirming, and of willing. The religious man, they maintain, uses his faculties in a manner that no longer tends to the progress of human culture. The scientific spirit is not only other than the religious spirit—it is, properly speaking, its negation. It originates through the reaction of reason against this spirit. Its triumph and the disappearance of the religious spirit are simply one and the same thing.

It is, then, less science and religion strictly so-called, than the scientific spirit and the religious spirit, that we have to bring face to face with one another.

We must further remark that the easy "separate-compartment" system, so much in vogue last century, is no longer implied in the present conditions. If the struggle is not only between two doctrines, but between two mental dispositions, it is quite impossible for a man who would be a person (*i.e.* a conscious being, one and rational) to allow equally, without comparing them together, the two principles over which there is so much wrangling in cultivated circles. And that which is inconceivable for the individual, is so, with greater reason, for the community—itself, also, a kind of conscious being; for its judgment depends less than that of the individual upon accidental circumstances. More than ever the question of the relations between religion and science is paramount and unavoidable.

I

RELATIONS BETWEEN THE SCIENTIFIC SPIRIT AND
THE RELIGIOUS SPIRIT

Formerly it was possible to deem the preliminary consideration of religion or of science a matter of indifference. This attitude can no longer be maintained to-day. Science has—to employ a current expression—become emancipated. While, in old days, her only certainty was that which particular metaphysical principles bestowed in enabling her to labour at the co-ordination of natural phenomena, she has since found in experience an appropriate and immanent principle, from which she derives, without other assistance than ordinary intellectual activity, both facts which are her working materials, and laws by the aid of which she arranges facts. It follows therefrom that, practically, in her origin and in her development, science is self-sufficing, and that the special mark of the scientific spirit is now shown in unwillingness to admit any starting-point for research, any source of knowledge, other than experience. To the scientist, therefore, science appears as something of primary and absolute importance, and it is useless to ask her to be reconciled with anything. She has vowed to be reconciled with facts and with them alone. If we wish to obtain a hearing we must accept her own standpoint.

Moreover, it is she especially who, in these days, takes the offensive. The human mind, there can be no doubt, is henceforward given over to science, whose certainty is imposed by an irresistible evidence. The problem of the relations between the religious spirit and the scientific spirit is presented to-day under the following form : Does the scientific spirit which, with some of its representatives, signifies the negation of the religious spirit, exclude it in reality ; or does it, in spite of certain appearances, leave us the possibility of that spirit ?

What, therefore, is the scientific spirit at bottom, and what are the consequences of its development in humanity ?

(a) *The Scientific Spirit*

Descartes, and especially Kant, regarded the scientific spirit as determined, in an immutable manner, by the logical conditions of science, and by the nature of the human mind. It was, with Descartes, a foregone conclusion to consider all things from a bias which allowed of their being reduced, directly or indirectly, to mathematical elements ; with Kant, it was the affirmation, *a priori*, of a necessary interconnection of phenomena in˙ space and in time. Armed with these principles, the mind advanced, with fresh ardour, towards the discovery of the Laws of Nature ; and the success which it obtained easily led to the belief that it was, from that time, in possession of the eternal and absolute form of truth. But this opinion was necessarily modified, when men came to examine more closely the methods of science, the conditions of her development and of her certainty.

To-day it seems to be quite established that the scientific spirit is not, any more than the principles of science, ready-made and given ; but that it is actually formed in proportion as science develops and progresses. On the one hand, it is the intellect which makes science, and the latter is not extracted from things in the same way as an element is extracted from a chemical compound. On the other hand, the product reacts upon the producer ; and what we call the categories of the understanding are only the totality of habits which the mind has contracted in striving to assimilate phenomena. It adapts them to its ends, and it is adapted to their nature. It is through a compromise that harmony is reached. And so the scientific spirit is no longer, henceforward, a bed of Procrustes, in which phenomena are supposed to be kept in order. We see the intellect, living and flexible, expanding and growing—not unlike the organs of the body—through the very exercise and effort that the task to be accomplished exacts from it.

Two ideas, brought into prominence at the time of the Renaissance, appear to have contributed to set the scientific spirit in the direction that it was thenceforward to take : on the one hand, desire to possess, at length, positive knowledge, capable of enduring and of increasing; on the other hand, ambition to influence Nature. Science believes that she can attain this twofold object through accepting experience as an inviolable and unique principle.

The scientific spirit is, essentially, the sense of fact as source, rule, measure, and control of all knowledge. Now, what science calls a fact is not merely a given reality : it is a verified or verifiable reality. The scientist who intends to resolve a fact, places himself outside that fact, and observes it just as every other thinking man, equally impelled by the sole desire of knowing, would do. In this way he sets himself to discern, to fix, to note, to express it by means of known symbols, and, if possible, to gauge it. In each of these operations the mind has an indispensable part; but this part consists in elaborating the datum so that it may be, as far as possible, admissible for all minds. While the primordial datum was hardly an impression, an individual feeling, the work of art which the scientific mind substitutes for it is a definite object existing for everybody—a stone that can be used in the building of impersonal science.

In this way is adapted to things, and scientifically defined by slow degrees, the ancient aspiration of the philosophical mind to know being in itself and the permanent substance of things.

Meanwhile the mind, reflecting on experience, asks if the latter only furnishes facts, and if it would not be possible, under the sole direction of this same experience, to pass beyond fact properly so-called, and to reach what is termed Law. Formerly laws were conceived as dictated by the intelligence in matter: it is a question, now, of inferring them from the simple facts. Not that they are found therein ready-made, and that we have only to extract them. But, in the same way as scientific fact is constructed by the mutual action and reaction of mind and of knowledge, so, perhaps, facts themselves are capable, through elaboration, of becoming laws.

One circumstance which, seemingly, we could not fail to encounter, has justified this ambition. If all the phenomena of Nature acted and reacted equally upon one another, they would form a totality of such complication and variableness that it would be, undoubtedly, for ever impossible to extricate laws therefrom. But it is found that, among the things which fall under our experience, certain combinations and certain connections, though still very complex, have a relative stability, and are obviously independent of the rest of the Universe. This circumstance has made possible the experimental induction, by means of which the mind—isolating two phenomena from the totality of things—determines a solidarity between them.

Thus is the once-metaphysical notion of Causality defined scientifically, through being adapted to given things.

That is not all : the mind, impelled by a third idea—that of Unity—has tried to discover if, from this very idea, it could not form a scheme applicable to experimental science.

Immediate knowledge of physical laws is piecemeal. A law is two phenomena interconnected, but isolated from other phenomena. By analogy and assimilation, the mind brings laws gradually together, through distinguishing them as particular and as general. And so it reunites after having separated ; and it is able to conceive, as an ideal, the reduction of all laws to a single law.

The Unity of the metaphysicians has thus become the scientific systematisation of phenomena.

It is by the aid of symbols, sometimes even of artifices, that man simplifies Nature in this manner ; but is not scientific fact itself (the starting-point of all these inventions) already a constructed symbol, an imaginary objective equivalent of the original fact ?

The scientific spirit is aware of the consequences that the increasing boldness of its ambitions involves.

Its object is always the same : to create in the human intellect a representation, as faithful and serviceable as possible, of the conditions of phenomenal appearance. But, in proportion as it recedes farther from concrete and particular phenomena, in order to consider or imagine general phenomena which offer remote consequences as alone verifiable, it acknowledges that its explanations, though they may be sufficient, are not on that account necessary ; and it only attributes to these vast conceptions the value of experimental hypotheses.

Experience, more and more extensive and profound, has not only assimilated the philosophical concepts of substance, of causality, and of unity. It has recovered from bygone thinkers a concept that dogmatic metaphysics and science had hoped to eliminate for good and all : the concept of radical change, of Evolution—partial or even universal. This was one of the great principles which the Greek physicists sought to estimate. Now, whether in our means of knowing, of noting, of representing, of arranging things, or in Nature itself, science, at the present time, no longer sees anything quite stable and definitive. Not only is a purely experimental science, by definition, always approximative, provisional, and modifiable ; but, according to the results of science herself, there is nothing to guarantee the absolute stability of even the most general laws that man has been able to discover. Nature evolves, perhaps even fundamentally.

In conjunction with things, the scientific spirit is henceforth itself subject to evolution. It is, in this sense, a spirit of relativity. It considers every explanation as necessarily relative, both to the number of known phenomena, and to the state (maybe a transient one) in which it actually finds itself. This relativity, moreover, does not impair its value, and in no way hinders that continuous addition of knowledge which is the first article of its method. For, although evolution be radical, it is not conceived, on that ground, as arbitrary and as scientifically unknowable. If the remotest principles of things are transformed, that very transformation must obey laws which are analogous to immediately observable laws, to experimental laws.

A further trait, linked with the preceding, characterises the scientific spirit as we now see it. It is, undoubtedly, no longer dogmatic, in the meaning which a metaphysician would give to that word. But it is, and tends to persevere in its being, after the manner of a living thing in which are accumulated countless natural forces. It regards itself as the supreme example of judgment and of reasoning. If, then, it continues to repel all metaphysical dogmatism, it re-establishes for its own use a kind of relative dogmatism actually based on experience. It believes in its power of unlimited expansion, and in its indefinitely increasing value. Consequently, whatever problem may be in question, it refuses to conclude with Dubois-Reymond : *Ignorabimus.* No one is justified in declaring, with regard to that of which we are ignorant to-day, that we shall always be ignorant of it. Moreover, do we not reach a decision which is to some extent positive, when we recognise that, what we do not know—even if we must always be ignorant thereof—is, in itself, knowable according to the general principles of our scientific knowledge ? The history of science proves that we are right in affirming a continuity between what we know and what we do not know.

That is why the expression "scientifically inexplicable," is, henceforward, devoid of meaning. A mysterious force, a miraculous fact, when we admit that the fact exists, is nothing else than a phenomenon which we do not succeed in explaining by the aid of laws that we know. If this impossibility is averred, science will be rid of it in order to seek other laws.

If, therefore, the laws which science propounds are, and continue, not absolute affirmations, but questions which the experimentalist puts to Nature, and which he is ready to state in modified terms if Nature refuses to be adapted to them, it is no less certain that the scientific spirit has a practically unbounded confidence in the postulate which all these questions imply ; this postulate is nothing else than the legitimacy and the universality of the scientific principle itself.

If such is the scientific spirit, can room be found, in human consciousness, for the religious spirit ?

(b) *The Religious Spirit*

One very simple way of settling the question would be to maintain that the scientific spirit is, by itself, the one essential of human reason—that all the ideas or tendencies by means of which the latter has succeeded in manifesting itself throughout the ages, have, from this time, their only verified and legitimate expression in the principles of science. This would mean that everything outside science would be, on that very account, outside reason ; and, as religion is necessarily other than science, it would be, *a priori*, relegated among those raw materials of experience which it is the special aim of science to transform into objective symbols capable of furnishing truth.

In order that the scientific spirit may admit the legitimacy of a standpoint in regard to things other than its own, it must not deem itself adequate to actual reason, it must recognise the claims of a more general reason. Of this latter it is, doubtless, the most definite form, but it does not exhaust its content. Is it clear, however, that the scientific reason has now taken the place, unconditionally, of that ineffable reason which men have, from all time, regarded as the special prerogative of their race ?

The scientific reason is reason in so far as it is formed and determined by scientific culture. Reason, taken in its fullest sense, is that outlook upon things which determines, in the human soul, the whole of its relations with them. It is the mode of judging that the mind assumes, in contact both with science and with life, as it gathers and welds together all the luminous and fruitful conceptions which spring from human genius.

Now, when we adopt, in this way, no longer the exclusively scientific standpoint, but the more general standpoint of human reason, we are able to inquire into the relations between the scientific spirit and the religious spirit without deciding the question in advance.

If science is, practically, self-sufficing, if she has, in experience, a kind of absolute and primary principle, does it follow that in the estimation of reason (no longer merely scientific, but human) she can be considered absolute? It is quite conceivable that a thing which, taken in itself, seems to be a whole, may, nevertheless, be in reality only a part of some vaster whole. All progress is made through developing, for its own sake, a part which, in fact, only exists by means of the whole to which it belongs. Science is within her right in not recognising any other being, any other reality, but that which she comprises within her formulas. But must we infer that reason, henceforward, can make no distinction between being as it is known by science, and being as it is?

Science consists in substituting for things, symbols which express a certain aspect of them—the aspect that can be denoted by relatively precise relations, intelligible and available for all men. She is based upon a duplication of being into reality pure and simple, and into distinct or objective representation. However determined she may be in pursuing the real into its smallest recesses, she remains an onlooker contemplating and objectifying things; she cannot, without contradiction, become identified with reality itself. Universality, necessity, and objectivity—the conditions of knowledge—are categories. To identify categories with being is to ascribe to their character of immovable exactness the absolute value which metaphysical systems attribute to being *a priori*. In real science the categories of thought are themselves mutable, seeing that they have to be adapted to facts regarded as a reality which is, *a priori*, distinct and unknowable.

To this irreducible duality science herself bears witness. For the two principles of the real—things and mind—are, for her, data which she cannot

resolve. When she considers them objectively from
her own standpoint, it seems to her, not only that
she assimilates them, but that she is able to reduce
them to one and the same reality. But this very
operation she can only effect if its conditions are
furnished to her; and these conditions are and
remain : firstly, things with which she cannot
provide herself; secondly, a mind, distinct from
these things, which shall consider them objectively,
and transform them so as to make them intelligible.
Things and mind—whatever else be their intrinsic
affinity or opposition—are together, for science, the
very being from which she gains distinction, and
which she cannot ignore if she analyses herself
philosophically, since she is only fashioned out of
the elements that she borrows from them continually.

Can we, at any rate, elaborate these elements, so
that they may become exactly conformable to the
exigencies of scientific thought ?

The scientific data which represent things, take from
their origin a character which does not seem assimilable
with science for the very reason that science desires
to regard being from an opposite standpoint. This
character is heterogeneous continuity, multiplicity
as a whole, which, in order to become an object, is
first of all translated by the senses and by the understanding into qualitative discontinuity and numerical
multiplicity. Science starts from this heterogeneous
multiplicity, which, for her, represents brute matter,
and applies herself to the task of reducing it to a
homogeneous continuum. She effects this reduction
through expressing qualities by quantities. Now, the
expression must, necessarily, preserve a relation to the
thing expressed ; otherwise it would be worthless.

Even though all trace of the discontinuity and of the heterogeneity of things should disappear in our formulæ considered apart, we could not be exempted from recollecting the relation of the formulæ to reality, and from referring to that relation when we had to apply these formulæ, and to appreciate, by means of them, the objects of concrete experience.

As to approaching the contrary problem, and proposing no longer to reduce the given diversity to unity, but, starting from unity, to extract diversity from it—that problem may be historical and metaphysical, but it is only in appearance approached by science; in reality, it is not scientific. A purely experimental science assimilates, reduces, unifies, but neither expands nor diversifies. That is why the trace of given diversity which continues in the reductions of science is itself irreducible.

Similarly, the strictly scientific mind—the subject of science, leaves standing, beyond itself, mind in general. In vain does science claim to reduce the mind to the rôle of a mere instrument, of a passive assistant: the mind works on its own account, trying to discover if there is in Nature order, simplicity, and harmony — distinctive marks that are clearly much more calculated to bring satisfaction to itself than to express the intrinsic properties of phenomena. And these notions, which direct the investigations of science, are not, in truth, purely intellectual notions: taken in their entirety, they constitute feelings, æsthetic and moral needs. Thus, feeling itself is linked with the scientific spirit, as exemplified among the scientists in its living and actual reality.

It follows from what we have just said, that, if science takes possession, in her own way, of things and of the human mind, she, nevertheless, does not lay hold of them altogether. Inevitably the being of things overflows the being which science assimilates, and the human mind outstrips the intellectual faculties for which she finds use. Why, then, should not man have the right to develop, for their own sake, those of his faculties which science only uses in an accessory manner, or even leaves more or less unemployed?

The impossibility of marking out an exact frontier between science and being, between the objective and the subjective, between abstract intellect and feeling, the necessary persistence of a middle zone in which these two principles are indistinguishable, establishes a continuity between the scientific world, in which being is reduced to empty and universal relations, and the living, thinking individual who attributes an existence and a value to his own being. Seen from afar, through the concepts that we substitute for them so as to enable us to dogmatise on their nature, abstract intelligibility (the special mark of science) and human feeling are opposed to one another. But in reality this separation does not exist; and, if science is a system of formulæ, in which individual reality ought no longer to have any place, it is, nevertheless, only created, developed, and maintained in individual minds, elaborating, in an endless progress, their impressions and individual ideas. And as, in fact, that which exists is not precisely science—an abstraction which only denotes an aim, an unconditioned, therefore an idea—but scientific study, which is always in the state of becoming real science, is not separable from the scientists; and shifting, subjective life will ever remain an integral part of it.

The individual, in science, seeks to systematise things from an impersonal standpoint. How could science, which is his working method, forbid him to seek, likewise, to systematise them from the standpoint of the individual himself? This kind of systematisation, indeed, would not admit of objective value, in the meaning that science gives to that phrase; but, if it satisfied feeling, it would respond to human needs which are no less real than the need of bringing things into conformity with one another.

Moreover, we must conceive different degrees in the systematisation effected from the standpoint of the individual. The lowest degree is the consideration of all things in their relation to a single self, taken as world-centre. Now, above this extreme individualism there is quite a ladder of systematisations in which things are related, not to a single individual, but to the several individuals who, in their totality, form a group, a company, a nation, humanity. Subjective systematisation can thus imitate, in its way, the universality of science. The latter disengages the universal from the particular, through abstraction and through reduction. An analogy to the universal can be drawn, in the subjective order, from the agreement of individuals, from the harmony which, out of their diversity, forms a sort of unity.

It is a systematisation of this kind that religion represents. She attributes a value to the individual, and considers him as an end in himself. But she does not allow him any other way of fulfilling his destiny than that of treating other individuals as, also, ends in themselves; accordingly, she exhorts him to live for others and in others. It is not the personality of a single person, but of all persons—each one being regarded as an end, and as, at the same time, sharing in a common life—which is the central idea to which all things ought to be referred.

It is only right, it would seem, to recognise that such a systematisation, at once subjective and concrete, is nowise excluded by the scientific spirit. Following the statement of La Bruyère, we have to do, here, with things that are different—not incompatible. Something more is still needed. It is not enough that a conception is possible, admissible without contradiction, to make us believe that we ought to adopt it. We must have, besides, some positive reason for considering it true. Can we, on behalf of religion, maintain a reason of this kind ?

.   .   .   .   .   .

Man ought to be allowed to consider the conditions, not only of scientific knowledge, but of his own life. Now, if there is, for human life as we observe and conceive it, a necessary foundation, it is belief in the reality and in the value of the individual.

Each of my acts, of my least words or thoughts, signifies that I attribute some reality, some worth to my individual existence, to its preservation, to its part in the world. Concerning the objective value of this judgment I know absolutely nothing ; there is no need for it to be shown me. If, perchance, I reflect thereon, I find that this opinion is, in truth, only the expression of my instinct, of my habits and prejudices—whether personal or inherited. In compliance with these prejudices, I am ready to assume a tendency to persevere in my own being ; to deem myself capable of something ; to regard my ideas as serious, original, useful ; to labour for their diffusion and adoption. All this would have no chance of withstanding an examination that was ever so little scientific. But without these illusions I could not live—at least in the human sense of living; and, thanks to these untruths, I am able to relieve distress, to encourage some of my fellows to support and to love existence, to love it myself, and to aim at making a tolerable use of it.

What is true as regards individual life holds good equally as regards social life. It rests on the opinion—scientifically futile—that family, society, country, and humanity are individuals which tend to be and to continue, and that it is possible and right to strive for the maintenance and development of those individuals.

However devoted to science we may be, the legitimacy and the dignity of Art lay hold of our imagination. But Art attributes to things properties that are inconsistent with those which science verifies. Art takes from reality any object whatsoever—a tree, a cauldron, a human form, the sky or the sea, and into that being of fancy it infuses a soul, a supernatural soul, the offspring of the artist's genius; and, by means of this transfiguration, it snatches away from time and oblivion that contingent and unstable form to which the laws of Nature only conceded a shadow of momentary existence.

Morality claims that one thing is better than another; that there are within us lower activities and higher activities; that we are able, at will, to exercise the latter or the former; that we ought to trust the instigations of a faculty (ill-defined and irreducible, moreover, to the purely scientific faculties) which she calls Reason; and that, through following her advice and obeying her commands, we shall transform our natural personality into an ideal personality. Of what value are all these phrases if science is the sole judge?

But even science herself, considered, not in the theorems that schoolboys learn by heart, but in the soul of the scientist, presupposes an activity irreducible to scientific activity. Why should we cultivate science? Why should we set ourselves tasks that become daily more arduous? Must we maintain that science is necessary for living, when we regard life as good and real? Are we quite certain that science will obtain for us a life more agreeable, more tranquil, more consonant with our natural liking for comfort and for least effort? Will it not, rather, be a life higher, nobler, more difficult; rich in struggles, in new feelings and ambitions; specially devoted to science, *i.e.* to disinterested research, to the pure knowledge of truth? What are the intense and superior joys of initiation in research, still more those of discovery, if not the triumph of a mind which succeeds in penetrating apparently inexplicable secrets, and which enjoys its victorious labour, after the manner of the artist? How can science be duly estimated save through the free decision of a mind which, dominating the scientific mind itself, rises towards an æsthetic and moral ideal?

Thus, whatever manifestation of life we consider, the moment that it is a question of conscious and intelligent human life, and not simply of a life purely instinctive and unaware of itself, we see implied other postulates than those which preside over the sciences. In a general way, while the postulate of science is this proposition : everything happens as if all phenomena were only the repetition of a single phenomenon, the postulate of life may be expressed as follows : act as if, amidst the infinity of combinations (altogether uniform from the scientific standpoint) which Nature produces or can produce, some possessed a peculiar value, and were able to acquire a tendency fitting them to be and to continue.

The mental operations which the use of this postulate implies can, it would seem, be determined.

In the first place, faith has to be specified. Not a blind faith. We have to consider the faith that is guided by reason, by instinct, by the sense of life, by example, by tradition ; but we do not find in any of these solicitations the scientific motive which would enable us to say : it is. As, clearly, it is a question of diverting her intelligence from the mechanical resultant of things, science cannot suffice here. The saying of St. Augustine, which made such an impression on Pascal, remains true : We labour for what is uncertain. For the thinking man, life is a wager. We do not see how it could be otherwise.

From this first condition a second follows. Faith, indeed, is not necessarily the passive acceptance of that which is. On the contrary, it is capable of taking for its object that which is not yet, that which does not seem bound to be, that which, perhaps, would be impossible without this very faith. That is why faith—with men in general, and especially with men of a superior mould—engenders an object of thought that is more or less new, an original intellectual representation, upon which it fixes its gaze. The man who would act, in his capacity as man, sets an end before himself. According to the daring and power of faith, this end is an ideal more or less lofty,

more or less distinct from the real. At first, faith
only sees its object dimly, far away and in the clouds.
But it strives to fix its meaning in conformity with
the need of the intellect and of the will. In fact, it
determines the object gradually, in proportion as it
strives to realise it.

Lastly, from creative faith, and from the object
which it sets before itself, proceeds a third condition
of action : love. The will, indeed, becomes enamoured
of its ideal object in proportion as, under the combined influence of faith and intellect, that object is
depicted in more beautiful and more vivid colours.

Faith, representation of an ideal, and enthusiasm—
these are the three conditions of human action. But
are they not, precisely, the three moments in the
development of the religious spirit? Do not these
three words express accurately the form that will,
intellect, and feeling take under religious influence?

Human life, therefore, on the side of its ideal
ambitions, partakes naturally of religion. As, undoubtedly, on the side of its correspondence with
Nature, it partakes of science—seeing that it depends
on science for the means of attaining its ends, we are
apparently justified in regarding life as the connecting
link between science and religion.

But does not the sense of life, combined with
science, suffice, exactly, to guide man's conduct,
without his needing to add thereto religion properly
so-called? Clearly, science, by herself, only furnishes
the means of action, and remains silent about ends.
But, in order to determine these latter, as reason
demands, we have, it would seem, in the bosom of
actual Nature, two standards more trustworthy than

all those which could be enjoined upon us by authorities said to be superior : instinct and the social conscience.

Instinct is a fact, a precise and positive datum. Whatever be its origin, it represents the tendency and the interest of species. To follow it, is, evidently, the chief obligation of anyone, who, according to the dictates of reason, desires to keep in harmony with Nature.

Besides being an individual belonging to a natural species, every man is member of a human community. This, again, is a fact ; for man is only man, a rational and free being, through having a share in that community. He ought, therefore, to comply with the conditions underlying the community's existence. And as, for each given community, at each given period, the conditions of existence are expressed by a totality of traditions, laws, ideas, feelings, which constitute a kind of social conscience, there is, for the individual who would be good for something, who would be himself in an objective and true sense, a second obligation to obey the rules of the community in which he lives, to be a submissive and active organ of that community.

What more does man need for the guidance of his life ? We are too much given to wrangling about ends. For a right-minded man they are plain, inasmuch as they are given. It is the means with which we are specially concerned, and science is ready to furnish them.

A rational doctrine, surely, and one which, followed conscientiously, would also be a singularly lofty one : Ὡς χάριέν ἐσθ' ἄνθρωπος, ὅταν ἄνθρωπος ᾖ.[1] What a worthy being is man, when he is truly man !

[1] Menander.

But can it be affirmed that this doctrine yields complete satisfaction to human reason? The latter asks not only for the rational, but for the best, whenever it is possible. And she calls upon us to make it possible.

Now, are we sure that the instinct which we find within us is a perfection that we cannot overstep? It could appear so, when we deemed it primary, immutable, sprung immediately from eternal Nature or from Divine Wisdom. But to-day, whatever be its origin and genesis, we regard it as acquired, contingent, modifiable. It is, for man, a fact doubtless, and relatively stable, but one that is, in the end, like other facts. Evolutionism no longer recognises any fact as sacred. Man, moreover, has learnt from science herself how to make use of Nature so as to outstrip her; how, through obedience, he may obtain the mastery over her. Why should he not make use of his instinct, instead of remaining subject to it? And then, where will he put the end, with respect to which instinct will be treated as means?

The social conscience is, also, the outcome of an evolution. Moral laws are no longer eternal. They are no longer divine revelations. They show us what results from the struggles of innovators against the laws and customs of their country and of their time. They are scarcely able, to-day, to maintain their authority. Be they ever so ancient, we cannot allow that they are still suitable for a society in which so many things have changed. Old things have only one right—that of disappearing, and of making clear room for new things. Are they recent? What power can be claimed for an institution which time has not proved, and which everybody recognises as

having originated through accident, through calcula-
tion, through lies, through impulses and passing
circumstances ? However worthy of respect may be
the ideas and laws of our own day, why should they
restrain our conscience to a greater extent than the
laws and the ideas of bygone periods bound the
conscience of our forefathers ? What is progress,
that lever of the modern mind, save the right of the
future over the present ? And what is genius save—
athwart the totality of ideas that link the individual
necessarily with his age—a vision, as it were, of new
ideas, which, most frequently, outstrip the mental
capacity of contemporaries ?

Certainly, every reasonable man reverences the
laws, customs, ideas, and feelings of his community
and of his time, just as he conforms to the instinct
of his kind ; but he can see, neither in the one nor
in the other of these two motives, ultimate rules
beyond which he has not the right to conceive anything. He finds, on the contrary, in his very reason
—with its indefinite search after what is better—an
incitement to make instinct and the social conscience
themselves subservient to the pursuit of higher ends.

Doubtless man could live without giving himself
any other end than life, but he is not so disposed.
He could limit himself to acting according to his own
pleasure, or to that of others ; but, if he reflects
thereon, this does not satisfy him. Nothing compels
him to go beyond himself, to seek, to will, to be.
He chooses to try his luck, to run a risk, to enter
upon a struggle. But Plato's saying remains true :
The struggle is noble, and the hope is great—καλὸν
γὰρ τὸ ἆθλον καὶ ἡ ἐλπὶς μεγάλη.

We cannot disguise from ourselves that, to strive

to surpass our nature is to believe ourselves free, and to be bent on acting as if we were so. And, as freedom does not consist in acting without reason, but, on the contrary, in acting according to that same reason, to suppose ourselves free is to believe that we can find in reason motives of action that are not mere physical laws, mechanically determinative. Is it really true that reason, and not a sort of æsthetic craving for the unknown and for heroism, invites us to enter upon the struggle of which Plato speaks; and through what combination of ideas are we induced to fling ourselves into a course, without being able, apparently, to see whither it will lead us?

Practice implies: firstly, faith; secondly, an object offered to that faith; thirdly, love of the object and desire to realise it. What do we find beneath these three elements, if we try to form a more or less distinct idea of them?

If we ask ourselves, in the first place, how this faith—necessarily involved in every conscious action —is fixed and justified, we find that it rests, wittingly or unwittingly, upon the idea and the feeling of duty. To believe, i.e. to affirm, not idly but resolutely, anything else than what we see or what we know, enjoins on reason an effort. This effort needs a motive. Reason finds that motive in the idea of duty.

Duty is a faith. It is trivial to declare that it is no longer duty if its fulfilment is proved inevitable or even desirable for reasons established by material evidence. Duty is faith *par excellence*. For every other belief we may allege the support of sensible reasons: utility, the example of other men, the affirmation of competent authority, custom, mode, tradition. Duty is quite compact in itself: it does not give any other reason than its incorruptible disinterestedness.

And, in spite of all the arguments by which clever people try to win her over, reason persists in feeling within her an affinity for this mysterious law. We do not succeed either in depriving duty of its suprasensible character, or in eliminating it from human life. Every time that a man, before acting, examines himself thoroughly with respect to the reasons which ought to determine his action, he encounters, sooner or later, the question of duty, and he is only satisfied if he can respond to it. And, before any authority whatsoever can be admitted, there must hover above it the universal, sovereign law of duty. The faith which presides over human life is nothing else, in short, than faith in duty.

This faith is no mere abstract notion : it is a living and productive power. Under the operation of duty the intellect conceives and engenders. It projects, before the eye of consciousness, forms which translate, into an imaginative and communicable language, the content of the idea of duty—in itself indefinable. Where the intellect has no other end than to know, the forms which it fashions are the representation of the influence exercised upon the senses of man by the action of external objects. We may suppose that, indirectly, these forms proceed from the objects themselves. But, if it is a question of some practical idea, some representation of an act, not necessary, but possible and convenient, the object can no longer be a simple image of given reality : it is a sort of invention. The mind, certainly, makes use of the resources which the external world and science offer ; it adopts the language of the medium in which it lives. Nevertheless, its operation is not a simple epiphenomenon, or a mechanical resultant of given phenomena ; it is an effective agency. Let us look at the artist in the act of creating : he starts from an idea that is, first of all, confused and remote ; and this idea by degrees comes nearer and stands out, thanks to the very effort that he makes to lay hold of it, and to realise it. Similarly, the writer seeks the idea by means of the form, while he bends the form to the expression of the idea. Vivified by faith, the understanding constructs, at first, a dim representation of the ideal ; and, gradually, it renders this notion more distinct through adapting thereto all that which, amid the resources at its disposal, seems fitted to translate and develop it.

The object which the intellect lays down as the expression and the foundation of the idea of duty is, necessarily, the grandest and most perfect that can be conceived : such it is bound to be, in order to explain the peculiar worth of this idea. This object, which springs from the depths of consciousness, transcends it infinitely : thus its appearance in the field of consciousness is a revelation. And this character cannot vanish, because, the object becoming ever greater and more exalted, in proportion as man strives to conceive it more adequately, the inequality between the real and the ideal continues to increase with the progress of reflection and of will, instead of becoming less.

The third condition of life is man's love for the ideal which he pictures to himself. Now, as with faith and with the ideal, so with love : when we examine it thoroughly, it carries us beyond Nature properly so-called. It is, between two distinct persons, a blending of existence which defies analysis.

There is, undoubtedly, a form of love, in which the individual only considers self, and has in view merely his own enjoyment. And love of this kind is little more than instinctive perception. But from this love, which, organised by the intellect, becomes egoism, man — in proportion as he rose towards humanity—learnt to distinguish, more and more clearly, another love, which we may call self-sacrificing love ; inspired by this latter, he would live, not only for himself, but for another, in another. It is love in the higher sense which Victor Hugo feels when he writes : " Madman, to believe that thou art not thyself!" Love makes of two beings a single being, while allowing personality to each one of them ; far more, while enlarging, while realising in all its power the personality of the one and of the other. Love is not an external bond, like a combination of interests ; it is not, moreover, the absorption of one personality by another : it is the participation of being in being, and, with the creation of a common existence, the completion of the being of those individuals who form that community.

If this is so, man's love for the ideal and perfect being that his reason anticipates, is already a sense of union with that ideal. It is the desire for a closer participation in its existence and in its perfection. It is that very perfection, in so far as it draws us towards itself. Self-sacrificing love, or the giving of self to ideal things (the "Eternal-Womanly" as Goethe called it), is a divine power which comes down to us, and which draws us upward towards the heights :

> Das Ewig-Weibliche
> Zieht uns hinan.

Thus, for him who seeks the hidden resort of faith, that resort is discovered in the idea and in the sense of duty as a thing altogether sacred. For him who fathoms the idea of progress (an object of faith), that idea implies the conception of ideal and infinite being. And the love of this ideal is, at bottom, the sense of a kinship with it, of an initial participation in its existence.

What does this mean, but that, at the root of human life, as such, lies what is called Religion?

To rise to the creative principle of life is not a necessity. We can live by mere instinct, or by routine, or by imitation; we can live, perhaps, by the abstract intellect or by knowledge. Religion offers man a richer and deeper life than purely spontaneous or even intellectual life : she constitutes, so to speak, a synthesis—or, rather, a close and spiritual union—of instinct and intellect, in which each of the two, merged with the other, and, thereby even, transfigured and exalted, possesses a fulness and a creative power which separate action could not yield.

II

RELIGION

It is true that many will dispute the position thus given to religion in human life. Only yesterday, they will say, it was allowable for religion to labour for the progress of humanity, because morality was more or less involved therein. But this solidarity was only a contingent and transitory fact. Historically, religion and morality originated and developed separately. And it is the very progress of morality which has compelled religion to adapt herself to it, and to make it her own. But just as, originally, they were independent of one another, so, at the present time, they are dissevered ; and morality, henceforward emancipated and become like other sciences, suffices, alone, for the guidance of humanity.

The question of the relations between morality and religion is, perhaps, too easily decided in theories of this kind. The psychological origins of morality are difficult to determine : Socrates was a profoundly religious man. From the fact that two living forms appear independent just when their history begins for us, it does not follow that they have separate origins : otherwise, the transmutation of the naturalists would be nonsense. And that which interests us for the ordering of our life is less identity or diversity of empirical origin than the harmony which is established between the ideas in human reason, as this latter advances towards perfection. What does it matter that religion formerly taught hatred, if now she teaches love ? What does it matter that morality, at first, condemned the religion of the theologians, if, seeking support in conscience, she afterwards rejoined and embraced the religion of the spirit ? Morality is not the negation of religion : between the precepts of the one and the commands of the other there is often but a difference of expression.

Religion, nevertheless, even where she coincides with morality, is distinguishable from it in many respects.

And, firstly, if the real precepts are, in great part, identical on both sides, a difference as regards foundation is made manifest. Many thoughtful people deem this difference unimportant. But the question

of foundation, which may be secondary for a writer
on ethics, is of great moment from the religious
point of view, seeing that religion is, above all,
practice, life, realisation, and that the foundation is
the principle of the realisation. What religion aims
at obtaining is, in the first place, effectual means, not
only with a view to knowledge, but with a view to
the real performance of duty. She believes that
pure ideas, however clear they may be, do not suffice
to move the will; that what produces being is being;
and she offers human virtue the support of divine
perfection, in order to help it to exist and to increase.

Religion, in the second place, as fully developed,
is the communion of the individual, no longer merely
with the members of his clan, of his family, or of his
nation, but with God as the Father of the Universe,
i.e. in God, with all that is or can be. Religion is,
henceforward, essentially universal. She teaches the
radical equality and brotherhood of all human beings;
and she offers, as motive for the actions of the individual, the conviction that, however humble he may
be, he can labour effectively for the coming of the
Kingdom of God, in other words for Justice and for
Goodness.

Lastly, religion purposes to train man through an
inward and substantial operation. It is not merely
external acts, habits, customs that she would reach—
it is the man himself, in the deepest source of his
feelings and thoughts, of his longings and desires.
Moralists declare readily that we do not love as we
wish, but as we are able. But religion enjoins love
itself; and she gives the power of loving.

It is true that the cold reason hesitates, regarding
these ideas as nothing else than exaggerations or

paradoxes. But it is remarkable that, in spite, or because, of her paradoxical appearance, religion has ever been one of the most powerful forces which have affected humanity. Religion has united and divided men, she has made and unmade empires, she has occasioned terrible wars, she has opposed spirit as an insurmountable hindrance to material might. In the sphere of individual conscience she has raised contests as dramatic as the wars between nations. She has braved and subdued nature, she has made man happy in wretchedness, miserable in prosperity. Whence proceeds this strange sovereignty, if not from a faith stronger than knowledge; from a conviction that God is with us, more effectual than all human aid; from a love stronger that all arguments?

. . . . . .

Is humanity getting ready to repudiate religion, in order to seek, through wide-spread experiences, some new guide? That is possible; for, if we cannot affirm that, in this world, even the most elementary forms are preserved without diminution, how is it certain that the higher forms and values will continue? There is nothing to prevent these values, not only from being transformed, but from being lost, or to prevent religion from sharing in the general fate. But it is also possible that, even among the most liberal and enlightened thinkers, religion will be maintained. For, hitherto, her vitality and her power of adaptation have exceeded all that we could imagine. And, in the moral order, we never know if a form of existence is definitively abolished, since, as a rule, human revolutions consist precisely in resuscitating dead things.

The life of religions, however, is not exempted

from the general law, according to which a living thing, if it would endure, must comply with the conditions of its existence. Vitality and flexibility are directly related. Buddhism in Japan is not the Buddhism of India; again, the Christianity of the Middle Ages was adapted to the philosophy of Aristotle and to the Roman idea of Empire. Probably, there will be the same adaptations in the future as in the past. Religion will subsist, if, while manifesting an intense faith, she remains in a relation of action and reaction with the ideas, the feelings, the institutions, and the life of human communities.

What, in existing communities, are the data which cannot be set aside?

In the first place, science, in its general conclusions, and especially in its outlook, has become imperative for human reason.

Similarly, if the morality of the philosophers is diverse in its principles, in its demonstrations, in its theories, it is not less true that there is, in our midst, a living and active morality, which, though still imperfectly defined, cannot be assailed. This morality, indeed, is derived less from reasoned doctrines than from traditions, customs, and religious beliefs; from the teaching and example of superior men; from habits which are created by life and by institutions, as well as by the influence of physical, intellectual, and moral conditions. It represents the experience of humanity.

Lastly, the form of social life in different countries is a third condition with which religions are obliged to reckon. Formerly they were essentially national. But a religion seems to us, now, all the nobler for soaring above the differences which divide humanity.

The coexistence of the spirit of universality with the necessary maintenance of the traditions and the feelings, of the mind and the life adapted to each nationality, is one of the problems which trouble the modern mind. On the other hand, the democratic régime, become general in modern nations, sometimes presents a hostile attitude towards the very principle of religion.

There is no apparent reason why religion should not be adapted to the above-mentioned conditions.

Either by evolution, or by the action of the media which she has traversed, religion—at one time so overburdened with rites, with dogmas, and with institutions—has, more and more, disengaged from this material envelope the spirit which is her essence. Christianity, in particular, the last of the great religious creations which the story of humanity shows, has, so to speak, neither dogmas nor rites as it is taught by Christ. It calls on man to worship God in spirit and in truth. This spiritual character has dominated all the forms which it has assumed. And even to-day, after the attempts to imprison it, either in political forms, or in texts, it continues, amongst the most cultivated peoples, an irreducible affirmation of the reality and of the inviolability of spirit.

Let religion display herself thus in the world, according to her own nature, as an altogether spiritual activity, aspiring to transform men and things from within, and not from without, by persuasion, by example, by love, by prayer, by fellowship of souls, and not by compulsion or by statecraft; and it is certain that she has nothing to fear from the progress of science, from morality, or from institutions.

Freed from the yoke of an immutable and dumb

letter, or from an authority which is not purely moral and spiritual, and brought back to herself, she becomes, once more, entirely living and flexible; capable of reconciliation with the whole of existence; everywhere at home, since, in all that is, she discerns an aspect Godward. What may appear to be at variance with modern ideas or institutions, is such and such external form, such and such dogmatic expression of religion—the trace of the life and the science of bygone generations; it is not the religious spirit, as we see it circulating through the great religions. For this spirit is nothing else than faith in duty, the search after well-being and universal love, those secret channels of every high and beneficent activity.

But, it will be asked, is the religious spirit, quite alone, without any visible form of manifestation, still religion—is it still a reality?

A distinction is here necessary. If the spiritual principle is conceived as obtained and determined, according to a purely objective method, by the elimination of all the material and definable elements of which the religious phenomena given in experience are composed, it is evident that, in this principle, there is no longer anything real, and that it is merely a word by which an imaginary residuum is designated. What is the personality of a man, if I claim to find it in what remains, after I have taken away from that man, regarded as an external phenomenon, all the elements which belong to him in common with other beings? That is why Kant's Categorical Imperative is only an empty abstraction for the critics who, instead of penetrating the philosopher's thought, understand his doctrine in an entirely objective and dogmatic sense. To seek spirit in matter, is to render its discovery impossible.

But, assuredly, the idea of duty is an active and potent idea, which bestows on the object in which we embody it an incomparable authority. And all the forces which prompt human activity, all the main causes of great historical movements, are thus "imponderables," which we picture through symbolical explanations, but which we shall never be able to comprise in formulæ.

The power of words has often been noted with amazement. And, in truth, the passionate glow and acquiescence, which could not be obtained from men through teaching them a clear and consistent doctrine, are created, straightway, through flinging them some such words as : liberty, country, empire, justice, the Will of God ! God with us ! Does this mean that, cleverer than the scientists, ordinary folk invest these words with clear ideas ? And must we suppose that the concepts suggested by these words are identical in all minds ? Much rather ought we to allow that these words are signals, which, whenever they appear, rouse and stir up, in people, a confused and floating mass of feelings, of ideas, of aspirations, of passions, which spread from individual to individual through a sort of contagion. There is thus created a power which will enrapture multitudes : this power is a tendency, an aspiration, a common spirit—it is not a clear and definite concept.

In this way there are principles, which, while they are essentially formal, are, at the same time, very positive and effectual ; and it may be imagined that Kant could readily consider the notion of duty as a principle of this kind. But Kant only attributed such a value to the notion of duty because he deemed it superior to empirical objectivity. He did not admit that it was a fact, in the sense in which the fall of a body is a fact : he saw therein a dictate of reason, *i.e.* of the purely free will.

Similarly, nothing hinders us from allowing that the religious spirit—so largely effective, and yet in itself so incomprehensible and indefinable—is a principle at once formal and positive, like the great impelling forces of history, like feeling, like life.

. . . .

Must we say, however, that religion is, exclusively, spirit and life, and that it neither can nor should be manifested in concepts and in material expressions ? What is, exactly, in point of religion, the relation of spirit to letter ?

A philosopher who applied himself, above all, to develop the spiritualistic principle, viz. Fichte, wrote as follows : *Die Formel ist die grösste Woltat für den Menschen,* Formal expression is, for man, the greatest of benefits. For man, soul and body are necessary. Mind cannot be realised without being incarnated in matter. Thus, even the Light, protested Mephistopheles, ought not to despise bodies.

> . . . da es, so viel es strebt,
> Verhaftet und den Körpern klebt.
> Von Körpern strömt's, die Körper macht es schön,
> Ein Körper hemmt's auf seinem Gange.[1]

Expel from religion every objective element, and you reduce her to an unintelligibility which will be confounded with the imaginations of the individual, and

---

[1] For, strive as it may, it continues fettered to bodies. It streams from bodies, it beautifies bodies ; a body impedes it on its way.

which will not even be characterised any longer as religion.

In fact, it is inadmissible that, in the inspiration which transforms a life, in the feeling which raises men above themselves, in what is called the soul of a nation, in the religious spirit which History shows us operating continuously, there are merely elements of a subjective and non-intellectual kind. It is only in certain old text-books of psychology that the soul's faculties are described as absolutely shut off from one another. The real soul is one; and, in each of its manifestations, it is quite whole—with its intellect and its imagination, as well as with its will and its spiritual activity.

Hence the concentration of the religious spirit, which is expressed by the idea of a religion without symbols, does not signify more than a phase: it is simply the condition of a fresh impulse.

In a general way, the mind only abandons one form in order to look for another. It leaves a form which has become false to it so as to assume one which, adapted to its internal progress and to its new conditions, will represent it more truly. It is in this sense that Kant shows the practical reason freeing itself, first of all, from the empirical laws which enslave it; then, in the second place, positing, as the immediate expression of its will, the notion of duty; lastly, seeking, in the third place, the means of effecting, out of human life in its entirety, the realisation of this notion.

The religious principle is not merged in the forms by which it was expressed in the past. Otherwise it would have a thousand contradictory aspects, and would be unthinkable. It is more and more revealed as the affirmation of the reality, the sublimity, and the creative power of spirit.

Its seat is, henceforward, conscience. No longer an external and material thing, it has become inward life.

It is an activity of the soul, whether of the soul of an individual, or of those ever-widening collective souls which it is able, itself, to create through individual souls. This evolution, due especially to the action of mystics, is now secured. But mysticism itself is subdivided into passive mysticism and active mysticism. The former is satisfied with retiring from the world, and with contemplating God; the latter, from the bosom of God, loves, wills, and shines. Now, in order to realise itself outwardly it must think and act. That is why the two elements of belief and practice, which, from earliest times, religion has added to feeling, are quite inseparable from it.

How are we to explain the moulds of thought or categories, by means of which the intellect perceives and receives phenomena? When we say that they originate from the double action of the mind and of phenomena, it is clear that we are giving, not an explanation of the fact, but merely a metaphorical representation of it. Similarly, and *a fortiori*, the inventions of genius, which not only outstrip facts, but dominate them, modify them, create them— setting up models which are, for them, unrealisable, are something else than the mechanical resultants of given phenomena. Accordingly, they appear to the human mind as revelations, as the effects of communion with a higher reality.

Whence came, asks Schiller, the mysterious maiden, who, each spring, transformed Nature and the hearts of men ?

> Sie war nicht in dem Tal geboren,
> Man wusste nicht woher sie kam.[1]

In like manner, religious inspiration is interpreted by conceptions which, for us, necessarily outrun experience, in that, relating to the very source of being and of life, they are presented as revelations. The conscious self regards them in this light : they will only operate within it, they will only exist, through being thus referred to a supernatural origin.

These conceptions, like all intellectual representation of an object, must be defined, determined in a formula, *i.e.* briefly, in an image. This image can only be a symbol. It has, in fact, been the prolonged endeavour of the religious spirit to dissolve the solidarity which linked it with things as actually given, and with the science of these things, in order to cherish aims that surpass them—aims that cannot be realised by Nature alone. If, now, the categories and preformed notions which we apply to things with a view to perceiving them, can only be irreducible symbols, if scientific knowledge itself remains invincibly symbolical, how would religion, which aims at representing the non-representable, escape from this law of the intelligence ? It would even seem that religious symbolism ought to constitute, somehow, a symbolism of the second grade ; for religion cannot, when her expressions clash with the affirmations of science, vie with her rival in the ability to enrich our knowledge. Religion has an object other than that

---

[1] She was not born in the valley. We knew not whence she came.

of science; she is not—she is not for us—in any way the explanation of phenomena. She cannot be affected by the discoveries of science, which relate to the objective nature and origin of things. Phenomena, from the religious point of view, are estimated according to their moral significance, to the feelings which they suggest, to the inner life which they express and which they rouse; and no scientific explanation can remove this character from them.

Not that the objective elements of religion : beliefs, traditions, dogmas, ought to be emptied of all intellectual content, and limited to a purely practical value. Kant attempted this radical separation of practice from knowledge—a kind of wager, to which he himself was unable to adhere. Deprived of every theoretical notion, practice would no longer have any value, whether religious or even human; and the mind does not permit the realisation of such a division. But there are, undoubtedly, in the mind two modes of knowledge : distinct knowledge, and vague, or, more particularly, symbolical knowledge. The idea which directs the studies of an artist, of a poet, of an inventor, of a scientist even, is a vague idea, which, perhaps, will never be completely resolved and made clear; nevertheless, it is a positive, active, efficacious idea. The human will and intellect are chiefly moved by such ideas. The mathematician, by his analyses, strives to overtake imaginative intuition, which presents itself to his thought as a revelation, and which is fixed and determined in proportion as he seeks to convert it into conceptual demonstration. The mind does not evolve truth : it posits it, it assumes it, in a necessarily vague manner; then it puts its hypotheses to the proof, and, through this very operation, renders them more and more distinct. Truth, for man, is hypothesis, sensibly verified and specified by fact.

Religious knowledge, which takes for its object, not what is, but what ought to be, cannot be determined after the manner of scientific knowledge; but if, independently of its practical value, it offers a symbolical meaning with which reason can be satisfied, inasmuch as the experience of science and of life has effected it, we are justified in saying that it possesses a veritable and legitimate intellectual content.

Such is the foundation of what are called dogmas, an integral element in all real religion.

The fundamental dogmas of religion are two in number: firstly, the existence of God, of a living, perfect, almighty God; secondly, the relationship, at once living and concrete, of this God with man.

It would be little consonant with facts to say that the idea of God is, at the present time, abandoned by human reason. Reason has withdrawn, more and more, from the idea of an external and material deity, who would only be a magnified substitute for natural beings. But, on the other hand, she applies herself, more and more, to notions which—brought together, defined and thoroughly examined—correspond quite surely with what the religious consciousness adores under the name of God.

Visible Nature is, throughout, dissociation, dispersion, dissolution, degradation, destruction. Now, we dream of universal preservation, concentration, conciliation and harmony. The development of one individual, according to the natural course of things, presupposes the destruction of certain others. The

Over-man of Nietzsche requires useful slaves.   Evil
is, in our world, a condition of Good—a condition
which appears to be indispensable.   Who created
this world?   Shall we say the Good, or the Evil;
God, or the Devil?   To God, virtue, love, perfection,
may be ascribed the saints, the meek, the just, the
self-sacrificing men.   But the devil has put into the
world hunger, suffering, hatred, envy, lust, falsehood,
crime, war; and, thereby, he has awakened the
activity of man and instigated his progress.   Science,
industry, social organisation, justice, art, religion,
poetry, education—all these marvels are only, in a
sense, the means invented by man for the purpose of
overcoming and forgetting the ills which surround
him.   Suppress the evil, and the good relapses into
nonentity.   Πόλεμος πάντων μὲν πατήρ ἐστι πάντων δὲ
βασιλεύς.[1]

But it is precisely against this law of Nature that
human reason protests.   She would like to be able to
fashion the good through the good, and not through
the evil; she resolves that the liberty, the well-being,
the virtue of some shall not be the misery, the bondage,
the depravation of others.   She attributes to all that
is, to all that has something positive and living in it,
an ideal form, a value, a right to exist and to develop.
She bestows an existence, even upon the Past which
is no longer, even upon the Future which, perhaps,
will not be.   She would maintain the free and natural
development of all forms of activity: science, art,
religion, private virtues, public virtues, industry,
national life, social life; communion with Nature,
with the Ideal, with Humanity.

Yet more, reason plans, among so many elements

---

[1] Strife is the father and king of all things.

which seem disparate, the introduction of unity, of harmony, of solidarity. She demands that every single thing shall be all that it is capable of being, in the ideal meaning of the word ; that it shall realise the maximum of perfection possible to it, and, at the same time, that it be one with the whole, and live by that very communion.

Is the realisation of such an aim possible ?

It must be clearly recognised that it exceeds the plan of Nature, whose passivity is indifferent to the intrinsic value of beings, if so be that, for Nature, there are beings. In like manner, it goes beyond the logic of our understanding, which, reducing things to concepts, can only identify them, or declare them incompatible. It would be especially inconceivable, if, with the dogmatic systems of theology, we only made appeal to the categories of eternity, of immutability, of static quality and unity.

But actual Nature—regarded from the standpoint of reason, if not from that of bare science—is not, perhaps, a mere immutable mechanism. Is it certain that, in her living reality, she contains only being, and not beings ? Life, if we consider it under its proper aspects, and if we look upon it as a reality, offers us the outline of a harmonious and relatively persistent union of substances and of properties, which mechanical forces, left to themselves, would never have formed.

By analogy with life, we are able to conceive a Being, in whom all that is positive, all that is a possible form of existence and of perfection, coalesces and subsists ; a Being who is one and multiple—not like a material whole, made up of elements placed side by side, but like the continuous and moving infinity of a mind, of a person. If this idea, which transcends experience, is not mechanically enjoined upon the understanding, it is, nevertheless, in complete harmony with human reason, as both the traditions of races and the reflections of thinkers testify. The Being which this idea represents is what the various religions call God.

The second fundamental dogma of religion is the living communion of God with man. This communion is thus defined by the Christian religion: "No man hath beheld God at any time; if we love one another, God abideth in us." In other words, God is love, and love is communion — the power of living in another. To love is to imitate God, it is to be God in a sense, it is to live in him and through him.

These ideas, which are at the heart of Christianity, convey nothing but what is very conformable to the aspirations of reason. The Being, in whom everything that deserves existence ought to be reconciled, merged and fixed harmoniously, is naturally conceived, both as a model that the intellect seeks to copy in the objects which it fashions, and as a source of moral energy, whence the will, striving after the best, can ceaselessly acquire renewed strength. To believe in God—to believe in the eternal union of all those perfections which the spatial and temporal world exhibits as incompatible, is, at one and the same time, to believe that this incompatibility is only apparent, and that a power exists through which the Good can become, in very truth, the condition and the means of the Good.

When we contemplate God as the union of perfection and of existence, as Love, Father, Creator, and

Providence, we recognise ideas which correspond to the aspirations of reason. These ideas, however, are not clear and distinct, and we do not see how they can become so. They are vague and symbolical ideas, very real, nevertheless, and very potent.

We must regard, as still more symbolical, the expressions by which the intellect seeks to render these notions more and more concrete, and, thereby even, more and more comprehensible for all, more and more fitted to determine the will. But these developments are justified, when they are conceived so as to become reconciled, in the living reason, with the essential conditions of our science and of our life. Do we not see that science, as the pure search for truth, and life, which seeks a reason for living, are themselves suspended in this Being, in whom alone existence gains a value and perfection a reality ?

We have, further, to distinguish as essential elements of religion, besides feeling and dogmas, rites and deeds—whether public or private.

It is impossible to consider deeds as a purely adventitious element of religion. Where do we find, in the human soul, that substance termed pure being, whose action, without any regulative effect, would be only a ray or an emanation ? We make use, here, of a metaphor drawn from sensible images. Far from our being able to regard deeds as thus, with man, a mere result, eminent psychologists maintain that feeling, inward disposition—what we call being, is only, in truth, the effect and psychical translation of exterior and motor activity. In any case, it is impossible for us to know if a given feeling is absolutely spontaneous, or if it owes something to the influence

of our actions upon our being. This influence, if it
is not, by itself, creative, is indeed very deep. It is,
therefore, quite reasonable that deeds and rites have,
from the earliest times, been considered a part of
religion. However spiritual the world's religions may
become, they will never be able to separate being from
doing, without detracting from the laws of human
nature. As long as religion shall endure, it will
comprise — as essential elements — practices, rites,
active and external manifestations.

Practices presuppose authority and obedience. It
is inconceivable how these principles can be struck off
from religion, any more, in fact, than from life in
general. But the religious authority is obviously
spirit, and spirit alone. Every other authority is
but an organ through which the authority of spirit is
manifested. Exclusively moral, the religious authority
can only be understood and obeyed by free consciences.

Religious rites do not constitute the end, but the
means. They ought to be adapted to further the
realisation of religious ends. Now these latter are :
purity of heart, self-renunciation, the establishment
of a community wherein each member shall exist for
the whole, as the whole for each member—wherein,
following the language of St. John, they all shall be
one, even as, in God, the Father and the Son are one.

Religion will thus preserve her ancient character
as the tutelary genius of human communities. She
requires the union of all consciences, therefore of all
men ; she aims at effecting between them a bond of
love, as the support, as the principle of the material
bond. In this way she will carefully preserve the
rites, which, handed down by so many ages and
peoples, are the incomparable symbols of the per-

manence and breadth of the human family. She will maintain them through infusing into them an ever deeper, more universal, more spiritual thought. To act, to feel, to vibrate together, during the accomplishment of a common task, is, according to reason herself, the secret of union. Tὰ κοινὰ συνέχει, said Aristotle.[1]

We should make religion an incomplete and still abstract idea if we were to confine it to beliefs and practices. Just as it starts from feeling, so it ends therein, for the object of dogmas and rites is both to express feeling and to determine it. The development of feeling is like a circle which only recedes from its starting-point in order to return thereto. It is not without significance that the psychologist and the moralist consider mysticism an essential element, and, perhaps, the foundation of religion. All intense religious life is mystical; and mysticism is the life-source from which religions, threatened by a formal and scholastic spirit, derive fresh vigour.

But there is an abstract and barren form of mysticism, as well as a positive and fruitful form. The first is that which endeavours to live entirely by feeling, believing itself freed from the tyranny of dogmas and practices. In isolating itself from the intellect and from activity, feeling is not raised, it becomes enfeebled. On the other hand, guided and enriched by thought and by action, feeling can, indeed, expand and display its creative property; it is then the active mysticism, so incomparably efficacious, which we find at the heart of all the great religious, moral, political, and social movements of humanity.

[1] Things that are common to all serve as a link.

Religious feeling, thus regulated and determined by belief and practice, may be described—in comparison with purely natural and philosophical virtue —as the transformation of tolerance into love.

Philosophers and politicians have found reasons for teaching men to tolerate one another. How could I rightly claim for myself a liberty that I refused to my fellows? But such reasoning is more formal than real. Have we proved that the liberty of others is as good as our own? Yes, perhaps, if by liberty we mean the bare ability to will, or not to will. But a liberty of this kind is an academic abstraction. All genuine liberty is bound up with the ideas, the opinions, the inclinations, the habits, which determine it. And that liberty is really better than another, which operates according to higher principles. How, then, can all forms of liberty claim the same right? Has error the same right as truth, vice as virtue, ignorance as knowledge? And do not all branches of learning to-day, moral as well as physical, claim an equal scientific certainty? If truth ought to tolerate error, it could only be for a time, during the delay granted to the latter for her instruction and correction.

In short, the principle of tolerance is an ill-gotten notion, the expression of a scornful condescension, the mental denial of what we seem to allow. It is not clear how tolerance would be justifiable, unless we admitted, in all things, another point of view than that of positive science.

But religion actually vindicates, beside the standpoint of science, the standpoint of feeling and of faith. For her, the value of liberty is not gauged in proportion to scientific knowledge. Individuality, as such—be it that of ignoramus or of scientist, of criminal or of honest man—has a special value. A world in which prevail personality, freedom to err and to do amiss, variety and harmony, is, for the religious man, better, loftier, more like divine perfection, than a world in which everything would be merely the mechanical application of a single immutable rule. The only way for the finite to imitate the Infinite is through endless diversification.

That is why, in his experience of other men, the religious man appreciates most of all, not the points wherein they resemble him, but the points wherein they differ from him. He does not simply tolerate these differences. They are, in his eyes, bits of the universal harmony, they are the being of other men ; and, thereby even, they are the condition attaching to the development of his own personality.

"Consider," said the shoemaker Jacob Boehme, " the birds of our forests ; they praise God, each one after its fashion, in all keys and in sundry ways. Do we find that God is offended by this diversity, and that he silences these discordant voices ? All forms of existence are dear to the Infinite Being."

Religion commands us to love others, and to love them for themselves. Bolder than philosophy, she makes love a duty—the duty *par excellence.* She calls upon men to love one another in God, *i.e.* to ascend to the common source of being and of love. Mutual love is natural between brethren.

.   .   .   .   .   .

In spite of their relations, science and religion remain, and must remain, distinct. If there were no other way of establishing a rational order between things than that of reducing the many to the one, either by assimilation or by elimination, the destiny of religion would appear doubtful.   But the struggles which contrasts engender admit of solutions other than those which science and logic offer.   When two powers contend, both of them equally endowed with vitality and with fertility, they develop and grow by that very conflict.   And, the value and the indestructibility of each becoming more and more evident, reason strives to bring them together through their conflicts, and to fashion, from their union, a being richer and more harmonious than either of them taken apart.

Thus is it with religion and science.   Strife tempers them both alike ; and, if reason prevails, from their two distinct principles—become, at once, wider, stronger, and more flexible—will spring a form of life ever ampler, richer, deeper, freer, as well as more beautiful and more intelligible.   But these two autonomous powers can only advance towards peace, harmony, and concord, without ever claiming to reach the goal ; for such is the human condition.

THE END